SCULPTING

WITH THE

ENVIRONMENT

—*A Natural Dialogue*

EDITED BY BAILE OAKES

VAN NOSTRAND REINHOLD
I(T)P™ A Division of International Thomson Publishing Inc.

New York • Albany • Bonn • Boston • Detroit • London • Madrid • Melbourne
Mexico City • Paris • San Francisco • Singapore • Tokyo • Toronto

Cover : S. Jacobs Design
Front cover photography : © Thea Litsios ;
  GESTATION : BAILE OAKES, 1990, PALISADES PARK,
  SANTA MONICA, CA

Back cover photography :
  © PETER ERSKIN: *SECRETS OF THE SUN*
  © PATRICIA JOHANSON: *FAIRPARK LAGOON*
  © JAMES TURRELL: *RODEN CRATER*
  © PETER RICHARDS: *THE SPRING*

Designers : Baile Oakes, Mark McGowen
Art direction : Sharon Jacobs
Executive editor : Wendy Lochner
Editor : Jane Degenhardt
Production editor : Anthony Calcara
Production Manager: Leeann Graham

Printed and bound in Hong Kong
First edition
For more information, contact:

Van Nostrand Reinhold
115 Fifth Avenue
New York, NY 10003

International Thomson Publishing Europe
Berkshire House 168-173
High Holborn
London WC1V 7AA
England

Thomas Nelson Australia
102 Dodds Street
South Melbourne, 3205
Victoria, Australia

Nelson Canada
1120 Birchmount Road
Scarborough, Ontario
Canada M1K 5G4

International Thomson Publishing GmbH
Köningswinterer Strasse 418
53227 Bonn
Germany

International Thomson Publishing Asia
221 Henderson Road #05-10
Henderson Building
Singapore 0315

International Thomson Publishing Japan
Hirakawacho Kyowa Building, 3F
2-2-1 Hirakawacho, Chiyoda-ku,
102 Tokyo
Japan

International Thomson Editores
Campos Eliseos 385, Piso 7
Col. Polanco
11560 Mexico D.F. Mexico

1 2 3 4 5 6 7 8 9 10 CP 01 00 99 98 97 96 95

Library of Congress Cataloging-in-Publication Data

Oakes, Baile
  Sculpting with the environment : a natural dialogue / Baile Oakes.
    p.   cm.
  ISBN 0-442-01642-5
    1. Environmental policy.   2. Social ecology.   3. Environment (Art)
  4. Earthworks (Art)   5. Astronomy, Prehistoric.   I. Title.
  GE170.025   1995
  363.7--dc20   94-19254
                                                              CIP

Contents

FOREWORD   I

ESSAYS :

    Suzi Gablik   3

    Fritjof Capra   6

    Thomas Berry   9

Ancient and Contemporary Art   13

Jody Pinto   24

Peter Erskine   30

Baile Oakes   38

Charles Ross   46

Nancy Holt   56

James Turrell   64

Robert Adzema   78

Phyllis Yampolsky   82

Donna Henes   86

Fern Shaffer and

    Othello Anderson   90

Juan Geuer   94

Patrick Zentz   100

Douglas Hollis   106

Peter Richards   112

Buster Simpson   120

Michele Oka Doner   126

Reiko Goto   132

Lynne Hull   136

Constance DeJong   140

William Jackson Maxwell   144

Patricia Johanson   150

Alan Sonfist   158

Agnes Denes   166

Sherry Wiggins   172

Mel Chin   174

Viet Ngo   178

Mierle Laderman Ukeles   184

Dominique Mazeaud   194

Newton Harrison and

    Helen Mayer Harrison   198

Andy Lipkis   208

Betsy Damon   216

Vijali   220

Tom Van Sant   228

AFTERWORD :

    Joanna Macy   237

ACKNOWLEDGMENTS :

    Baile Oakes   238

ARTISTS' ACKNOWLEDGMENTS

    AND RESUMES   240

This book is dedicated

with much Love and Gratitude

to my Wife, my Parents, and my Grandfather

for the special gifts of Life they bestowed upon me.

TO MY PARTNER IN LIFE, KATHLEEN MURRAY OAKES,

for the adventurous dance she is taking with me

and for the treasures of life she has brought me through our children

TO THE MEMORY OF MY MOTHER, THE LATE PATRICIA OAKES BANNON,

for the gift of love she gave so naturally

TO MY FATHER, ROBERT BANNON,

for his support, love, and caring throughout my life

AND TO THE MEMORY OF MY GRANDFATHER, THE LATE FORREST OAKES,

who opened the world of the river to my soul ...

Foreword

All of our lives are forever linked

to the health and well-being of

the life of the Earth.

All of our actions influence

this vital relationship.

My goal with this book is

to demonstrate how

the visual language of art

can expand our dialogue

and understanding of

our vital relationship

within the living systems

of our planet home.

≈

Foreword / Baile Oakes

The purpose of this book is to present the scope of past and current public art projects that help us understand our relationship to our biosphere—Earth. Since I am a sculptor whose interest is public design, I have created a forum for other artists in this field who address our perception of our relationship to the biosphere. The book covers approaches to design that help us recognize our place within the natural laws of the planet, and discusses rituals that foster celebration of this relationship. It also features art that serves as reclamation—healing some of the damage that we have visited on natural systems. The opening of the book presents a historical perspective, explaining how art has been used to express ecological concerns throughout the ages. It serves as a brief comparative study of contemporary artists working in this field and pre-Columbian cultures who integrated art, architecture, and the sacred in their study of their relationship to the Earth and the Cosmos.

From the time of earliest recorded history, art has been used to point the way to the continued health and survival of our species. Most of these works were symbols of hope and education concerning the cycle and resources of the Earth that assured the well being of the people. Through the ages this teaching function of art has evolved through many religions and into the detachment of modernism. We presently find ourselves so removed from a perception of our place in the natural order of the world that we view humanity and technology as entities separate from the Earth and its other life forms.

The dialogue throughout this book focuses on humankind's interrelationship with Nature. Today, the environmental crisis is an unmanageable conflict between those espousing human centered values and those who emphasize the need to preserve the life supporting systems of the planet. It is not likely that this conflict will be eliminated until we understand that human-centered values include preserving the Earth and nurturing all its life forms. Unless we are able to make the connection—to draw the biosphere and its systems into our own self image—ours will be a species intent not only on self-destruction but the elimination of most other life forms.

We do not currently have the time or financial luxury of expending our energies on abstract arguments. Our visual language needs to communicate directly concerning relevant issues and incorporate into our infrastructure ever-present reminders of our vital relationship within the living systems of the Earth. This book concerns itself with projects that are crossing over traditional lines. Artists, architects, scientists, planners and other design professionals who are working together to create systems that once more inspire, educate, and offer a fresh hope that positive solutions can be found that will help us to develop a new perspective of our place in the balance of life on the planet. This shift of perspective will help us all to manifest a healthy and prosperous global environment and community.

I hope this manuscript can foster a reevaluation of the management of our financial and natural resources. Many of the projects featured herein would add greatly to the cultural wealth of our society, but have not been brought to fruition because their creators are limited by whatever funds they can slowly acquire. These projects are monumental in scale, but the resources they need are really only a drop in the bucket compared to the funds our society expends on minor public works projects. Artists need to be considered as essential to the team of any infrastructure project as planners, architects, and engineers. Our society has the ability, time, and financial resources to move into a sustainable future. However, for our effort to succeed it needs to be a complete cultural commitment to develop sustainable systems for living.

I have not followed the traditional road for introductions to a book on art—focusing on the historical perspective of this genre. Since the book is comprised of artists who demonstrate the importance of using the visual language of the arts to help us understand and establish a new paradigm by which we view the Earth as ourselves, I asked a cultural historian, a physicist, and a critic to submit essays that would set the tone for the spirit that infuses the work that follows.

I know that these projects need to be understood as one person's decision to be part of a solution for our collective health and well being if the book is truly to succeed as an educational and inspirational tool. For this reason it was important to me to have each artist tell their own story as to the intention and purpose of their work in the style of a first person narration. My hope is that the individuals reading this book will be able to identify with the artists' voice on a personal level, and view them simply as individuals like themselves. I hope that this will inspire others to look into their careers and service in life and determine what decisions they can make to help contribute to healing our biosphere. For change in our society is all a matter of the solutions that each of us contribute on a day-to-day basis to the problems that lie before us. My hope is that this project will help serve as a catalyst to release the power of growth within individuals and their community, for it will take vast numbers of people to affect the metamorphosis that we so desperately need.

In the summer of 1991, I stood before a review committee to present a visual arts plan for the redevelopment of a city's convention center. I asked the city to take this opportunity to use visual arts to inspire a fresh understanding of our interrelationship with our planet. I was unsuccessful in this presentation, but the experience proved to be the genesis and inspiration for the book before you. It is my hope that this book will reach those who control the infrastructure development in our country and convince them of the powerful role visual arts has in helping us reestablish a balance with the living systems of our planet. While we exploit resources that should be sacred, we do not take advantage of the creative resources of individuals that can help us preserve our future prosperity. Art can be used as a tool to bring us closer to our planet, to help us look at the Earth and see ourselves. It is time we empower our artistic resources, and renew our dialogue with the Earth.

BAILE OAKES, *Sculptor.*

Suzi Gablik

The Ecological Imperative

Suzi Gablik lectures widely

and writes in the areas of

cultural philosophy and criticism.

Her books include

Has Modernism Failed?,

The Reenchantment of Art,

and the forthcoming

Conversations Before the

End of Time.

She has taught at the

University of the South

in Sewanee, Tennessee,

the University of California

at Santa Barbara,

Virginia Commonwealth University

in Richmond, and was a

C.C. Garvin Endowed Professor

at the College of Arts and Sciences

at Virginia Tech.

≈

What is it about human beings in Western culture that permits us to pursue activities that threaten our very survival? What is it that is so important to us that we are apparently willing to destroy the planet—and ultimately ourselves—to get it? Why do we persist in these practices even after we realize their self-defeating futility?

When I first encountered these questions posed by deep ecologist William Keepin, in an essay in *ReVision Magazine*, they reverberated so deeply with the crisis in my own soul about what is happening to our world that I was stunned. For a considerable time now, it has seemed evident that some form of unexamined, self-destructive, psychological dynamic is functioning at the root of Western industrial civilization, whose dysfunctional ideas and beliefs are now promoting its annihilation. One of these beliefs is that human well-being depends on science, technology, and industry rather than on a harmonious and symbiotic relationship with the natural world. Another is the belief that we must maximize growth and economic development at whatever the cost, even if we devour this land and the Earth's resources as we go—a process we have been taught to identify as "progress." But the great danger now, according to deep ecologist Joanna Macy, is that we block so much feedback, both through official secrecy and through psychological denial, that we feel the crisis is too big to let in. A major part of Macy's work during the last fifteen years has been an effort to help us stop blocking feedback. She calls it "despair work." "Because of the extraordinary circumstances we are confronting now, at this juncture of history," Macy stated recently in an interview, "there's a chance for wholesale transformation. Clarity and firmness of intention can have much more effect than more stable times." I believe that among many artists today, we are beginning to see the emergence of a new clarity and firmness of intention concerning the environment that was not there before.

A world view, or paradigm, is a set of cultural beliefs about the world. These beliefs are powerful in a society since they influence the way we think, what goals we pursue, and what we value. The socially dominant paradigm is seldom stated explicitly, but it conditions us to want certain things and to respond in certain ways to what we want. Our society's view of the world is oriented towards manic production and consumption, maximum energy flow and mindless waste—at the expense of poorer countries and of the environment. Most institutions in our society, including the art world, have echoed its self-assertive and consumerist values, to a point that is now threatening the health of individuals, of society, and of the ecosystem in which we live.

Changing paradigms means breaking through this cultural trance and suspending the whole dysfunctional world view of our culture, in order that a more coherent relationship may be constructed between human civilization and the natural world. For many artists today, this is now the critical issue that must be addressed in their art. It means exploding the humanist notion of the autonomous individual as the solitary center of all meaning, and replacing it with a sense of human dependence on a stable climate, fertile soil, living rivers and forests, and a sustainable biosphere.

When people strive to create a new paradigm, they must first take time to identify and clarify what its implicit assumptions will be. For artists who are trying to change paradigms, the first step in this process is to become conscious of how much they have internalized the values and dictates of the old paradigm, based on a competitive and power-driven professionalism, combined with an art-for-art's-sake philosophy that has disenfranchised art from any social role. The remapping of the modernist paradigm, happening now throughout our entire culture, requires alterations in the framework and context in which we do our work. For many artists, this means nothing less than a total reassessment of the meaning and purpose of art. Performance artist and writer Guillermo Gomez-Pena states: "Most of the work I'm doing currently comes, I think, from the realization that we're living in a state of emergency. I feel that more than ever we must step outside the strictly art arena. It is not enough to make art." Chicago painter and photographer Othello Anderson comments similarly: "Carbon and other pollutants are emitted into the air in such massive quantities that large areas of forest landscapes are dying from the effects of acid rain. Recognizing this crisis, as an artist I can no longer consider making art that is void of moral consciousness, art that carries no responsibility, art without spiritual content, art that places form above content, or art that denies the state of the very world in which it exists." The inward focus and isolation chamber of the studio are today being challenged by the broader context of political, social, and environmental life. "We've been very alienated from our resources," states California eco-artist Newton Harrison, "but our time of grace is over. The idea that technology is able to buy us out of our problems is an illusion. We are going to have to make vast changes in our consciousness and behavioral patterns because if we don't we won't be here."

Most artists spend their time making "normal" art, in the sense of administering to the existing paradigm, and following its ideals of individualism, aesthetic freedom, and self-expression. Within this model, they do not see themselves as paradigm-makers whose ideas and activities can actually shape the culture itself. As a secular society of professionals, our only object of dedication is our specialized pursuit, and the most crucial questions affecting the future of the planet are left to experts, while the welfare of the whole is left to the workings of the market and to bureaucracy. The beliefs we have subscribed to—that the problems of art are purely aesthetic and that art will never change the world—are beliefs that have diminished our capacity as artists for constructive thought and action. Arthur C. Danto has referred to this state of affairs as "the disenfranchisement of art," for the hidden constraints of a neutral, art-for-art's-sake philosophy is that it has led to cultural powerlessness. Disembodied aesthetics relieves us of conflict and responsibility, but at a price. It doesn't train us for the larger struggles of our society, or give us experience that can be applied to larger issues. When a crisis arises that does not fall within our limited routines or interests, we are without resources.

Whether or not art has the power to change the world is not a relevant question anymore, since the world is changing already. Things are moving into a new mode because they have to; cultural awakening is being triggered by stress. The real question is how, as artists (and principal carriers of creativity in our culture), we can learn to balance our artistic preoccupations with the demands on us for greater social responsibility. It seems as if our creativity must now be evaluated in terms of world problems, and what it can offer to their solution. Our potential for social, environmental, and political action needs to be released from the feelings of inadequacy, cynicism, and despair which are blocking it, and from an aesthetic ideology that has crippled art by restricting the scope of its vision. Beneath our aesthetic theories also lie tacit assumptions about selfhood that quietly operate to sustain the status-quo. Our prevailing paradigm of selfhood—radical individualism—demands absolute independence for the artist, and has created a social order in which the self is experienced only as private and separate from others and from the world. However, as Richard Shusterman says in *Pragmatist Aesthetics*, "the premise that aesthetic creation is necessarily individualistic is a questionable romantic myth nourished by bourgeois liberalism's ideology of individualism, and one which belies art's essential communal dimension." If certain tacit assumptions about selfhood define the practice of art, then this revised self-image, from seeing ourselves as individual passive victims to being active agents of transformation in the community, is the single most important factor in changing the paradigm.

To develop a broader vision will mean evoking new images of what it means to be an artist. It will mean letting many of our cherished notions break down—letting go of our narrower vision of brisk sales, well patronized galleries, good reviews, and a large, admiring audience—in order to experience that larger transforming power, which is the truly significant and essential power of art to change things. To effect such a shift at the core of our thinking requires that we look at art in terms of purpose rather than in terms of style: to ascertain where one is, how one got there, how now to proceed, and to what end. To see ourselves as paradigm-makers, to modify the framework itself, is to become ourselves the impresarios of change, the orchestrators of culture and consciousness.

The ecological destruction happening on the planet needs no introduction here. No one these days can be unaware of the complex problems of water degradation, toxic waste, species extinction, soil and forest depletion, acid rain, and the greenhouse effect. Time is running out with respect to many of these environmental threats. Nor is it easy to deal with issues that bring deeper and deeper levels of anxiety to us all. The precondition for any human effort is a vision of success. One way to make art into a culturally useful tool might be to infiltrate images of hope—images that can empower us into the collective unconscious. To create belief in a coherent, resonant society again we need to feed a new symbolic order into the social hologram, like seed crystal that can take root. This is the primary accomplishment of the artists included in this book. Like Joanna Macy, they are committed to "despair work"—that is, to lifting the denial and repression about what is happening to our world. Symbols are evocative; they are accumulators, transformers, and conductors of psychic energies, so they have a most important and therapeutic function. Symbols set into motion unconscious psychological processes; they have an integrating value. In our present situation, reconnecting art with life and with the natural environment is a matter of absolute priority. We have the freedom to choose other courses, but for each of us at the present time, this is the biggest challenge to our creativity in the deepest sense of the term.

Suzi Gablik

Suzi Gablik, *Critic.*

Fritjof Capra

The New Vision of Reality

For physicists at the beginning of the century, the new quantum view of reality was by no means easy to accept. The exploration of the atomic and subatomic world brought them in contact with a strange and unexpected reality. In their struggle to grasp this new reality, scientists became painfully aware that their basic concepts, their language, and their whole way of thinking were inadequate to describe atomic phenomena. Their problems were not merely intellectual but amounted to an intense emotional and, one could say, even existential crisis. It took them a long time to overcome this crisis, but in the end they were rewarded with deep insights into the nature of matter and its relation to the human mind.

The dramatic changes of thinking that happened in physics at the beginning of this century have been widely discussed by physicists and philosophers for more than fifty years. They led Thomas Kuhn to the notion of a scientific paradigm, defined as "a constellation of achievements—concepts, values, techniques, etc. —shared by a scientific community and used by that community to define legitimate problems and solutions." Changes of paradigms, according to Kuhn, occur in discontinuous, revolutionary breaks called paradigm shifts.

Today, twenty-five years after Kuhn's analysis, we recognize the paradigm shift in physics as an integral part of a much larger cultural transformation. The intellectual crisis of the quantum physicists in the 1920s is mirrored today by a similar but much broader cultural crisis. The major problems of our time are all different facets of that crisis, which is essentially a crisis of perception. Like the crisis in quantum physics, it derives from an outdated worldview, inadequate for dealing with the problems of a globally interconnected world. At the same time, researchers in several scientific disciplines, various social movements, and numerous alternative organizations and networks are developing a new vision of reality that will form the basis of our future technologies, economic systems, and social institutions.

What we are seeing today is a shift of paradigms not only within science but also in the larger social arena. To analyze that cultural transformation I have generalized Kuhn's definition of a scientific paradigm to that of a social paradigm, which I define as "a constellation of concepts, values, perceptions, and practices shared by a community, which forms a particular vision of reality that is the basis of the way the community organizes itself."

The paradigm that is now receding has dominated our culture for several hundred years. During that time it has shaped our modern Western society and has significantly influenced the rest of the world. This paradigm consists of a number of ideas and values: the view of the Universe as a mechanical system composed of elementary building blocks; the view of the human body as a machine; the view of life in society as a competitive struggle for existence; the belief in unlimited material progress to be achieved through economic and technological growth; and—last, not least—the belief that a society in which the female is everywhere subsumed under the male is one that follows a basic law of Nature. During recent decades all of these assumptions have been found severely limited and in need of radical revision. And indeed, such a revision is now occurring.

The new paradigm may be called a holistic world view—seeing the world as an integrated whole rather than a dissociated collection of parts. It may also be called an ecological view, if the term "ecological" is used in a much broader and deeper sense than usual. Deep ecological awareness recognizes the fundamental

Fritjof Capra is founder and president of the Elmwood Institute, an educational institution dedicated to fostering ecological literacy. Ecological literacy, as defined by the Elmwood Institute, consists of three components: systems thinking, knowledge of the principles of ecology, and the practice of ecological values.

During 1993, Elmwood is concentrating on two core programs: Ecoliteracy—design of an ecologically oriented Kindergarten-12th grade curriculum and development of collaborative learning communities; and EcoManagement—promotion of ecologically conscious management and sustainable business through publications, lectures, and seminars.

His books include The Tao of Physics, Turning Point, *and* Belonging to the Universe.

≈

interdependence of all phenomena and the fact that, as individuals and societies, we are all embedded in (and ultimately dependent on) the cyclical processes of Nature.

The new paradigm may also be called a systemic view, or systems view, of the world. In my way of using these terms, "ecological" and "systemic" are synonymous, "systemic" being merely the more technical, scientific term. "Holistic," however, is a slightly different concept and somewhat less appropriate to describe the new paradigm.

There are several differences between "holistic" and "ecological" (or "systemic"). A holistic view of say a bicycle means to see the bicycle as a whole, to understand the interdependence of its parts, etc. An ecological view of the bicycle includes all that and adds to it the perception of how the bicycle is embedded in its natural and social environment—where the raw materials that went into it came from, how it was manufactured, how its use affects the natural environment and the community by which it is used, etc. This distinction between "holistic" and "ecological" is even more important when we talk about living systems, for which the connections with the environment are much more vital.

Finally, the term "holistic" may seem to suggest that the new paradigm deals only with the whole and no longer with the parts. This is, of course, incorrect. Although there is a clear shift of emphasis from the parts to the whole, the parts are still important. For that reason "systemic" or "ecological" seems to be a better term for the new paradigm.

The sense in which I use the term "ecological" is associated with a specific philosophical school and, moreover, with a global grassroots movement known as "deep ecology," which is rapidly gaining prominence. This philosophical school was founded by the Norwegian philosopher Arne Naess in the early seventies with his distinction between "shallow" and "deep" ecology. The distinction is now widely accepted as a useful terminology for referring to a major division within contemporary environmental thought.

Shallow ecology is anthropocentric. It views humans as above, or outside of Nature, as the source of all value, and ascribes only instrumental, or use value to Nature. Deep ecology does not separate humans from the natural environment, nor does it separate anything else from it. It does not see the world as a collection of isolated objects, but rather as a network of phenomena that are fundamentally interconnected and interdependent. Deep ecology recognizes the intrinsic values of all living beings, and views humans as just one particular strand in the web of life.

Ultimately, deep ecological awareness is spiritual, or religious, awareness. When the concept of the human spirit is understood as the mode of consciousness in which the individual feels connected to the Cosmos as a whole, it becomes clear that ecological awareness is spiritual in its deepest essence. It is therefore not surprising that the emerging new vision of reality, based on deep ecological awareness, is consistent with the so-called "perennial philosophy" of spiritual traditions—whether we talk about the spirituality of Christian mystics, that of Buddhists, or the philosophy and cosmology underlying the Native American traditions.

The connections between the new paradigm in science and the basic ideas in spiritual traditions are studied in transpersonal psychology. This school of psychology originated in California in the 1960s and is concerned, directly or indirectly, with the recognition, understanding, and realization of nonordinary, mystical, or "transpersonal" states of consciousness.

The link of these transpersonal experiences with the awareness of deep ecology has become more and more apparent over the last few years. In fact, a new book by one of the leading deep ecologists, Warwick Fox, is titled *Toward a Transpersonal Ecology*.

Besides deep ecology, there are two other important schools of ecology: social ecology and feminist ecology (or ecofeminism). In recent years there has been a lively debate in philosophical journals and the alternative media about the relative merits of deep ecology, social ecology, and ecofeminism.

I would like briefly to characterize each of these three schools of thought and suggest a framework for their integration into a coherent ecological vision.

Deep ecological awareness seems to provide the ideal philosophical and spiritual basis for an ecological lifestyle and for environmental activism. However, it does not tell us much about the cultural characteristics and patterns of social organization that have brought about the current ecological crisis. This is the focus of social ecology.

The common ground of the various schools of social ecology is the recognition that the fundamentally antiecological nature of many of our social and economic structures and their technologies is rooted in what Riane Eisler in *The Chalice and the Blade* has called the "dominator system" of social organization. Patriarchy, imperialism, capitalism, and racism are examples of social domination that are exploitive and antiecological. Among the different schools of social ecology there are various Marxist and anarchist groups who use the respective conceptual frameworks to analyze different patterns of social domination.

Ecofeminism could be viewed as a special school of social ecology, since it, too, addresses the basic dynamics of social domination within the context of patriarchy. However, its cultural analysis of the many facets of patriarchy and of the links between ecofeminism and ecology go far beyond the framework of social ecology.

Ecofeminists see the patriarchal domination of women by men as the prototype of all domination and exploitation and of its hierarchical, militaristic, capitalist, and industrialist forms. They point out that the exploitation of Nature, in particular, has gone hand in hand with that of women who have been identified with Nature throughout the ages. This ancient association of woman and Nature interlinks women's history and the history of the environment, and is the source of a natural kinship between feminism and ecology. Accordingly, ecofeminists see female experiential knowledge as a major source for an ecological vision of reality.

So far, I have emphasized perceptions and thinking. If that were the whole problem, the paradigm shift would be much easier. There are enough brilliant thinkers among the proponents of the new paradigm who could convince our political and corporate leaders of the merits of systemic thinking. But that's only part of the story. The shift of paradigms requires not only an expansion of our perceptions and ways of thinking, but also of our values. And here it is interesting to note a striking connection between these changes in ways of thinking and of values. Both of them may be seen as shifts from self-assertion to integration. These two tendencies—the self-assertive and the integrative—are both essential aspects of all living systems. Neither of them is intrinsically good or bad. What is good, or healthy, is a dynamic balance. What is bad, or unhealthy, is imbalance—overemphasis of one tendency and neglect of the other. In the old paradigm, we have been overemphasizing the self-assertive values and ways of thinking and have neglected their integrative counterparts. So what I'm suggesting is not to replace one mode by the other, but rather to establish a better balance between the two.

With that in mind, let's look at the various manifestations of the shift from self-assertion to integration. As far as thinking is concerned, we are talking about a shift from the rational to the intuitive, from analysis to synthesis, from reductionism to holism, from linear to nonlinear thinking.

As far as values are concerned, we are observing a corresponding shift from competition to cooperation, from expansion to conservation, from quantity to quality, from domination to partnership.

FRITJOF CAPRA, *Physicist.*
REPRINTED WITH PERMISSION FROM *Elmwood Quaterly. Fall, 1992*

Thomas Berry

The Bush

Thomas Berry is a historian

of cultures with special concern

for the foundation of cultures

and their relations with

the natural world.

He has studied the languages and

cultures of India and China

and has participated in the

educational program of the

T'Boli tribes in Mindanao

in the Phillipines.

He is the author of

The Dream of the Earth *and*

the Universe Story,

and served as president of the

American Teilhard Association

for the Human Future.

Presently he is director of

Riverdale Center, a research center

in New York devoted to the

study of a viable mode of

human presence upon the Earth.

≈

I was a young person then, some twelve years old. My family was moving from a more settled part of a southern town out to the edge of town where the new house was still being built. This house, not yet finished, was situated on a slight incline. Down below was a small creek, and across the creek was a meadow. It was an early afternoon in May when I first looked down over the scene and saw the meadow. The field was covered with lilies rising above the thick grass. A magic moment, this experience gave to my life something, I know not what, that seems to explain my life at a more profound level than almost any other experience I can remember.

It was not only the lilies. It was the singing of the crickets and the woodlands in the distance and the clouds in a clear sky. It was not something conscious that happened just then. I went on about my life as any young person might do. Perhaps it was not simply this moment that made such a deep impression upon me. Perhaps it was a sensitivity that was developed throughout my childhood. Yet as the years pass, this moment returns to me. Whenever I think about my basic life attitude, the causes that I have given my efforts to, and the whole trend of my mind, I seem to come back to this moment and the impact it has had on my feeling for what is real and worthwhile in life.

The experience, it seems, has become normative for me throughout the entire range of my thinking. Whatever preserves and enhances the meadow is good, what is opposed to the meadow or negates it is not good. My life orientation is that simple. It is also that pervasive. It applies in economics and political orientation as well as in education, religion, and everything else in life. What is good in economics is what keeps this meadow intact. What is bad in economics is what diminishes the capacity of this meadow to renew itself each spring and provide a setting in which crickets can sing and birds can feed. So in jurisprudence, law, and political affairs, what is good is what recognizes the rights of this meadow and the creek and the woodlands beyond to exist and flourish in their ever-renewing seasonal transformation.

Religion too, it seems to me, finds its origin here in the deep mystery of this setting. The more a person thinks of the infinite number of interrelated activities that take place here, the more mysterious it all becomes. The more meaning a person finds in the May-time blooming of the lilies; the more awestruck a person might be in simply looking out over this little patch of meadow land. It had none of the majesty of the Appalachian or the western mountains, none of the immensity or the power of the oceans, nor even the harsh magnificence of desert country; yet in this little meadow the deep mystery of existence is manifested in a manner as profound and as impressive as any other place that I have known in these past many years.

It seems to me we all had such experiences before we entered into an industrial way of life. The Universe, as manifestation of some ultimate mystery, was recognized as the ultimate referent in any human understanding of the magnificent yet fearsome world about us. Every being achieved its full identity by its alignment with the Universe itself. With the indigenous peoples of the North American continent, every formal activity was first situated in relation to the six directions of the Universe: the four cardinal directions combined with the heavens above and the Earth below. Only thus could any human activity be fully validated.

The Universe was the world of meaning in these earlier times, the basic referent in social order, in economic survival, in the healing of illness. It was the deep source of poetry and art and music. The drum made audible the heartbeat of the Universe itself, and this established the rhythm of dance whereby humans entered into the very movement of the natural world. The numinous dimension of the

Universe impressed itself upon the mind through the vastness of the heavens and the power reveled in the thunder and lightning, as well as through the springtime renewal of life after the desolation of winter. Then too, the general helplessness of the human before all the threats to survival revealed the intimate dependence of the human on the integral functioning of things. That the human had such intimate rapport with the surrounding Universe was possible only because the Universe itself had a prior intimate rapport with the human.

This experience we observe even now in the indigenous peoples of the world. They live in a Universe, in a cosmological order, whereas we, the peoples of the industrial world, no longer live in a Universe. We live in a political world, a nation, a business world, an economic order, a cultural tradition. Even more significant in its consequences is the fact that we live in cities, in a world of concrete and steel, of wheels and wires, a world of business, of work. We no longer see the stars at night or the planets or the Moon. Even in the day we do not experience the Sun in any immediate or meaningful manner. We live in a world of highways, parking lots, shopping centers, and malls. We read books written with a strangely contrived alphabet. We no longer read the book of the Universe.

Nor do we coordinate our world of human meaning with the meaning of the Cosmos. We have disengaged from that profound interaction with the natural world that is inherent in our very nature. Our children do not learn how to read the Great Book of Nature, or how to interact creatively with the seasonal transformations of the planet. We no longer coordinate our human celebration with the great liturgy of the heavens.

We have indeed become strange beings, so completely are we at odds with the planet that brought us into being. We dedicate enormous talent and knowledge and research to developing a human order disengaged from and even predatory on the very sources whence we came and upon which we depend at every moment of our existence. We initiate our children into an economic order based on exploitation of the natural life systems of the planet. To achieve this, we must first make them autistic in their relation with the natural world about them. This occurs quite easily since we have ourselves become autistic toward the natural world and do not realize just what we are doing. Yet if we observe our children closely in their early years, and see how they are instinctively attracted to the experiences of the living forms around them, we will see how disoriented they become in the mechanistic and even toxic environment that we provide for them.

Recovering an integral relation with the Universe, the planet Earth, and the North American continent, needs to be a primary concern for the peoples of this continent. While a new alignment of our government and institutions and professions with the continent itself in its deep structure and functioning cannot be achieved immediately, a beginning can be made throughout the educational programs. Especially in the earlier grades of elementary school, new developments are possible. Such was the thought of Maria Montessori in the third decade of this century.

In speaking about the education of the six-year-old child, she notes in her book, *To Educate the Human Potential*, that only when the child is able to identify its own center with the center of the Universe does education really begin. For the Universe, she says, "is an imposing reality . . . an answer to all questions. We shall walk together on this path of life, for all things are part of the Universe, and are connected with each other to form one whole unity." This it is what enables "the mind of the child to become centered, to stop wandering in an aimless quest for knowledge." In this manner the child learns how all things are related and how the relationship of things to each other is so close that "No matter what we touch, an atom, or a cell, we cannot explain it without knowledge of the wide Universe."

The difficulty is that with the rise of the modern sciences we began to think of the Universe as a collection of objects rather than a communion of subjects. We frequently discuss the loss of the interior spiritual world of the human with the rise of the modern mechanistic sciences. In reality, the more significant thing is that what we lost was the Universe itself. We achieved extensive control over the mechanistic and even the biological functioning of the natural world, but this control was itself deadly in its consequences. We have not only controlled the planet in much of its basic functioning, we have, to an extensive degree, extinguished the life systems themselves. We have silenced so many of those wonderful voices of the Universe that spoke to us of the grand mysteries of existence.

We no longer hear the voices of the rivers or the mountains, or the voices of the sea. The trees and meadows are no longer intimate modes of spirit presence. Everything about us has become an "it" rather than a "thou." We continue to make music and write poetry and paint and sculpt and design, but this generally becomes an aesthetic expression simply of the human, and in time loses the intimacy and radiance and the splendor of the Universe itself. We had, in the accepted Universe of these times, little capacity for participating in the mysteries that were celebrated in the earlier literary, artistic, and religious modes of expression. For we could not live in the Universe in which these were written. We could only look on, as it were.

Yet the Universe is so bound into the aesthetic experience, into poetry, music, art, and dance, that we cannot entirely avoid the implicit dimensions of the natural world, even when we think of the art as "representational" or "impressionist" or "expressionist" or as "personal statement." However we think of our art or literature, its power is there in the mystery communicated most directly by the meadow or the mountains or the sea or by the stars in the night.

Of special significance is our capacity for celebration, which inevitably brings us into the rituals that provide the coordination of human affairs with the great liturgy of the Universe. Our national holidays, political events, heroic human deeds; these are all quite worthy of celebration but ultimately, unless they are associated with some higher level of meaning, they tend toward the affected, the emotional, and the ephemeral. In the political and legal orders we have never been able to give up invocation of the more sublime dimensions of the Universe to witness the truth of what we say. This we observe especially in court trials, in inaugural ceremonies, and in the assumption of public office at whatever level. We still have an instinctive awe and reverence, and even a certain fear, of the larger world that always lies outside the range of our human controls.

In this regard we might learn wisdom from the instructions given by a senior bushman of Africa to a young boy concerning his conduct in relation to the natural world, an instruction recorded by Laurens Van Der Post: "Remember, Little Cousin, that no matter how awful or insignificant, how ugly or beautiful it might look to you, everything in the bush has its own right to be there. No one can challenge this right unless compelled by some necessity of life itself. Everything has its own dignity, however absurd it might seem to you, and we are all bound to recognize and respect it as we wish our own to be recognized and respected. Life in the bush is necessity, and it understands all forms of necessity. It will always forgive what is imposed upon it out of necessity, but it will never understand and accept anything less than necessity. And remember that, everywhere, it has its own watchers to see whether the law of necessity is being observed. You may often think that deep in the darkness and the density of the bush you are alone and unobserved, but that, Little Cousin, would be an illusion of the most dangerous kind. One is never alone in the bush, one is never unobserved."

This final phrase is a sobering thought to a generation that has so profoundly subverted the inner constitution of the planet. We have tried to make everything referent to the human as the ultimate referent for meaning and value, but this has led only to catastrophe for ourselves as well as for a multitude of other beings. We must hope that we finally begin to recognize that the Universe itself is, in the phenomenal order, the only self-referent mode of being. All other modes of being in their existence and in their functioning are universe-referent. This has been recognized through the centuries in the religious rituals of the various traditions.

From Paleolithic times humans have coordinated their ritual celebrations with the various transformation moments of the natural world. Ultimately the Universe throughout its vast extent in space and its transformations in time was seen as a single multiform celebratory expression. No other explanation is possible for the world that we see around us. The birds fly and sing and perform their mating rituals. The flowers blossom. The rains nourish every living being. Each of the events in the natural world is a poem, a painting, a drama, a celebration.

Dawn and sunset are the mystical moments of the diurnal cycle, the moments when the numinous dimension of the Universe reveals itself with special intimacy. Individually and in their relations with each other, these are all pure expressions of the ecstasy of existence. Moments when the high meaning of existence is experienced. Whether in the gatherings of indigenous peoples in their tribal setting or in the more elaborate temples and cathedrals and spiritual centers throughout the Earth, these moments are celebrated with special observances. So too in the yearly cycle, the springtime is celebrated as the time for renewal of the human in its proper alignment with the universal order of things.

The proposal has been made by Christopher Norden that no effective restoration of a viable mode of human presence on the planet will take place until such ritual rapport of the human with the Earth community and the entire functioning of the Universe is reestablished on an extensive scale. Until this is done, the alienation of the human will continue, despite the heroic efforts being made toward a more benign mode of human activity in relation to the Earth. He finds the source of his confidence that the present is not a time for desperation but for hopeful activity in the writings of indigenous peoples such as James Welch, N. Scott Momaday, Leslie Silko, and David Seals, all authors with profound understanding of the ritual rapport of humans with the larger order of the Universe.

In alliance with such authors as these, I would give a certain emphasis here to the need to understand the Universe primarily as celebration. The human I generally identify as that being in whom the Universe celebrates itself and its numinous origins in a special mode of conscious self-awareness. The fact that spontaneous forms of community ritual, such as the All Species Festivals inaugurated by John Seed, have already been developed gives promise for a future with the understanding, the power, the aesthetic grandeur, and the emotional fulfillment needed to heal the damage that has already been wrought upon the planet.

As a final note I would suggest that the task before us is one of the entire planet and all its component members. While the damage done is immediately the singular work of the human, the healing cannot be the work simply of the human, any more than the illness of some one organ of the body can be healed simply through the efforts of that one organ. Every member of the body must bring the healing. So now the entire Universe is involved in the healing of the damaged Earth, especially, of course, the forces of the Earth with the assistance of the light and warmth of the Sun. As the Earth is in a sense a magic planet in the exquisite presence of its infinitely diverse members to each other, so this movement into the future must in some manner be brought about in ways that are ineffable to the human mind. We might think of a viable future for the planet less as the result of some scientific insight, or as dependent on some socio-economic arrangement, than as creating a symphony, or as renewed participation in the vast cosmic liturgy.

THOMAS BERRY, *Cultural Historian.*

Ancient and Contemporary Art

Overlooking the Urubamba River
Machu Picchu, Peru

Before the advent of electricity, it was common knowledge that the Moon rose approximately an hour later each evening and that the full Moon rose at sunset. Today few people in developed countries are aware of this simple phenomenon. We understand that some of the ways that we produce electricity cause pollution of the air, ground, and water; but few of us realize that light pollution is robbing us of our connection to our heritage, myths, and spirit.

Ancient peoples based their creation myths on celestial phenomena, many contemporary religions speak of "God who dwells in the heavens," and scientists today search the Cosmos with ever more powerful telescopes seeking information about the origin of the Universe. However, ambient light has severed the connection to the Universe for people in cities around the world. As we become isolated from the rest of the Universe, we lose our roots, a basis of the meaning of our lives and a connection to each other.

Our ancestors found meaning in observing the order of the movement of the Sun, Moon, and stars. The regularity of their presence and motion conveyed a sense of immortality. These celestial entities were named as gods and their presence in the sky were interpreted as eyes that could see and know all of the activities of the mortals below. There was a reverence for these entities and our ancestors' religions were based upon the understanding of the structure and meaning of the Earth and its relationship to the Cosmos.

In our technological age, we search for the meaning of our existence amidst the technological marvels that comprise the structure of our culture. For the most part we have forgotten the foundation upon which these technological marvels rest and without which technology and we could not exist. This foundation consists of the same phenomena that our ancestors revered. The life-sustaining relationship between the Earth, Sun, Moon, and stars.

Past cultures integrated light and shadow events into the everyday structures that sustained their communities and lives to mark the consistency of the cosmic order. These cultures practiced an art form that traces its roots at least six thousand years back. It is one we can learn a lesson from. Many contemporary artists have begun to create public works that once again bring a sense of cosmic order into our lives. The following section touches on a few examples of ancient art as well as some contemporary work inspired by the same concerns.

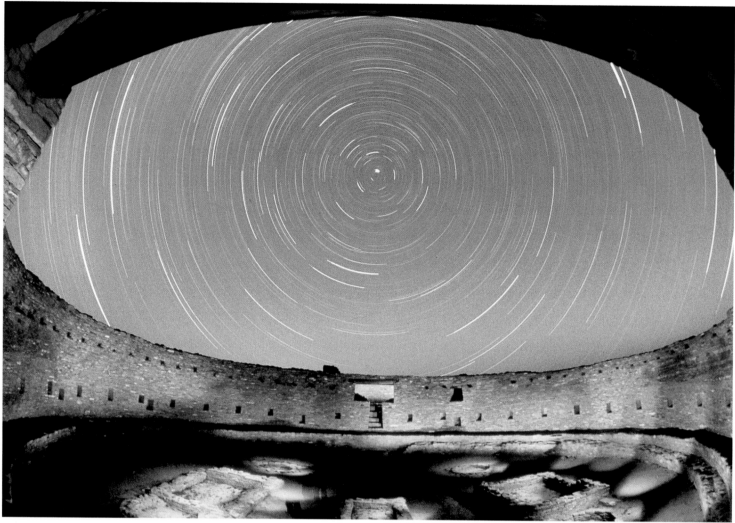

Casa Rinconada/Star Axis

Chaco Canyon rests in the San Juan basin of northwestern New Mexico. Through it cuts a wash whose stream was the agricultural lifeline of the Anasazi culture that flourished there for about two hundred years. Anasazi is a Navajo word meaning "Old Ones." However, the Hopi are the descendants of these early people, and they prefer the name Hisatsinom when referring to their ancestors. For reasons unknown, the Hitsatsinom left Chaco within one generation.

The Hisatsinom performed their ceremonies in subterranean chambers known as kivas. For them—and for their Pueblo Indian descendants—kiva walls marked the limits of sacred space. The kiva's layout reflects the cosmology of this culture. The kiva's connections with the Underworld associate it with the idea of creation and birth. As an architectural space, the kiva parallels the idea of the womb, the place from which we are born or emerge into the world.

With the creation myth designed into its architecture, the kiva might be expected to incorporate alignments that reflect cosmic order. The main features of the kiva attest to the Hisatsinom concern to keep things in balance. They viewed the world as being made up of four quadrants that were defined by the intersection and relationship of the cardinal directions. The four large posts that held up the roof of the kiva represented these four quadrants and the entry door of the kiva was precisely aligned to celestial north. Thus one entered from the direction of the spirits and the dead. Upon entering and especially upon leaving the kiva, people were reminded of their relationship to the eternal star—the perceptual center of the cosmos. The plan of the kiva was tied to the order of space and the direction of time.

Casa Rinconada
Entry is aligned to the North Star.
Highlighted areas of the floor
locate the posts that supported the roof.
Chaco Canyon, New Mexico
1000–1200 A.D.

Photo: Mark Nohl courtesy New Mexico Magazine

New Mexico is also the home of a contemporary work of art currently under construction by the artist, Charles Ross. Ross's concern is to build a monument that will place us into a physical relationship with the order of the Cosmos. Over the years his work has led him to the precession of the North Star. Polaris has not always been the pole star. As the Earth revolves on its axis, it wobbles just as a top at play. However, unlike a top, it takes 26,000 years for the Earth to complete each of these cycles which point its axis into different areas of the sky.

The major component of Ross's *Star Axis* will be a stainless steel tunnel, large enough to enclose a stairway that will lead visitors eleven stories up to the top of the mesa. From the bottom of this tunnel, the minute orbit of Polaris will appear to entirely fill the opening at the other end. The visitors' perception of the opening will appear to enlarge as they progress up the stairs. There will be a past and future date engraved into each of these steps indicating when Polaris filled this perceived opening. Thus a visitor can stand on a step and view the orbit of Polaris as it appeared when people first came to this continent or how its orbit will appear hundreds or thousands of years into the future.

Star Axis will serve as a doorway to a broader understanding of our place in the Universe.

Machu Picchu / Gestation

Machu Picchu offers an ideal location for observing the relationship between architecture and the study of the Cosmos by an ancient civilization. Most of its precise stone work architecture is still intact because it was never discovered by Spanish conquistadors and was abandoned sometime after the conquest for unknown reasons. It is nestled in the mountains overlooking the Urubamba River and is believed to have been built in the fifteenth century as the estate of the Inca ruler Pachacuti. In this sense, it was a planned community, incorporating everything that the ruler needed to oversee his empire. A principle concern would have been a temple—facilitating contact with the Sun god, one of the principal deities of the Inca.

Dave Dearborn has researched extensively in Machu Picchu in order to determine whether any of the architecture could have been used for these purposes. The following information has been provided by his research, writings, and photography.

Torreon
Overview showing stone
and Winter Solstice sunrise window
Below:
Stone pegs on exterior of
Winter Solstice facing window
Machu Picchu, Peru
1500–1600

A prominent building facing the eastern horizon is the Torreon. One of its dominant features is a curved wall that comprises the east and south wall of the building. The interior of the building is dominated by a large stone that is carved from the bedrock upon which the building rests. The stone is carved flat and smooth with the exception of a small plateau in its southwest quadrant whose cut face forms a precise straight edge that is perpendicularly aligned with a window in the eastern wall of the building.

In the fifteenth century, the Pleiades would have been seen through this window during the time of the Winter Solstice. Just preceding the Winter Solstice, this constellation would have appeared to be rising over the mountains a little before sunrise, and could have been regarded as the herald of the approaching rebirth of the Sun. Each day as the solstice approached, the constellation would have risen a little bit earlier and would have been higher in the sky at sunrise. This assumption is reinforced by the high regard that modern Andean cultures have for the role of the Pleiades as a herald of the coming solstice.

This window also frames the rising Sun of the Winter Solstice. The exterior wall that frames this solstice facing window has four carved stone pegs which protrude from the four corners of the window. These pegs are flat on top and rounded on the bottom and Dearborn has argued that they could have easily supported a shadow-casting device which could have precisely predicted the day of the coming solstice.

A frame could be fashioned to support a plumb line in the window opening. In the days before the solstice, the shadow cast by this line would be a few degrees off parallel with the face of the plateau in the stone. Each day this angle would decrease until it was exactly parallel with this stone formation on the day of the Winter Solstice. The movement of this line could be measured and a priest could predict from its movement the exact day of the solstice. The valley in which the building is located is often shrouded in fog, so being able to predict the solstice would have been very important.

Torreon

Interior
Shadows cast by plumb line and horizontal
line during solstice season sunrise
demonstrating alignment
and measurement for predicting
the day of the Winter Solstice

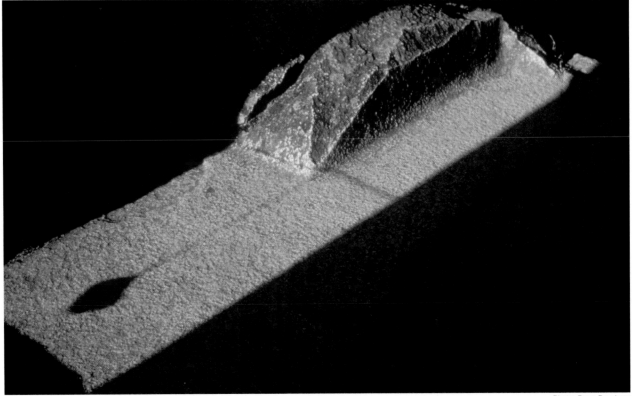

Photo: Dave Dearborn

**Torreon
Pachacuti Inca
Sunrise Winter Solstice
June**
Machu Picchu, Peru
1500–1600

One way of measuring this angle and dating the Inca calendar would have been to stretch a taught string across the middle part of the window and to measure the daily movement of the shadow cast by the plumb line as it moves across the shadow cast by this horizontal string. These shadows would interact with one another from approximately May 12th until August 1st. These times of year were important to the ancient Inca. The days around May 12th marked the beginning of their year. Around August 1st was the day when the Earth opened, became fertile, and the planting of the crops began. Thus the stone could have been used by the priests to bring order and understanding to this important time of the year.

This simple building served as a foundation upon which the Inca based their calendar and therefore all important events that brought order, balance, and meaning into their lives.

In our culture, the solstice bears the same significance as it did for the Inca, yet the event today goes unnoticed for the most part. The day that marks the rebirth of the life giving power of the Sun has been appropriated by different religions and used to mark the special events that are part of the foundation of their respective belief systems. However, all the various religious events make a singular reference to the coming of the light.

Gestation
Baile Oakes
Sunset Winter Solstice
December

Santa Monica, California
1990

Gestation in Santa Monica, California, like the Torreon, marks the rebirth of the Sun. It too is designed as a sanctuary. But unlike the Torreon, which was in all probability reserved for the nobility or the priesthood, *Gestation* is a public seating area where all are invited to take a rest and enjoy the view of the life giving elements of the water, sunlight, and earth. It is part of the community fabric, heralding the approach of the Winter Solstice and marking the day of the event.

Gestation is located on the edge of the continent and its central opening frames the elements of water, sunlight, earth, and air—the dynamic relationships that foster creation, regeneration, and birth. The form of the sculpture grows from this circular central opening into a structure that allows visitors to enter the form and rest within its quiet embrace.

From the perspective of looking southwest toward the horizon line of the ocean and sky, the central element of the sculpture appears to close, forming a thin vertical aperture. When the Sun appears in the top of this aperture, it announces the beginning of the solstice season. Each day the Sun will appear lower in this aperture until the day of the Winter Solstice. On this day the Sun sets exactly in the middle of this opening, marking the celebration of the rebirth of the life of the Sun—the conception of the coming birth of Spring.

Photo: E. C. Krupp, Griffith Observatory

Photo: E. C. Krupp, Griffith Observatory

Burro Flats/Dark Star Park

Places where rock art or architecture participate in an important celestial event were, for our ancestors, sacred. . . Naturally, we associate the sacred with religion, but among traditional peoples a sense of the sacred is really a recognition of the world's structure. This cosmic order induces reverence and awe because it seems to be what makes existence and life possible.

—E. C. KRUPP, *Echoes of the Ancient Skies*

E. C. Krupp, Director of the Griffith Observatory in Los Angeles, has studied light and shadow effects around the world. The following account of Chumash and the previous account of Hitsatsinom traditions has been researched and, in some places, condensed from his writings.

Traditional peoples relied on the sky to inform them of the cyclical time that governed their growing and hunting seasons and therefore their very lives. They needed displays to commemorate the passage of time and one of these symbolic displays can be found in southern California in the Santa Susana Mountains, north of Los Angeles—the traditional land of the Chumash people. The Chumash were hunter-gatherers but had an advanced social order and understanding of celestial phenomena. Their religious life was organized by the 'antap, an important cult whose officers comprised an elite component of Chumash society.

Among the 'antap were astronomer-priests, astrologers of a sort, each known as 'alchuklash, who were responsible for maintaining the calendar and determining the proper times for various ceremonies. The Chumash year started at the Winter Solstice, and the Summer Solstice marked the year's halfway point. They saw the Summer Solstice as a time when the year and things were divided in half.

Photo: Nancy Holt

Dark Star Park
Nancy Holt

Shadow alignment of poles and spheres
with a pattern set into the ground
9:32 A.M., August 1st
Founding date of the city of
Rosslyn, Maryland
1984

The 'alchuklash conducted elaborate ceremonies to mark the solstices, and sought out light-and-shadow events in naturally occurring rock formations where the cycle of Nature and the divine were revealed. One of these sites can be found at Burro Flats in the Simi Valley just on the other side of the ridge from where Rockwell International tested the rocket engines that sent man to the moon.

There, at sunrise on the Summer Solstice, a horizontal rock slab casts its shadow onto a large rock set into the ground. The shaman has elaborated on this naturally occurring light-and-shadow event by carving mortars into the bedrock in a pattern that resembles a bear paw, and a line of cupules into the vertical rock slab. These cupules are in line with the rising Sun of the solstice and the tip of the slab's shadow rest in the mortar at the center, while it bisects one of the large mortar receptacles in the bear paw pattern. This ritual container is divided in half by sunlight and shadow during the Summer Solstice season.

This private shamanic event can be considered analogous to the 'alchuklash's public ceremony in which a ritual basket is brought out and filled by offerings to the Sun.

A contemporary light-and-shadow effect can be found in *Dark Star Park* in Rosslyn, Maryland. Artist Nancy Holt incorporated a shadow alignment into her design of the park. The shadows cast by a grouping of spheres and poles align with asphalt patterns on the ground at approximately 9:32 A.M. on August 1st of each year, the date that William Henry Ross acquired the land that become Rossyln. Holt's design merges historical time with the cyclical time of the Sun. Her simple gesture aligns the city and those experiencing the park with the dance of the cosmos.

Jai Singh's Observatories / James Turrell's Autonomous Spaces

In 1719 Maharaja Jai Singh and the Mogul Emperor of India, Mohammad Shah, witnessed an argument among the court's counselors concerning whether the planetary positions favored an imminent expedition by the emperor. The next day, Jai Singh informed Mohammad Shah that he had decided to take it upon himself to construct an accurate naked-eye observatory in order to educate the people and put to rest any future debates that were based on faulty tables and calculations.

By 1724 A.D., Jai Singh had completed India's first large scale astronomical observatory in Delhi. The beauty of these instruments is that they enabled both amateurs and professionals to make accurate astronomical observations. Jai Singh also used these instruments to reform the imperial calendar and create accurate astronomical tables.

The emperor richly rewarded Jai Singh for his work by granting him two provinces to govern. Jai Singh used the opportunities afforded by his new position to build four other observatories in Mathura, Varanasi, Ujjain, and Jaipur. His work became one of the greatest scientific building accomplishments of the century and astronomers from around the world came to witness its marvels.

The manifestation of Jai Singh's instruments go far beyond the pure function of the work. Jai Singh was able to create sculptures with his architectural statements. He was sensitive towards the inherent geometrical balance that arises from earthing the movement of the Cosmos in form.

His Giant Equatorial Sundial, the Brihat Samrat Yantra, in Jaipur can exist as pure sculpture. However, it is also the most precise sundial in the world. The base of its right-angled triangle is 144 feet long, and the hypotenuse rises at an angle

Brihat Samrat Yantra
Giant Equatorial Sundial
Jai Singh
Jaipur
1730

Mishra Yantra
Composite Instrument
Jai Singh
Delhi
1724

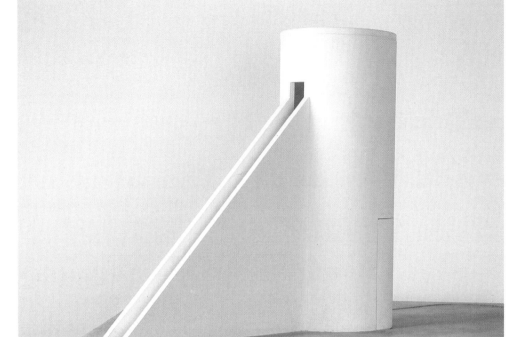

Straight Up
James Turrell

Model for Skyspace, camera obscura,
and instrument that marks solar noon
on the Winter Solstice
1989

that is the same degree as the latitude of Jaipur—27 degrees. The triangle is flanked by two quadrants, each fifty feet in radius, which are graduated in hours, minutes, and seconds. The shadow of the hypotenuse serves as the gnomon, and travels about thirteen feet in one hour along the quadrants. The shadow's movement is further divided into 2.4 inches each minute, which is further subdivided by thirty fractions, each standing for an ultimate accuracy of two seconds.

Upon entering the observatory in Delhi, the visitor comes across a unique heart shaped yantra, the Composite Instrument, Mishra Yantra. This astronomical device contains five different instruments and is a beautiful example of form following function. Its five instruments are as follows: the Meridian Wall Instrument, Dakshinovritti Bhitti Yantra (which indicates zenith distance, altitude, meridian pass time, and rising and setting time of stars and planets); Small Equatorial Sun Dial, Laghu Samrat Yantra; the Cancer Zodiac Instrument, Kark Rashivalaya; the Amplitude Instrument, Agra Yantra; and the Stable Fixed Instrument, Niyat Chakra Yantra (which comprises the center of this instrument and can be used to calculate midday at four other observatories around the world).

Jai Singh's instruments use the beauty of pure geometrical design to appreciate and measure the movement of the heavens. James Turrell's work deals with the actual perception of the light filling a space in such a way as the light feels to be tangibly present. The ceiling of *Straight Up* is a *Skyspace* open to the sky. The closure of the space helps to extend our perception to the infinite space beyond. The building is also designed as a camera obscura. There is a small hole in the floor below the *Skyspace* that has a proportional relationship with a lower chamber of the space. This relationship projects images of the clouds and, during the equinox season when the Sun is at solar noon, an image of the Sun onto the sand covered ground floor of the tower. The stairway that serves as an entry into the upper *Skyspace* is also designed to align with the Sun at solar noon on the Winter Solstice. The noon solstice Sun casts its light through the *Skyspace* and doorway, down the stairs and onto the bottom plate at the entry to the building.

Both Jai Singh's and James Turrell's spaces are formed by our perception, and extend our sensing into areas where our eyes are not adequate. They help us obtain a sense of wonder from normally unimpressive events and heighten our awareness of the mysteries of the light that falls upon the Earth.

Jody Pinto

Much of the inspiration for my work has come from my background: my Irish grandfather who was a glass-blower, my Italian grandmother's garden, my story-telling parents, and weaving in, around, above, and below, the exciting, mysterious absurdities of the Old and New Testaments, learned in a frog green uniform at a French Catholic school.

My work is a synthesis of systems and ecologies, an exploration of differences and similarities: the glass-blowing furnace of my grandfather and my grandmother's garden.

In the late sixties and early seventies, I made work about systems that I perceived as ecologies—the relationships between body, land, and language. Given the political atmosphere of the time, I often represented these systems/ecologies as wounded, yet capable of healing or being healed. Language served as trace, track, and diviner for the equivalency of body and land. The experiences of those years had a tremendous impact on me.

In 1972 I founded a group in Philadelphia called Women Organized Against Rape. It was the first rape crisis center to establish itself as a link and monitor within the system of hospital, police, and court. It was and still is a grass-roots organization. Afterwards, my work moved from the studio into the empty land-fills and abandoned buildings of the city and the public forum.

Papago Park/City Boundary

In 1990 landscape architect Steve Martino and I entered a competition sponsored by the cities of Phoenix and Scottsdale, Arizona, to design a gateway for Papago Park that would also serve as a boundary marker between the two cities. Before I knew of the competition, I saw Steve's work on television and magazines. I was impressed by the fact that he had worked with Ronald Gass, one of the first people to take samplings and seedlings from the desert and encourage nurseries to grow them. I thought to myself: I would like to work with Steve someday.

Six months later I received an invitation to enter the Papago Park/City Boundary competition. I sent Steve my slides and asked him to join me. We met for the first time when we were selected as finalists. Touring the site, we decided to do a project that involved regeneration. We could see the park had a dying ecology, and during the course of our research were astounded to learn that, through ecological degradation, it had lost its status as a national monument. The park was once Papago Saguaro National Monument. Today, only a handful of saguaros remain alive—no new ones have survived in fifty years.

The park's ecology declined primarily as a result of improvements to recreation facilities. The park had allowed itself to be defined by user requirements at the cost of its own survival. The "improvements" decimated a once flourishing and varied plant community: the cholla cactus was removed in the 1930s, soon followed in the 1940s by other mother plants like bursage, which once provided shelter for seedlings, insects, and other life forms that activated the desert food chain. The disruption in the park's ecology and food chain eventually caused a further decline in plant and animal species, until the fox was no longer evidenced at the site. With the

Jody Pinto has created a

a work with Steve Martino that

gently integrates with the natural

systems of its desert environment.

A monument that respects

and utilizes ancient

water harvesting techniques

to bring new growth and life to a

biologically threatened park.

≈

Photo: 1940 Charles Felming
Photo: 1990 Eric Scudder

Papago Park Site
Demonstrating degradation of desert flora
Phoenix, Arizona
1940–1990

Papago Park / City Boundary Project

Boundary line of Phoenix, Scottsdale, and
entrance to Papago Desert Park
View of tree form with seven water harvesting
terraces and vertical solistial markers
1992

Jody Pinto

24 / 25

absence of the fox, the rabbit population exploded. Most of the bases of the saguaro and other cacti were eaten away by rabbits whose own food source had been disrupted.

We thought it ironic to design a gateway for a park that had a dying ecology. So, although the competition did not require it, we provided a master plan to control the rabbit population, reapportion recreation facilities, and redesign the land use that these facilities appropriated.

Steve and I felt it was important to choose a form for our design that would recall the civilizations that existed previously in the area. The tree form is a universal symbol of life and regeneration. We mutually agreed to use it as our primary design motif. I remembered during our site introduction a historian mentioning that the cultural genesis of the area had been passed down through seven civilizations. This fact immediately touched me, for the number seven holds great importance for many cultures around the world and is linked with the achievement of higher forms of consciousness and creation itself. I felt then that we had to incorporate the number in our design. This worked out easily with the tree form: seven branches became seven terraces, and seven vertical markers formed our axis of alignment.

Early on we also decided to extend the concept of boundary; the term "alignment" was much more encompassing and in keeping with the nature and spirit of our project. "Gateway" was the terminology used in the call to artists. Rather than deal with gateway in the literal sense, we interpreted it in our project as a spiritual opening, celebrating all of the ancient water harvesting processes that were used to make survival possible in the desert.

**Papago Park
Rain Water Irrigation System**
Channel in tree stem before a rainfall

Dry irrigation terrace
Flowering ocotillo

The seven cultures that inhabited the area in the past all relied on harvesting rainwater for food production and survival. They based their canal systems on the original Hohokom irrigation system, which once spanned an area of 800 miles. The Hohokoms laid the groundwork, and each civilization that came after used and adapted the system for itself. Many of the canals that exist today are based on the Hohokom system. "Hohokom" means those who are gone. The Pima consider themselves to be the descendants of these people.

The design is itself a functional farming and irrigation system that collects and distributes rainwater. This time the crop is the desert itself. The tree form is composed of seven desert farming terraces. The fundamental principle of the terrace design reflects basic farming methods of all civilizations in the desert. The technique relies on human intervention to capture natural storm run-off and divert it for agricultural benefits. This concept has remained constant from the earliest inhabitants' simple check dams for farming to the sophisticated, computer-monitored delivery systems in place today. The tree's wall structure diverts the natural flow of storm water through the stem of the plant to the seven farming terraces.

**Papago Park
Rain Water Irrigation System**

Tree stem fills with rainwater

Rainwater flowing from tree stem onto terraces

Water harvesting terraces
Desert life being restored

Jody Pinto

The street intersection on which the gateway stands is not just a traffic intersection, but also a symbolic meeting of Nature and spirit. Since Papago Park has a dying ecology, we based our design on an alignment with the Summer Solstice, the longest farming day of the year. Thus, the design calls attention to and celebrates the basic life forces of the desert and its timeless methods of survival and regeneration.

The project collapses time, creating a regenerated present through the use of past technology. The process itself of regeneration and alignment becomes the gateway and boundary. We envisioned the project as the first step in restoring the former glory of the late national monument. The ancient methods of irrigation are used as a learning and teaching device for the public.

We used vertical markers to break the skyline and indicate to the traveler a major crossroad. They serve as anticipatory cues for the project, not unlike the anticipatory markers of ancient solar shrines that preceded Summer Solstice celebrations. In redefining "Gateway" and "Boundary," we focused our attention on place and process.

Having formerly been a marshaling area for a road-widening project, the site was badly abused when we first came to it. The highways sliced through the land and interrupted the natural washes, which in turn ran onto the highways. We recontoured the land to take advantage of the washes that developed back in the area of the buttes. Thus, storm runoff was diverted into the channel of the stem and out into the terraces. We removed existing plant material, including trees which were then nurseried and replanted after construction. The cacti was salvaged from a road construction project, and the area was replanted with a mix of indigenous seed. The stone used for construction was reject material from a local gravel quarry of the Yavapai on Fort McDowell Reservation.

The selection and arrangement of elements used in the project empower it with meaning, memory, and a distinct sense of place. Five of the seven markers align with sunrise on the Summer Solstice. The other vertical elements align through the base of the tree form to the surrounding modern day cities, the Native American ruins of Casa Grande, and the prominent geologic feature of the area, Squaw Peak.

Projects like ours are often didactic in nature. Signs instruct visitors what to expect and how to interpret what is present. Steve and I felt it was important to avoid this. We wanted to encourage people's curiosity, to instill a sense of mystery. We wanted people to explore the project in order to understand what it took to regenerate the desert. We wanted them to discover on their own the solar movements and their relationship to our daily life and that of the planet. Visitors move through the project the same way the former civilizations moved through their monuments. They encounter the vertical elements long before seeing the actual tree form.

For Steve and me, the empowerment of the project has begun to take place in the communities of Phoenix, Scottsdale, and Tempe. On the day of dedication, June 21, 1992, at 5:00 A.M., the arts commissions expected about 40 people. Between 400 and 500 people, entire families, came to watch and take part in the solstitial alignment celebration. Later that year and again in 1993, the "Tree of Life," as it is referred to locally, served as the final destination for a candlelight procession to commemorate those lost to AIDS. Candles were placed along the tree form, illuminating the Tree of Life in the desert evening. The spectacle was a moving testament to the fact that public ritual is still a requisite in our society and that art has the potential to become central in the ritual functioning of our communities.

Photo: Steve Martino

Papago Park
Vertical stone markers

Papago Park

First year after completion
1992

Below:

Papago Park

Second year after completion demonstrating
regeneration of desert flora
1993

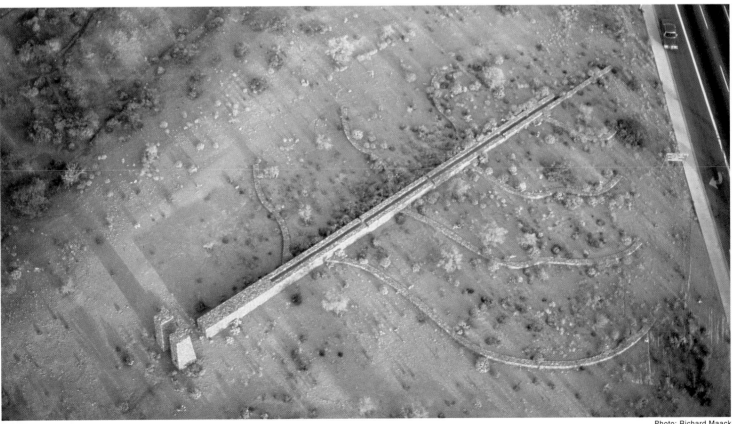

Jody Pinto

Peter Erskine

Secrets of the Sun—A Participatory Solar Spectrum Installation

Secrets of the Sun, Melennial Meditations I (S.O.S.) is a site specific, interactive artwork about the beauty and dangers of solar radiation: the beauty of the rainbow and the horrors of global warming, ozone depletion, and mass species extinction. *S.O.S.* uses the emotional impact of art to address the full range of Nature, from its most elemental expression as pure light to its most complex expression as global ecology.

For millennia people have worshipped the Sun for its warmth, light, and capability for producing food. In modern times we have come to take the Sun for granted. The Earth is solar powered, yet we are largely unaware of our dependence on our star. We just throw a switch. I turn on my TV or my light. I open my refrigerator. All these simple, normal, modern human acts are changing the climate and destroying the ozone layer with possible catastrophic consequences for the global ecology.

Now is the second time in one and a half billion years that the predominant species has the ability to change the world's climate. Stromatolite, a blue green bacteria, lived in a world with no free oxygen in the air or water. It excreted oxygen, but it created so much in the environment that it became extinct, poisoned by its own waste. Sound a little familiar? Of course, its demise was also the beginning of a whole new chapter in creation.

At the present rate of destruction, the ozone layer, which protects all life from invisible ultraviolet radiation, could be gone in one hundred years. It took Nature three billion years to create the ozone layer. Without its protective shield no life can exist on the surface of the Earth. Many experts believe we have only until the year 2000 to reverse the trend. But if we are to survive, the public must be aware of this information. People are drawn to beauty, and ignore the invisible. Out of sight, out of mind! With these thoughts in mind, I decided to make visible and invisible sunlight the theme of my art .

In December 1989 I began a series of tabletop experiments with prisms, mirrors, and spectrum sunlight in a small model. Within a few weeks I foresaw enormous possibilities. However, just after I would set something up, the sunlight would move off the mirrors and I would lose the spectrum effect. The Earth wouldn't stand still for me!

I realized that I needed a heliostat (a Greek word meaning Sun-stop), a mirror device, that would track the Sun to keep a consistent beam of light on a prism in my studio. Then I would have a fixed solar spectrum rainbow I could use as "paint" for my new work.

In order to make the heliostat I had to learn more about the Solar System. I had to learn which way the Earth rotated on its axis, how it tilted from one season to the next, and the shape of its orbit.

Early in 1990 I saw parallels between my solar spectrum experiments and the global ecological crisis, but I couldn't figure out how to combine them in my work.

Then in April of 1990 I heard the "Mass for Endangered Species" on the radio. This was a Palestrina Requiem Mass with a resonant bass voice over it reading the official list of the world's threatened and endangered mammals and birds. It

Secrets of the Sun is a traveling site specific installation that reveals to us the incredible beauty of our life-giving star. However, the message within the beauty strives to awaken the understanding that our current lifestyle is damaging the life-sustaining balance between solar radiation and Earth's ecosystems.

≈

stopped me dead. The radio station put me in touch with Bruce Odland and Paul Klite of "Terra Infirma," a group of environmental sound artists. I got a tape of the Mass and combined it with the spectrum light. It clicked! Bruce, Sam Auinger from Austria, and I went on to collaborate on both the Rome and Berlin installations of *Secrets of the Sun.*

Rome Installation

I was offered the chance to exhibit *Secrets of the Sun* in Trajan's Markets in the Imperial Forum in Rome in 1992. This was the first time a site specific contemporary artwork would be installed in the Forum. The installation was organized by the city of Rome and the International Solar Energy Society: Italian Section.

The markets have lasted for 2,000 years, yet now their existence is threatened by acid rain and traffic fumes that are dissolving the ancient Roman marble. This damage is compounded by the vibrations of the traffic shaking the buildings apart. For me, Trajan's Markets became a poignant symbol of what we could lose because of environmental destruction today.

It was an unimaginable opportunity, but I had to raise all the money to pay for the show. I spent four months trying to raise funds and got nowhere. The prospects for the show were growing dimmer when artist Lita Albuquerque introduced me to Fred Weisman, Los Angeles businessman, art collector, and philanthropist.

Fred's art collecting and patronage had never extended to California light and space art. However, while standing in the spectrum light of *S.O.S.* in my studio, he told me he wanted to help the Rome installation in any way he could. As he has done many times before in his business career, Fred took a substantial calculated risk, this time with environmental art. The Frederick R. Weisman Art Foundation eventually funded the installation, including the design, construction, and transportation of the complex solar equipment.

Then, only a week before I was to ship the equipment to Rome, the Teresa and H. John Heinz III Foundation came through with a grant to cover unforeseen installation expenses in the Forum as well as funds to seek future venues for the traveling installation.

After the Rome show closed, the city of Berlin offered to organize a *Secrets of the Sun, Millennial Meditations I* installation as part of their bid for the 2000 Olympics. The exhibition opened in Berlin on the Summer Solstice and closed on the Autumnal Equinox of 1993.

Although both the Rome and Berlin installations were site specific, they had many common elements. First, all of the visitors had to sign a "Damage Waiver" before entering the solar spectrum rooms. This presented an opportunity for people to reframe their thinking, take ecological responsibility, and see their actions from a new point of view. They could see themselves as part of the problem, as well as part of the solution.

Next, visitors were asked to don a "protective" white jumpsuit which had social, health, and technical connotations. Donning the white suit gave one an entirely new physical appearance as well as a new mental attitude. The viewers became a canvas for the solar spectrum colors.

Once in their protective suits, Rome visitors walked outside past the heliostat, solar electric photo voltaic panels, and an array of mirrors. The heliostat, with a 10 by 15 foot mirror, tracked the Sun all day; the solar panels generated all the electric power for the installation; and the mirrors reflected the heliostat's fixed beam of sunlight onto prisms in the darkened exhibition rooms.

Several rooms inside Trajan's Markets contained slowly changing spectrum sunlight, sound, and sculpture. No filters or artificial lights were used in *Secrets of the Sun*, and the spectrum hues were some of the most intense, saturated colors that could be seen outside of a physics laboratory. The spectrum was reflected throughout the space, and the resulting color mix was caused by forty mirrors. Twenty mirrors had environmental texts silk-screened onto their surfaces. The mirrors provided a meditated, illusory experience of the space, and the text changed color as the spectrum scanned across it.

Secrets of the Sun
Room of Reflected History
Trajan's Markets

Ancient marble statues and mirrors that
reflect the solar color spectrum
Rome, Italy
1992

Secrets of the Sun
Spectrum Vapor Chimney Room
Trajan's Markets

Rome, Italy
1992

Peter Erskine

One of the spaces contained a Spectrum Vapor Chimney Room where clouds of pure water vapor burst into color, illuminated by the spectrum light. The "Mass for Endangered Species" played in the background, and a large mirror with environmental text silk-screened onto its surface stated that we are in the midst of the greatest mass species extinction since the dinosaurs. An L.E.D. display set into the mirror kept a count of the number of species that became extinct during the exhibition—one every fifteen minutes, about 2900 a month.

« One archway enclosed an array of marbles—architectural fragments
excavated from the Forum. Light from above struck the marbles and
created a dazzling multi-colored array of precious jewels that hypnotically

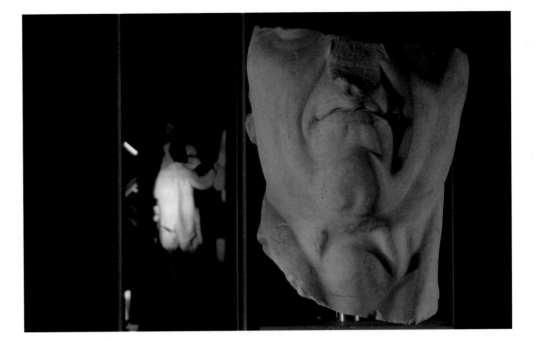

**Secrets of the Sun
Room of Reflected History
Trajan's Markets**
Rome, Italy
1992

turned from ruby red to magenta to aquamarine green to deep amethyst
as we watched. If a cloud moved in front of the Sun, the vision faded
and the fragments turned grey.

Was it real? Gradually the sunlight reappeared.
Pale pastel colors grew brighter and deeper as the clouds rolled away.
The exhibition continued in the Room of Reflected History.
This room was lined with mirrors and four larger than life classical
marble sculpture fragments. Two large male torsos—one dressed in
armour, one in a toga—faced two giant heads—an emperor and an empress.
The deep folds of the toga, the creases in the emperor's face, the curls of
the empress's hair were saturated with intense rainbow color.
Ancient marble sculptures that we see today are pure white but in Roman
times they were brightly, even garishly, painted. Hair, eyes, lips, clothing
were yellow, blue, red, purple. *SOS* brushed the ancient art with brilliant
color that appeared startling modern but reached far back into the past. »
—GRETCHEN WOELFLE, *Art Critic*

**Secrets of the Sun
Room of Questions and Answers
Trajan's Markets**
Rome, Italy
1992

The Room of Questions and Answers
completed the circle of visitor involvement and responsibility that began with
the signing of the "Damage Waiver" and
the wearing of the white suits. This room
invited people to make comments and
suggest possible solutions to environmental problems in Rome and the rest of
the world. I saw the Room of Questions
and Answers as a means to empowering
people to make changes in their environment and realize that things will get
worse if they do not act. I also wanted visitors to describe their reactions to
S.O.S.—their comments are useful to me
in developing future *S.O.S.* installations.

Peter Erskine

Secrets of the Sun:
Millennial Meditations
Trophy Room with Extinction Wall
Berlin, Germany
1993

The Berlin Site

In Berlin, *S.O.S.* was installed at the Haus der Kulturen der Welt (House of World Cultures) in the Tiergarten, a building with a perfect North-South celestial orientation. A huge walk-in *S.O.S.* Sundial indicated true solar time, and immediately connected visitors with the larger forces of the Solar System.

There were no Roman bricks, sculptures, or even interesting spaces to work in, so we created a cave in the lobby of the building with black theatrical velvet. Bruce Odland called the piece "electronic cave art of the future."

After the ritual circumambulation of the solar equipment, white suited visitors entered the velvet cave. First they saw the Spectrum Vapor Chimney Room, a reminder of the terrible fossil fuel pollution in Northern and Eastern Europe.

Then they entered the Grove of Dead Trees, where leafless trees became multicolored ghosts of nature lost. Thirty percent of Germany is covered with forests, and one half of the trees are dead or dying.

On the extinction wall of the Trophy Room, silhouettes of endangered species of fish, mammals, reptiles, and birds vanished from view. These sculptures threw the long shadows that our future casts, shadows made from mixing millions of colors of solar spectrum light. The mirrors with environmental quotes mixed up the images of the animals, the shadows, and the visitors.

Odland and Auinger's environmental sound installation called *Lost Neighborhood* mixed live sounds of the fossil fueled traffic outdoors with the digital tapes of "talking trees," "crying fish," and "clocks gone crazy." They used the massive parabolic curve of the building's roof to create a solar-powered, architectural loudspeaker that floated their urban resonances over the heliostat.

**Secrets of the Sun
Grove of Dead Trees**

Text on mirror:

"The green prehuman Earth is a mystery
we were chosen to solve, a guide to the
birthplace of our spirit, but it is slipping away.
The way back seems harder every year.
If there is danger in the human trajectory,
it is not so much in the survival of our own
species as in the fulfillment of the ultimate
irony of organic evolution: that in the instant
of achieving self-understanding through the
mind of man, life has doomed its most
beautiful creations. And thus humanity
closes the door to its past."

— by Edward O. Wilson, *Biologist*

Berlin, Germany
1993

A Solar Solution

The final message of *Secrets of the Sun* is that every person is equal under the Sun. We are all part of the problem and we can all contribute to the solution.

The Sun can fry us, but it also sends to Earth 35,000 times the energy we burn in fossil fuels each day. Solar energy is clean, universal, and plentiful for the next four billion years. It is a big part of the environmental solution that has been ignored.

Secrets of the Sun asks questions about who we are as a species, where we come from, and where we are going. *S.O.S.* employs the most advanced optical physics and solar technology to reveal the full range of the visible solar spectrum. Yet the whole phenomenon fades away when a cloud passes before the Sun. We are ultimately dependent on Nature.

Baile Oakes

My service is predicated on my belief that the developed world is in the midst of a life-threatening crisis. A crisis originating from the fact that we view ourselves and our technology as entities separate from the Earth and its life systems. We destroy other life forms and natural systems because of our unwillingness or inability to see them as our very selves. Visual arts and design have always played a vital role in helping to convey the dreams and aspirations of civilizations. Since we currently view ourselves as entities separate from the Earth and its life systems, it follows that most of the infrastructure we design and build to support ourselves removes us from a relationship with the Earth. I aspire to have my work in the field of public art demonstrate ways to begin to reverse the trend by incorporating into our infrastructure ever-present reminders of our vital relationship within the living systems of our planet.

With my earlier work I strove to create forms that would evoke the sense of balance and growth that is inherent in the natural world. My hope was that these works would help bring to the viewer a sense of the dynamic balance inherent in Nature that sustains all life. I have always been in awe of what I refer to as the "visual chord"—the visual equivalent of a great acoustic chord evoking a feeling of balance and harmony. Some great works of art and architecture strike this chord within me, bringing a sense of peace to my soul. My goal was to find this "chord" in my work.

After my wife, Kathleen, and I conceived our first child, I began to feel that abstract efforts to reach people and raise consciousness by using form alone lacked the direct communication that critical situations require. I felt that I needed to bring a more direct sense of dialogue and communication to my work with art. I wanted my work to bring attention to the forces that encompass us, the forces that our lives depend upon.

Gestation

During the gestation period of our first child, I designed a sculpture for the city of Santa Monica for Palisades Park. A park that defines the border of the city, continent, and ocean. I wanted to create a sculpture that would address the dynamics of this meeting place, and at the same time, invite the public into an intimate dialogue with the work. I wanted the sculpture to be one you could enter, sit and play within, a nurturing sanctuary. I also wanted it to serve as a beacon to foster an understanding of the basis of all life on the planet: the cycle of the Sun.

I was fortunate to have a patron, Nora Clow, who believed in the worth of the project and offered the city a matching

The primal forces

of life are the inspiration for

my work as a sculptor.

I aspire to describe and demonstrate

natural phenomena and

the cycles of life on our planet

in such a manner as

to place us in direct relationship

with the forces of our world.

≈

Gestation
Palisades Park
Newly installed before the wood aged
Santa Monica, California
1990

grant to fund the development and placement of the sculpture. The remaining funds were raised by the Santa Monica Arts Foundation with the majority of support coming through the generosity of Peter Norton and the Norton Family Trust.

Palisades Park marks a meeting place of air, water, land, flora, and fauna. The earliest moments of organic creation resulted from the interaction of the life of the sea with the rich minerals of the Earth and the gases of the atmosphere. I wanted to create a sculpture that would symbolize this dynamic of all life: creation, regeneration, and birth. The circle was chosen for its historic symbology of the infinite nature of life and time. The progression of the ribs of the sculpture from the initial core circle represents for me the constant progression of the growth in ourselves, the Earth, and the Universe: a segment of the infinite continuum of life.

The sculpture is constructed of Port Orford Cedar. I chose an organic material that when left unfinished would take on the hues and textures of the surrounding trees of the site. Cedar is one of the most durable outdoor materials, easily out-distancing steel in withstanding the elements. With proper drainage, unfinished cedar will last hundreds of years.

I did have reservations about using this material because of the present depletion of the Oregon cedar forests. The fact that all the wood I used was harvested from damaged dead fall in the forest made it a little more environmentally friendly, though environmental concerns were not what motivated the small mill I worked with. In the late 1980s our government wholesaled all the available standing cedar trees as unmilled logs to international buyers in order to make the trade deficit balance sheets look a little bit better. The policy not only accelerated the deforestation in the area but forced the closure of most of the small local mills. It basically turned this part of Oregon into a third world country, exporting valuable resources which, if managed properly, could have created sustainable forestry and jobs by supporting small local mills and cedar product manufacturing. Instead, the rampant cutting of the trees necessitated the closure of the forests to protect species that relied on the few remaining stands of cedar in the area. In my heart, the sculpture is dedicated to the memory of this incredible and squandered resource.

I have oriented *Gestation* so that the large circular opening that makes up the interior of the sculpture will frame the horizon meeting of land, ocean, and air—the trilogy of the genesis of organic life. As a person walks past *Gestation*, the large central opening will appear to close, until what is left of the opening is a thin vertical aperture perpendicular to the horizon. The sculpture is installed precisely to allow this thin aperture to frame the setting Sun when it meets the horizon on the Winter Solstice. The Sun will appear in the top of the aperture as the day of the Solstice approaches, and will each day move gradually down the aperture until, on the day of the Solstice, the setting Sun meets the ocean. On this day it reminds those present of the important event that nurtures all of our lives on Earth—the conception of the rebirth of Spring.

Gaia

In 1988 I was asked by the county of Santa Barbara to design a playground for Tucker's Grove Park. I had several objectives in mind. I wanted to create an environment for children that would encourage imaginative, creative play activities and help challenge their manual skills. I also wanted to incorporate an underlying theme for the structure of the playground that would evoke the feelings of the Earth's elements. What resulted is a play environment comprised of the trilogy of mineral, water, and organic growth.

The mineral element is represented by a granite slide in the form of a truncated cone. The cone has a slope that is steep enough to allow children to slide down its face, but shallow enough to allow them to climb up the slope to the top. There is no platform from which they can fall, and they can slide down from the top in any direction. The sides of the cone are faced in a light colored granite and the top is rose. The form gives the impression of a breast—a symbol for the mineral nourishment that sustains all organic life on our planet.

The organic growth of our world is represented by the "Tree Limb Jungle Gym." This climbing structure is built of oak tree branches that the county

Gestation
Above:
Sunset, Winter Solstice
Below:
Sunset, 2 weeks before the Winter Solstice
Santa Monica, California
1990

Photo: Theadora Litsios

Gaia
Tucker's Grove Park

Tree Limb Jungle Gym frames
the Stone Slide in the background
Santa Barbara County, California
1988–1989

Gaia

"S" Form Shells provide the
children with a quiet play area

trimmed from its trees as part of a tree maintenance program. The structure allows children to create a wide variety of imaginative games while at the same time developing their motor skills. Tree-climbing demands every hand and foot of a child be involved in constant activity, causing angles and spatial relationships to change every moment. Climbing through the structure's maze of branches gives children the experience of climbing through trees, though they don't get higher than six feet off the ground. Special care was taken to create open areas within the configuration for the children to discover. These areas in the sand evoke a sense of enclosure within the flowing movement of the limbs. Because no two limbs are painted the same color, the children can visually discern each individual branch as their eyes follow the forms on a visual roller coaster ride.

The currents of the wind and water are represented by "S-form Shells." This area provides a space for children to slow down a bit. Play activities involving sand, games of hide-and-go-seek, and some climbing take place here. All of us like to discover those out-of-doors areas that provide a sense of shelter and protection while at the same time being open to the sky. The most important aspect of the "shells" is this sense of enclosure that they offer children, this special protected place to play, right in the middle of other activity. Children can be in their space behind the shell, and all Mom or Dad have to do to keep an eye on them is glance over the top.

Baile Oakes

Photo:Mike Pahos, Santa Barbara County Parks Department

Whether the children consciously "get" the symbolism of the Earth elements in the forms, materials, and textures of the playground is irrelevant. We are all sensual beings, and children are especially sensual. So, for them to feel the hard surface of the granite and see its faceted structure, for them to touch the movement of the trees and allow their eyes to flow over the weaving limbs, for them to sense the fluid movement of the shells and relax in their quiet embrace is "getting it" enough for me. Education and learning do not need to be didactic. We are all creatures of our environment, and we are constantly influenced by our life experiences. It is my hope that the children's interaction with the elemental forms of the playground will spark in them a sense of their shared heritage.

Gaia
Tucker's Grove Park
Stone Slide,
Oak Tree Limb Jungle Gym,
"S" Form Shells
Goleta, California
1989

Silver Sands Park

In 1990 I was asked by the city of Palm Desert, California, to design a park on six acres of land that was at the time unused. I contacted Brian Spangle, landscape architect with The Hudson-Pacific Alliance, because of our past collaborations on other park designs. We worked together on the initial conceptual stages of the park. Brian was also responsible for the specifications of the finished design.

We believe that part of the purpose for city parks is to help us maintain a vital link to our natural world within the context of a metropolitan development. With the Silver Sands Park project our goal was to use the architecture of the landscape to facilitate enjoyable recreation while presenting to the community some of the natural laws that define this desert environment and make all life possible.

The park site is triangular in shape, surrounded on two sides by housing developments and on the third side by a golf course. The south and west views from the site reveal a panorama of a range of mountains. I decided to use earth mounds to define the use areas of the park because I wanted to visually and acoustically buffer the visitor to the park from the noise of the street and the distractions of the surrounding development. These earth berms allow the visitor to immediately enter into a relationship with the natural elements that comprise the park and serve to frame the vistas to the greater desert mountain ranges beyond. The berms embrace the visitor within the desert icons of mountain, stone, sand, palm groves, oasis, and sky. They define meandering pathways that draw the visitor through a sequence of interactive experiences of stark and barren, lush and thick,

Silver Sands Park
Model
Palm Desert California
1990–

dry and wet desertscapes. The plantings are of the vanishing desert's flora, displayed in ecologically correct biomes which clad the park's forms with greens and greys and demonstrate the evolution of plant life in a desert environment. Situated along these paths are small native palm oasis that provide the visitor with cool places to relax.

A *Solar Calendar Irrigation System* at the central oasis designates the heart of the park, and ties the park to the theme of the life-giving marriage of water, sunlight, earth, and air. The central pool is fed by canals extending from the east and the west, oriented to the rising and setting Sun of the Winter and Summer Solstices

Silver Sands Park
Solar Calendar Irrigation System
Central Oasis
Model
The canals radiating out to the east and west
from the central pool are aligned
to a solstice or equinox sunrise or sunset.
Palm Desert, California
1990–

and the Fall and Spring Equinoxes. On the these important days, the corresponding source canals glow with the golden light of the Sun's rays. The canals of the north and south axis feed the central pool's overflow to terminal ponds that allow the water to seep into the earth, sustaining the surrounding plantings.

The *Solar Calendar Irrigation System* is situated dead level with only a few inches of precious water filling the configuration. Water flows from the source canals at seasonally adjusted rates that take into account the rate of water evaporation and the irrigation needs of the vegetation fed by the terminal ponds. The central oasis sustains a grassed area shaded by native palm tree groves of *Washingtonia filifera* that cool the desert's environment for the park's visitors. The sand areas between the supply canals accentuate the preciousness of the water as a resource, and provide a play area where children can explore both sand and water.

I grew up in New Orleans where people depend upon levees to hold the water out of the city. I grew to love these earthen boundaries and the clear delineation they made between areas of my world. I would often lie at the bottom of the grassy slopes and look up them to the sky, with its dance of the clouds, Sun, Moon, and stars. It is the tranquillity and knowledge of this stage set that I wanted to bring to the park visitors with the *Sky Crater.*

The sky can be regarded as a vessel that carries to us the resources of oxygen and fresh water. I wanted to use the *Sky Crater* to emphasize this special relationship that we all too often take for granted.

Solar Calendar Irrigation System
Looking southwest from the canal that marks the sunrise of the Summer Solstice toward the canal that marks the sunset of the Winter Solstice

Silver Sands Park
Small oasis with native palms, *Washingtonia Filifera* and irrigation pool

**Silver Sands Park
Sky Crater**

Model
Palm Desert. California
1990–

The crater exterior will be formed of rock, barren of vegetation, an expression of the pure mineral life of the Earth. A visitor exploring the form discovers at its far side a spiral access ramp to the top of the crater. At the ramp's apex, the visitor finds a grassy bowl below. Descending into the bowl, he or she sees that the crater's lip obscures all surrounding landforms, vegetation, and man-made objects. All that can be seen is the domed ceiling of the day and night skies, alive with the dance of clouds, Sun, Moon, and stars. The visitor is alone with the heavens in a unique vessel that communicates the celestial elements in a profound, personal way.

Silver Sands Park operates on many different experiential levels. As an open space within the city, it affords public recreation. The environment reminds visitors of the unique qualities and values of their desert home. The water effect is an amenity, a calendar, an irrigation system, and—four days a year—an evocative event. The *Sky Crater* is a sculpture, a stage, and a very personal experience for those who discover its secret. The park contains the rock, water, sand, sky, and flora that nurtures this environment. Its goal is to draw attention to the forces of life that shape our planet, while nurturing each visitor's presence and role in the balance of Nature.

If my service in life instills in people a little more reverence for the forces of life that drive our planet, then I have succeeded with my intentions.

**Silver Sands Park
Sky Crater**

As one proceeds down into the bowl, the rim will eventually obscure all other surroundings, leaving one alone with the sky

Charles Ross

Our society has launched itself on a vast program of discovering the universe, yet there is little in our daily lives to remind us that we are beings of the stars. The cosmic link that is every human's birthright is not much honored in modern times and the human soul gets restless from lack of looking up. There is a need for art and architecture to speak more of our cosmic connection.

New technology gives vivid images of planets, atoms, and galaxies. But our discoveries tend to remain impersonal and abstract, lacking a human dimension. They are not yet integrated into the visible culture. Growing interest in ancient monuments and their star alignments reveals our nostalgia for how earlier civilizations embraced the Cosmos through art and architecture. Exploring the Universe is not exclusively a scientific endeavor. Art can also serve as a doorway to a sense of the energy and spirit in space.

My art has shown me that it is possible for us to recall our intimacy with the stars. We are, after all, made of star stuff. Light is the agent of our contact with atoms and galaxies. The light that scientists study to gain a measure of the Universe is the same light that falls on our skin. In working to transpose elements of light, time, and energy into material form, I've come to realize that we contain a cellular memory of our personal connection with the Cosmos.

My work deals with looking into light. It creates windows through which to view aspects of the larger natural order—giant prism columns and walls, solar spectrum skylights, solar burns, star map paintings, and the Earth/Sky sculpture, *Star Axis*. Each work offers a point of reference to the position of our planet and ourselves in the light of space. Some works give direct experience while others serve as artifacts revealing forms and structures contained in light.

Prisms and Solar Spectrum Skylights

Living in San Francisco in 1965, I created the first large scale prism—approximately eight feet high and eighteen inches on a side. Information from a dream helped me to invent a process that made building large scale prisms financially possible. It was around Thanksgiving. By the end of the week I sent most of my earlier work to the dump.

The prism columns are optically clear, and to my knowledge, they are the largest prisms ever built. Minimal in form, they yield maximal experience. Acting as "cracks in the world," they offer a view of another dimension of the everyday environment. An energy dimension made entirely of color and light.

In 1967 I moved to New York City where I joined the Dwan Gallery. I also helped found the first artists' co-op loft building at 80 Wooster Street, in the old manufacturing area now called SoHo. At this time, I began to create site specific prism works that project the solar spectrum.

By placing groups of large scale prisms under clear glass skylights I was able to project huge bands of spectrum into the architectural spaces below. Each prism is tuned to the Sun for a specific time of day and season. The spectrums evolve continuously throughout the day, expanding into bright washes or contracting into

Solar Prism Installation
Plaza of the Americas
Dallas, Texas
1985

brilliant bands of solar color as they move through the space, propelled by the turning of the Earth.

The spectrum covers everything in its path with a primal iridescence, transforming the identity of space and objects. People who stand in the rays of the large spectrum say they feel as if they are greeting an old friend. They experience a sense of instant recognition, as if remembering their being from light itself.

Changing by the hour, day, and season, the work is never exactly the same. After a few overcast days, the spectrum suddenly reappears like a new discovery. It is a natural event brought indoors. Like light breathing.

My largest spectrum commission to date is installed at the Plaza of the Americas in Dallas, Texas. Thirty-five prisms, each eight-and-a-half feet long, and sixteen inches on a side, are placed in three different locations throughout the atrium. Here the spectrum sweeps across pedestrian walkways and down staircases. Glass elevators move through the spectrum; gardens light up in it; ice skaters dance in the spectrum; and on weekends, one can dine in the spectrum. The work also gives the space specific Winter, Summer, Spring, and Fall identities, all orchestrated by the Earth's orbital motion.

Harvard Business School Chapel

In 1972 the architect Moshe Safdie asked me to create a spectrum work for a synagogue he was building in the old city of Jerusalem. It would have been my first architectural commission, but disputes within the client organization killed the project. Nineteen years later, in the Spring of 1991, I heard from Moshe again. The work planned for the synagogue was still very much alive in his mind. But he wanted to take it a step further and bring it to a new location—the Harvard Business School Chapel.

Inside the chapel, I wanted to create a sense of Cosmos within the sanctuary. As the work unfolded, a unique and dramatic interaction developed between the spectrum and the curved walls of the architecture. When the spectrums move down these curved surfaces, they evolve from lines of light to swords of light, to a kind of iridescent drapery, landing on the floor in blocks of pure color.

Photo: Gary Langhammer

Solar Prism Installation
Plaza of the Americas

35 prisms located in three different
locations throughout the atrium
Dallas, Texas
1985

Harvard Business School Chapel

Boston, Massachusetts
1993

Charles Ross

The location for the work caused its timescale to be somewhat limited. Both Moshe and I wanted the spectrum to last longer, so we asked solar architect Tom Hopper to create a tracking system for the prisms. The system realigns the prisms so they meet both morning and afternoon Sun, and doubles the length of some of the spectrum events by slowing their speed down the walls. The tracking structure looks as if it belongs to the work. It becomes a natural element derived from the requirements of Sun and site.

Solar Burn
Chateau D'Oiron
Loire Valley, France
1993

The Year of Solar Burns

In 1971 I decided to create a solar work that was the opposite of the spectrum pieces. Instead of using a prism to disperse sunlight, I used a large magnifying lens to condense the light into a single point of raw power.

Everyday for one year, I placed a wooden plank under the lens so that as the Sun passed across the sky it would burn its mark across the plank. Changing weather patterns acted as an iris, modulating the burn. Sunny days created a broad smoke flare; passing clouds left unburned interruptions; and cloudy days produced blank boards. The process was like farming—harvesting the day's "burn" in the evenings, and sowing a new blank board. It yielded a portrait of sunlight, drawn by the Sun itself.

Then came the big surprise—the *Solar Burn Spiral*. We discovered the double spiral figure by following the curvature of the burns as they were placed end to end in chronological order. This spiral is similar to the double spirals found in the rock

drawings and carvings of many ancient peoples, including the Anasazi of Chaco Canyon, New Mexico. Now recognized as a solar figure, to my knowledge, the true meaning of this archetypal form remained unknown in modern times until it appeared again, renewed in the Solar Burns.

The first burn work was done on my rooftop in New York City. From the sunny skies of New Mexico in 1992, I gathered a new version of the Year of Solar Burns. Commissioned by the French Ministry of Culture, it is now installed in the Chateau D' Oiron, a fifteenth-century castle in France's Loire Valley. The work fills all four walls of the Chateau's Salon Verte from floor to ceiling, and the double spiral created by these burns has been carved into the terra cotta floor.

Star Axis

The Solar Burns led me to a new awareness of the Earth's movement in space, and launched my interest in naked eye astronomy. All along, my work kept bumping into the geometry of Precession—our changing star alignment created by the dance of the spinning Earth. It dawned on me that it was possible to create a monumental work revealing both past and future star alignments in this 26,000-year cycle.

Star Axis is both Earth/Sky sculpture and naked eye observatory. It is under construction atop a small mesa where the Sangre de Cristo Mountains meet the eastern plains, eighty miles from Santa Fe, New Mexico. Standing eleven stories high and a tenth of a mile across, *Star Axis* provides a place of heightened focus where an individual can experience the movement of the Universe in relation to his or herself.

A Theater of the Sky Played in Light to Time

A slow wobble gradually shifts the Earth's axis toward and then away from Polaris. As the axis points to other regions in the sky, Polaris moves around the pole in ever-widening circles of sky, eventually relinquishing its place as the North Star. Each of these circles can be seen as a celestial marker in human history.

At the center of the *Star Axis* site, an inverted cone has been carved deep into the capstone and lined with rock masonry. Within this cone a stainless steel tunnel will rise eleven stories and be placed exactly parallel to the Earth's axis. The tunnel focuses on the celestial pole in order to sight and frame the motions of Polaris. Inside the tunnel, stairs rise to the top of the sculpture, emerging above the mesa through a granite pyramid whose shape is derived from the seasonal angles of the Sun.

Visitors will enter the tunnel from the bottom of the cone and walk up the stairs in perfect alignment with the Earth's axis and its outward extension to the stars. Wherever one stands within the tunnel, the circle of the sky framed by the opening represents Polaris's precise orbit for a particular period of history. Dates engraved in each stair identify the years. Thus, the visitor can stand in the orbit of Polaris as it existed for the pyramid builders, Leonardo da Vinci, or as it was in the Stone Age and will be again 13,000 years in the future.

To find the right setting for *Star Axis*, I began an intensive four-year search in 1971 throughout the southwest. In addition to the technical requirements, there was another more mysterious quality that I needed but could not describe at the time. Somehow, I kept returning to the mesas of New Mexico. Later I realized that the powerful Spirit of this land gave me a feeling of standing on the boundary between Earth and Sky. Here, both elements have equal weight, and you can see the curvature of the Earth as you look out to the ocean of light that plays across the plains.

Top: **Star Axis**
View from a stair within tunnel
Dated millinia in the future

Right: **Viewing Precession of the North Star From Inside the Star Tunnel**

Bottom: **Model of Star Axis**

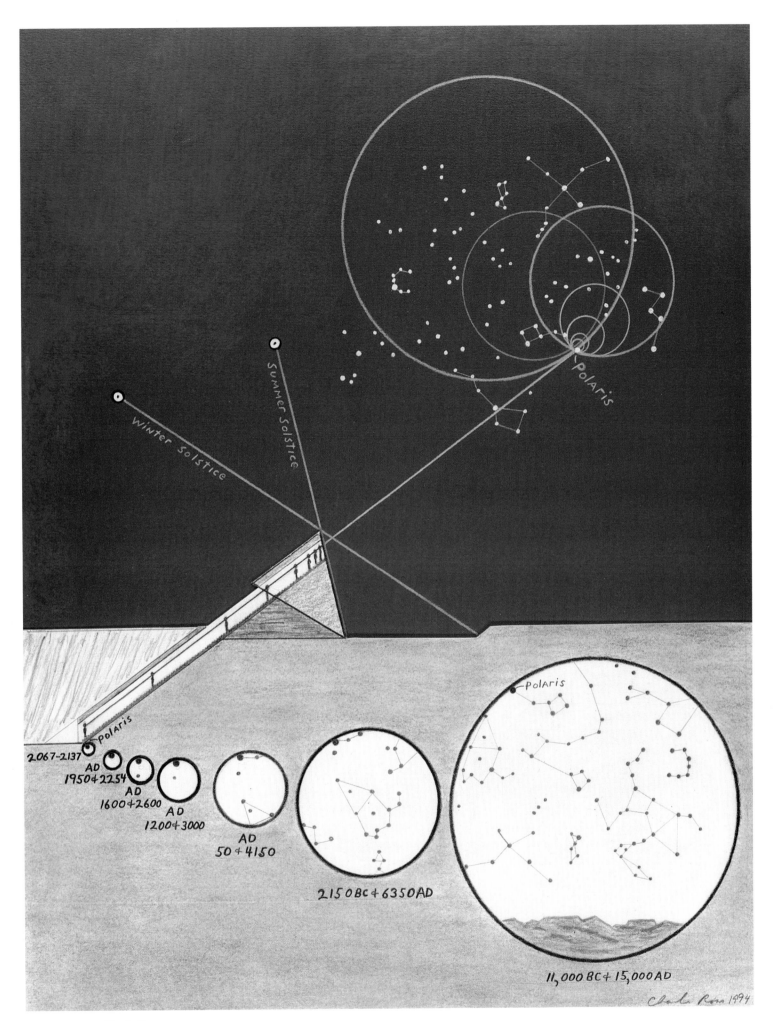

Charles Ross

Only an hour and a half from Santa Fe, *Star Axis* also marks a boundary between civilization and wilderness. The site is isolated, yet easily accessible. Large ranches surround the pristine landscape, where the dark night's sky lets you see the outline of the Milky Way. One doesn't have to reject the modern world to remember one's being in the stars.

As of today, I have been working on the project for twenty-two years. In some ways, the work had to be this slow because each element of *Star Axis*—every shape, every measure, every angle—was first discovered in the stars, and then brought down into the land. Star geometry anchored in earth and rock. The project constantly evolves. I never finalize blueprints until we are ready to build each section. *Star Axis* should feel like it has grown from the Earth—that is was not imposed but found in place.

I think of the Earth-to-star axis as an energy matrix that can be experienced in sculptural form. Larger orders of reality become visible by "earthing" them in form. *Star Axis* distills the geometry of time into a physical environment. By entering the Earth to reach the stars,one can see and feel how the human form is scaled to fit the Cosmos.

People often ask how I'm able to keep going on the project. Big projects that are meant to be done keep feeding you energy. *Star Axis* has always fed me ideas and a lot of energy. It plans to be done, and its completion is now in sight.

Star Axis
Site
Looking South

Right:
Star Axis
Site
View from the base of the tunnel showing
3.5-hour time lapse of Star Trails
Its axis will be precisely
in line with celestial north

Nancy Holt

For twenty-five years I have made large scale, outdoor, site-specific sculptures. Each work evolves out of its site with consideration given to the topography, built environment, and local materials, along with the psychology, sociology, and history of each place. Some of these works are system sculptures that channel natural elements such as water, air, or electricity. Other works have astronomical aspects, such as alignments with the North Star, the Moon, or the sunrises and sunsets on the equinoxes and solstices.

Sun Tunnels

Sun Tunnels is in northwestern Utah on land I bought specifically as a site for the work. The forty acres are in a large, flat valley with saline soil and very little vegetation. It's land worn down by Lake Bonneville, an ancient lake that gradually receded over thousands of years—the Great Salt Lake is what remains of the original lake today. From my site you can see mountains with horizontal lines where the old lake bit into the rock as it was going down. The mirages are extraordinary; you can see whole mountains hovering over the Earth, reflected upside down in the heat. The feeling of timelessness is overwhelming.

Time is not just a mental concept or a mathematical abstraction in Utah's Great Basin Desert. Time takes on a physical presence. The rocks in the distance are ageless; they have been deposited in layers over hundreds of thousands of years. Only ten miles south of the *Sun Tunnels* site are the Bonneville Salt Flats, one of the few areas in the world where you can actually see the curvature of the Earth. Being part of that kind of landscape and walking on earth that has never been walked on before evokes a sense of being on this planet, rotating in space, in universal time.

The following projects of

Nancy Holt address her interest

in the cyclical time of Nature.

She feels that time in Nature

helps one to come to that

place in perception that

is out of measured time.

It is these spaces between

the measured time,

when time drops out

and becomes nonexistent,

that is of interest to her.

≈

Sun Tunnels
Great Basin Desert, Utah
Begun 1973, completed 1976

**Sun Tunnels
Sunset Summer Solstice**
Great Basin Desert, Utah
1976

By marking the yearly extreme positions of the Sun on the horizon, *Sun Tunnels* indicates the cyclical time of the solar year. The tunnels are aligned with each other and with the angles of the rising and setting of the Sun on the days of the solstices, around June 21st and December 21st. On these days the Sun is seen on the horizon centered through tunnels. Actually, around the Summer Solstice the Sun can be seen through the tunnels for many days, the sunlight glowing bright gold on the tunnel walls.

The four concrete tunnels are laid out on the desert in an open X configuration, 86 feet long on the diagonal. Each tunnel is 18 feet long and has an outside diameter of 9 feet, 2.5 inches, and an inside diameter of 8 feet.

The configuration of holes in the upper half of each tunnel corresponds with a constellation, either Capricorn, Columbia, Draco, or Perseus. The four diameters of the holes vary from 7 to 10 inches, relative to the magnitude of the stars to which

Sun Tunnels
Great Basin Desert, Utah
Interior of tunnel

they correspond. During the day, the Sun, a star among stars, shines through the holes, casting a changing pattern of pointed ellipses and circles of light on the bottom half of each tunnel. The shapes and positions of the areas of light differ from hour to hour, day to day, and season to season, relative to the positions of the Sun. The spots of warm light in the cool, shady tunnels are like stars cast down to Earth, inverting the sky, turning day into night. And on many desert nights, moonlight shines through the holes, casting its own paler pattern.

Since the two grants I received from the National Endowment for the Arts and the New York State Council for the Arts covered only one-third of the total cost for making *Sun Tunnels*, I had to finance the rest with my own money. This meant making business deals to keep the cost down, which did not come easily to me and was often exasperating. I don't have any romantic notions about testing the edges of the world that way. It's just a necessity. It doesn't lead to anything except the work.

I wanted to bring the vast space of the desert back down to human scale. I had no desire to make a megalithic monument. The panoramic view of the landscape is too overwhelming to take in without visual reference points. The view blurs out rather than sharpens. When you stand at the center of the work, the tunnels draw your vision into the landscape, opening up the perceived space. But once you're inside one of the tunnels, the work encloses and surrounds you, and the landscape is framed through the ends of the tunnels and through the star holes.

The material and color of the tunnels is the same as the soil in the landscape they are a part of. The inner substance of the concrete—the solidified sand and stone—can be seen on the insides of the holes where the core drill cut through and exposed it.

The local people and I differ on one point: If the land isn't suitable for grazing, or if it doesn't have water, or minerals, or shade, or interesting vegetation, then they think it's not much good. They find it strange when I camp out at my site, although they say they're glad I found a use for the land. Many of the area residents who came to my Summer Solstice campout had never been in that valley before. So by putting *Sun Tunnels* in the middle of the desert, I have not put it in the middle of the residents' regular surroundings. The work paradoxically makes available, or focuses on, a part of the environment that most of the people who live nearby wouldn't normally have paid much attention to.[1]

Annual Ring

Saginaw, Michigan
1981

Annual Ring

This sculpture was commissioned by the General Services Administration (GSA) for the Federal Building in Saginaw, Michigan—a very successful, experimental building, heated by the Sun's energy, which is supplied by massive solar collectors visible from *Annual Ring.*

The site I selected for the work was a large grassy circle, comprising most of a small park, which was built on top of the half underground, two-storied Federal Building. From the streets in the heart of the city, the top half of *Annual Ring* is visible, drawing visitors up the tree-lined steps through the planted terraces to the little elevated park. There, away from the busy downtown activity, they experience a quiet, meditative place open to the sky.

The sculpture is made of one-inch square steel bars curved to form a 15-foot high, 30-foot diameter hemisphere with four circular openings. The bars come together at the top in a 10-foot diameter ring, with 3 vertical bars omitted on the south side to create an entryway. Encircling the hemisphere midway is another ring formed of a horizontal bar welded between the vertical bars. In all, there are approximately 800 welds in the sculpture.

Since *Annual Ring* is an open enclosure containing more empty space than material, visitors standing within the work often have the sensation of being both simultaneously inside and outside, airily contained in an open hemi-globe. Anytime there is sunlight, they can also observe the shadow patterns cast by the rings and radiating bars slowly moving on the ground inside the sculpture.

A plaque at the site explains that at solar noon on the day of the Summer Solstice, when the Sun is at its yearly zenith in the sky, the Sun shining through the ring at the top of the dome casts a circle of light onto a ring in the ground. At that moment, because of the distance of *Annual Ring* from the equator, the Sun is not directly overhead, causing the circle of sunlight and the ring in the ground to be off center.

The opposing eight-foot diameter rings on the sides of the hemisphere indicate east and west, and consequently frame the Sun rising and setting on the Spring and Fall Equinoxes. The angle of the North Star from the ground center of the sculpture is aligned through the center of the smaller, six-foot diameter ring. From inside the sculpture you can see the North Star framed in the middle of this ring. By an extraordinary coincidence, the North Star is centered through the small ring when I stand in the middle of the ring on the ground that marks solar noon on the Summer Solstice.

As always, I spent considerable time researching contractors—surveyors, engineers, astrophysicists, steel fabricators, riggers, concrete workers, and landscapers. Usually there are only one or two contractors in each specialty who see making a sculpture as a challenge and as a way to have their work appreciated as an end in itself. For the steel fabrication I decided upon Koehler Brothers, a family-owned company in Saginaw since 1850. With such strong local roots, the company workers wanted to make a contribution to their community and took pride in their work.

Before breaking ground for construction, I always take the time to meet with community leaders and make my proposals public through exhibitions, lectures, and interviews with the press. In this case I prepared the way by contacting the director of the Saginaw Art Museum. Through him, an exhibition of my work, including my proposal for *Annual Ring*, was organized at the museum, and press conferences and interviews were planned.

Unfortunately, before I had a chance to expose the proposal to the public, controversy about this commission flared up on the front page of the local newspaper. The Chicago office of the GSA released fragmented information to the press without checking first with its Washington headquarters. The public learned only that an unnamed New York artist had received thousands of dollars to create a sculpture in Saginaw. Since the city had a 20% unemployment rate, the expenditure of federal money for art met with resistance. However, after I explained to city council members, and later to the public, that the money would go to local contractors, the community did come around to supporting the sculpture.

Annual Ring
Interior illustrating solar shadow,
North Star ring, Equinox ring

Annual Ring
Alignment during solar noon
Summer Solstice

Sky Mound

In 1984 the Hackensack Meadowlands Development Commission (HMDC) invited me to visit a 57-acre landfill in the New Jersey Meadowlands—a vast, open, marshy area in the heart of the New York/New Jersey metropolitan area. The landfill is a place where sky and ground meet, where you can track the Sun, Moon, and stars with the naked eye, and where you have 360-degree panoramic views of Manhattan, Newark, the Pulaski Skyway, networks of highways and train tracks, old steel turn-bridges, and here and there decaying remnants of the Industrial Revolution. As soon as I saw the site I knew that I wanted to transform the landfill into a park/artwork.

The feeling of awe I frequently feel standing on top of the landfill is similar to the wonder I experienced on the huge American Indian mounds in Miamisburg, Ohio and in the Cahokia site along the Mississippi River in Illinois. Both kinds of human-made mounds were built to meet vital social necessities, but here the similarity ends. Landfills result, of course, from the essential need to rid ourselves of the used-up, cast-off materials of our culture, while American Indian mounds derived from deep spiritual, social, and ritualistic needs.

My proposal for *Sky Mound* incorporates the entire 100-foot-high landfill, top and side slopes, and integrates into the artwork the vernacular of landfill closure: methane recovery wells, a surface water drainage pond, mounds created from dispersal of fill from site construction, a methane flare, an access road, and vegetative cover for erosion control.

Using the latest innovative technology to close the landfill, a leachate collection system, a land drainage system, and a thirty-foot-deep slurry wall around the perimeter of the landfill were constructed in 1988–89. The invisible (below ground) slurry wall prevents the decomposing garbage from spreading beyond the landfill and contaminating the surrounding environment. In 1991 a lined stormwater retention pond, essential to the artwork, was completed. The rest of the area on top of the landfill was covered with a plastic liner made of recycled plastic soda bottles, then graded with eighteen inches of earth, and seeded. The liner helps to contain the gas within the landfill and reduce the formation of leachate by decreasing the absorption of rainwater.

The methane gas generated by the decomposition of the organic garbage in the landfill is being collected and used as an alternative energy source for the community, supplying about ten percent of the gas used locally. The methane gas recovery system, completed in 1990, was collaboratively designed by the engineers and myself to be part of the artwork. The looping pipe arches of the system (both functional and nonfunctional) will radiate out from the center of *Sky Mound*'s "lunar area"

**Sky Mound
Plan**

Sun viewing area with pond
and two star mounds

and indicate the extreme orbital positions of the Moon—the major lunar stand-stills—which occur every 18.61 years.

From the center of the "solar area" of *Sky Mound*, the Sun will be seen rising and setting on the solstices and equinoxes, framed on the horizon by the large earth mounds and tall steel posts at the edge of the landfill. At solar noon on the Summer Solstice, a circle of light, cast through a steel structure, will fit exactly into a steel ring in the ground. The angles of the sunsets and sunrises during the solstices and equinoxes, as well as the north-south axis, are also marked by eight rays that expand out from the solar center and run down the sides of the landfill.

A methane flare, evoking local oil refinery flares, will emerge from a pipe on top of a mound on the southwestern edge of the landfill and burn brightly on certain holiday evenings. Globe vents spinning at the ends of pipes around the lower slopes of the landfill will make the wind visible, and a steel measuring pole at the bottom of the landfill will allow observation of the settling of the landfill over the years.

Since these features and the mounds, posts, and rays will be visible from the New Jersey Turnpike on one side of the landfill and the Amtrak and NJ Transit trains on the other, *Sky Mound* will be viewed by the millions of travelers who pass by it annually. From jets flying low over it on their way to Newark Airport, the star-burst of radiating paths and mounds will be visible. For those desiring to have an experience of the work from the top of the landfill, the HMDC Environment Center will offer tours of *Sky Mound*. Eventually it will be open to the public all the time.

Various bushes have been planted in an irregularly shaped pattern around the perimeter of the pond, and the water has been stocked with fish. Hopefully, *Sky Mound* will attract many of the large variety of birds in the Meadowlands. Ducks, geese, and egrets have already been sighted there. Next to the pond, on the southern edge of the landfill, alignments of tunnels and stairways in two "star mounds" will indicate the rising and setting of two of the brightest stars, Sirius and Vega.

Since the star, Sun, and Moon alignments are all to the distant horizon, they will not be altered as the landfill settles. I was well aware of the degree to which landfills settle after visiting other landfills in the New York/New Jersey area. Consequently, in *Sky Mound* I am using basic forms, such as earth mounds, ponds, and graveled and vegetated areas that will settle along with the landfill.

Sky Mound is being constructed in two stages. The first phase consists of only those elements of the *Sky Mound* project required for the closing of a landfill, such as the methane collection system and the pond. This phase is now completed, and the costs, paid by the state, are estimated at $11 million. The second phase, the construction of the remaining nonfunctional sculptural elements, was to have been completed by the fall of 1992, funded by grants from the NEA, the New Jersey State Council on the Arts and a New Jersey state environmental bond. However, in

**Sky Mound
Sunrise on the Equinox**

1991 to accommodate some technological studies at the site, the construction of *Sky Mound* was postponed indefinitely.

Trash piles have been with us for thousands of years, as far back as archeologists have traced. With a friend who is an archeologist, I once visited a cave home of the Anasazi, the earliest known human beings in the Southwest, in a high butte in northwestern Utah. There at the base of the butte, just below the cave, I saw my first prehistoric trash—a large pile of broken pottery, fish and animal bones, shells, and such. Another excavated refuse pile, several feet deep, fills the back of the cave. Even in ancient Rome, despite its many advancements in engineering, human waste, refuse, corpses, and carcasses were dumped in open pits around the city, and when the pits were full, nearby moats were often used.

Today's landfills, then, have a long heritage. Around the globe there are millions of these shunned earthen forms—forgotten trash heaps, relegated to the realms of the unconscious. By the end of the century, with more reliance on improved methods of recycling and incineration, laws will go into effect to prohibit the use of landfills for garbage disposal. These heaps of rubbish will be seen as the artifacts of our generation, our legacy to the future. So there is no escaping our responsibility for making these mounds of decaying matter safe by using the latest closure technology, and eventually reinterpreting and reclaiming them, giving them new social and aesthetic meanings and functions.

**Sky Mound
Moon Viewing Area**

1. With a few additions and changes the text for *Sun Tunnels* has been excerpted from my article, "Sun Tunnels," in *Artforum*, pp. 32–37. April, 1977.

Nancy Holt

James Turrell

I am interested in light because of my interest in our spiritual nature and the things that empower us. My art deals with light itself, not as the bearer of revelation, but as revelation itself.

I am interested in using light as material—not light in glass, scrim, or Plexiglas—but light in the space itself, without traditional physical form. One of the difficulties of using light as a medium is that there isn't yet a tradition of using it in our culture, even though it is no more unusual to use it than stone, clay, steel, or paint. There is a rich tradition in using light as a subject in painting, but the artwork is not light—it is a record of seeing. My wish is to use light as the material, not the subject, to affect the medium of perception. It is used in a nonvicarious manner.[2]

I strive for the same internal quality an individual gets looking into a fire—not thinking in words but just drifting off. I try to evoke that kind of high beta brain wave activity because it is a more universal language than the spoken word. One with primitive roots that we are very familiar with, particularly in the dream.

Our perception of this world's light changes when we leave the ground in an airplane and fly through the sky. Some of my work focuses on the kind of sky spaces that you can enter into through flight and the idea of the journey into these spaces, when consciousness moves into and inhabits the sky. There are people who have inhabited the space of the sky for some time—the Tibetans in the Himalayas, the Hopi on top of the mesas. The Hopi live near the cloud base of the summer cumulus which passes closely overhead. In a true sense they actually inhabit the sky.

Our ability to perceive the sky is directly related to the expansion of territories of the self. At night in the city, light pollution closes off access to the stars. It physically limits the extension of our territory into the Universe and psychologically encloses our world. When we cannot see the stars any longer, it will be the beginning of the end. We will isolate our planet and no longer recognize ourselves as part of the Universe.

My interest in flight, the journey, and the sky is not much different from the Peter Pan syndrome of many artists. We do not wish to grow up because we want to have a life where the imagined can be as "real" as that which is commonly agreed upon as reality. The expansion of this shared reality, by including the imagined as real, seems to create a clear purpose for the solitary acts of my journeys of self.

Flying out of South-East Asia, over Tibet and amongst the Himalayas, I saw great mountains, jungle, and beautiful terrain on journeys that expanded the territories of self. The more extraordinary experience you have in flight, the more you realize the difficulty in passing on the experience to others. It would be easier to send others on the flight itself. The role of the Bodhisattva, one who comes back and entices others on the journey, is to some degree the same as that of the artist. This is where I began to appreciate an art that could be a nonvicarious act. The subject of my work is your nonvicarious seeing. You are not looking at a record of my seeing.

When I went to Japan, especially to Suwanose, an active volcanic island, I felt to be on a living surface. The Earth was a living skin. The aerial view reveals the vitality of the Earth and the passing and re-emerging of cultures. I remember earthquakes in California, but on Suwanose the ground shook daily. Volcanoes, of course,

James Turrell understands

that seeing is not done

with the eyes.

His Roden Crater *will*

provide possibilities for

those moments of alignment

when we suddenly experience

the Universe as an unbroken whole. [1]

≈

Roden Crater

Northeast view

Land purchased in 1979
Project begun in 1982

Flagstaff, Arizona
1986

connect to the center of the Earth with molten magma. The moment I saw the chain of volcanic islands south of Japan, I knew I wanted to find a volcano to work with. Volcanoes and islands have a terrestrial "thingness" to them. Likewise, my interest in the perception of light is in giving it thingness, just as a physical object has presence. I give light thingness by putting limits on it in a formal manner. I do not create an object, only objectified perception. By putting into question physicality and "objectness," the work may reveal more about physicality than any physical object.

Roden Crater

The spaces I encountered in flight encouraged me to work with larger amounts of space and with a more curvilinear sense of the space of the sky and its limits.

If you stand on an open plain you will notice that the sky is not limitless, but has a definable shape and a sense of enclosure, which is referred to as celestial vaulting. If you lie down the shape changes. Clearly, these limits are malleable. I looked for a hemispherically shaped, dished space, between 400 and 1,000 feet above a plain, in order to work with the limits of the space of the sky. The plain would provide the opportunity for celestial vaulting. The dish shape would affect changes in the perception of the size and shape of the sky. The height above the plain was important so that the slight quality of concave curvature to the Earth experienced by pilots at low altitudes would increase the sense of celestial vaulting after you emerged from the crater space. I also wanted a high-altitude site so that the sky would be a deeper blue, which would increase a sense of close-in celestial vaulting from the bottom of the crater.

I flew all the western states looking for a site, and found *Roden Crater*, a volcano on the edge of the Painted Desert. Rather than impose a plan upon the landscape, I decided to work in phase with the surroundings of the volcano. Driving across the desert, the site is approached from the west. The road makes a half circle on the north side of the crater and comes up a ravine on its northeast side. At the top of the ravine you reach a walkway that follows the circular rim of the fumarole

James Turrell

(secondary vent of the volcano) on the northeast side of the crater. The walkway is approximately 250 feet above the plain, and gives the first sense of the expansion of space. From here, a trail proceeds up the side of the fumarole. At the top of the fumarole there will be several different spaces, which are themselves pieces that work with the space of the sky. Some of the events in the spaces might occur daily, some during equinoxes and solstices, and others will be very infrequent. From the spaces on top of the fumarole, a tunnel extends 1,035 feet. As you proceed up the tunnel you will be able to see only sky.

Roden Crater
North northeast aerial view
Flagstaff, Arizona
1982

Roden Crater
Northeast aerial view
First stage shaping of crater bowl
1989

The entrance from the tunnel into the crater is made through an intermediate space, and as you emerge into the space of the open sky, the sense of enclosure will recede.

At *Roden Crater*, I did not want the work to be a mark upon Nature, but to be enfolded in Nature in such a way that light from the Sun, Moon, and stars empowered the spaces. Usually art is taken from Nature by painting or photography and then brought back to culture through the museum. I wanted to bring culture to the natural surround as if designing a garden or tending a landscape. I wanted an area where you had a sense of standing on the planet, an area of

Roden Crater

Model
South southeast view
1987

exposed geology like the Grand Canyon or the Painted Desert, where you could feel geologic time. Then, in this stage set of geologic time, I wanted to make spaces that engaged celestial events in light. The sequence of spaces leading up to the final large space at the top of the crater magnifies events. The work I do intensifies the experience of light by isolating it and occluding all other light. Each space essentially looks to a different portion of sky and accepts a limited number of events. This is the reason for the large number of spaces at the crater.

I wanted people to advance from the floor of the desert up into the sky. This is the reason for the tunnels leading to the top. Advancing from the east or the west, the path up into the bowl describes a stepped or truncated pyramid that arrives at a bowl at least 600 feet above the surrounding terrain. In this top space, the sky literally changes shape as you move about the crater. Lying down in the top crater space you can notice the shape of the sky change. After you walk out of this space and up to the top lip of the crater and then look out over the horizon, you will notice the Earth slant beneath and towards you. People flying between 600 and 3,000 feet notice the Earth curving beneath them the wrong way. This sense of concave curving below balances the sense of the convex curving of the sky above. The volcano, the bowl-shaped space above the plain, provides the possibility for this conjunction. [3]

In the crater, there are situations that are very similar to naked eye observatories like Tycho Bray and Jai Singh. The spaces have a sense of being designed from the outside in—the architectural form of the interior is completely dictated by the events in the sky or the space outside the architecture itself. By isolating light and occluding all other light, you can make an event that is normally not seen or unimpressive into something quite amazing.

All fourteen spaces at *Roden Crater* can be accessed by wheelchair. Ramps are quite elegant, and in some instances they are the best access for everyone. However, in some places I need a sharp breakoff to create an imaging aperture. So you cannot go every way with a wheelchair, but all the spaces are accessible.

Roden Crater

South view
Shaping of crater bowl
1989

James Turrell

Space That Sees

I have been working in other locations on a series of "autonomous spaces" that help me refine the spaces that I will be creating at the crater. Part of this work consists of a *Skyspace* series that address our perception of the sky that is directly overhead. I constructed one of these *Skyspaces* at the Israel Museum in Jerusalem. Since it is constructed into a hillside, it relates very strongly to spaces in the crater. I built with stone and found out that unpolished stone remains warmer. In the crater, there are some spaces where you lie down on the stone and it can get quite cold. The quality of the space and where you sit, how you feel, and how comfortable it is are all important, and need to be worked out before I begin to realize them in the crater.

    Space that Sees is the first work I have done that is on the scale and the level of finish as my work at the crater. You go underground to see the sky. It is not the very

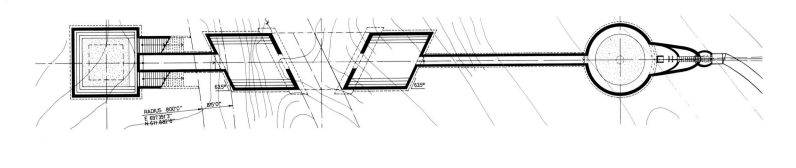

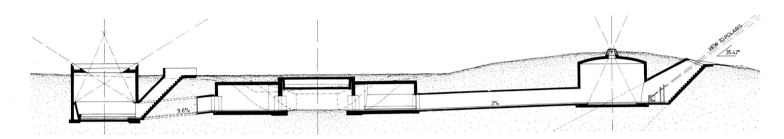

first place you would expect to see the sky upon going into a hillside. *Skyspaces* help me present a situation where the space of the sky is brought into contact with the space we are in. The sky is no longer out there, away from us, but in close contact. The plumbing of visual space through the conscious act of moving feeling out through the eyes became analogous to a physical journey of self as a flight of soul through the planes. [4]

Crater Spaces: North Space

The middle of the North Space is the main arrival point for the crater. Cars are left a couple of miles away, and visitors are shuttled to the location. The area to the south of the entry is a *Skyspace*.

The light inside the space is worked with the light outside. The interior light changes from the predominance of light coming from the outside during the day to the predominance of light coming from the inside during the night. The greatest change is noticed at the cusp of the change from day to night, or from night to day. Going from day to night, at first there is light but there is no presence. As the exterior light is reduced, there is a predominance of light on the inside. The space then encourages you to be a bottom dweller at the bottom of an ocean of air. The sky is no longer out there, but it is right on the edge of the space you are in. The sense of color is generated inside you. If you then go outside you will see a different colored sky. You color the sky. The work is about your seeing, not mine. At night the amount of light in the space allows one to see several planets and a few stars, but there is a blackness of depth and softness that is unparalleled, because it has no surface. It arises simply out of the contrast between the inside of a space where there is light and a space where there is none. [5]

In the opposite direction from the *Skyspace*, across the entry, you come to a camera obscura that projects whatever is directly overhead onto a white sand floor. I am interested in creating a passive space that senses. Nonpassive or aggressive sensing would be something like radar where you send out a signal and irradiate an area to see what comes back. It is like talking to someone to elicit a response, as opposed to just quietly observing. My spaces are themselves seeing; they are sinks of information—one needs to perceive them in order for them to be revealed. This is best demonstrated by the camera obscura space. You get a live image, and the space is seeing whether you see what the space is seeing or not. You become a witness to its sight. The space has formed up a consciousness that is reflective on your seeing.

Adjacent to the camera obscura space is a seat that directs your sight to the North Star. This element is the most important feature of the North Space. Generally we see the Sun go up and over us when in fact the Sun is relatively still and the Earth is turning. I wanted to create a space that would give the sensation of the Earth turning, instead of the sky rotating over your head. It is like when you are stopped in a train and the train next to you moves and you feel as if you are moving.

In the North Star Space there is a reclining seat that positions your view line directly to celestial north through an arrangement of two uprights. One is a ring, and the other one closer to you blocks out all light except your view of the area around celestial north. By looking through these uprights you will discern your movement around the North Star. The only thing you have to lock onto are the stars that seem to stay still, but as they seem to stay still, you find that you begin to lean. And you can straighten out, but you will begin to lean again. You feel yourself turning in relation to the rest of the Universe, and this is in fact the case.

As you proceed east from the North Space, you come to the East Space, the first water space that you will encounter at the crater. In addition to several practical reasons for incorporating the use of water it is also used to extend short-lived events. For example, by reflecting the sunrises off water at low angles of incidence, I can extend the imaged phenomenon to be twice its length of time.

The top of the crater is about 18 acres. We had a five inch rain in 1993, which is the equivalent of almost 8 acre feet of water falling inside the crater bowl. So I need a cistern tank that can hold about 4 acre feet of water with a system for overflow into a large pipe down the tunnel, in the event a rain like that comes again.

During construction, the large pours of concrete will need to have cooling coils put into the mass to slow down the cure. I will then be left with these coils within the concrete that I plan to run water through to moderate the temperature of the water in some of the spaces. If more heat is needed, I can bring the water through some of the black rock masses of the crater, thereby utilizing the solar gain of the crater. In this way, I believe we can maintain the water at about 78-80 degrees year round.

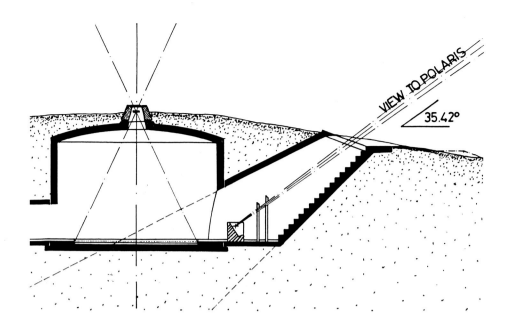

Roden Crater
North Space

Detail of camera obscura
and North Star seat
1994

East Space

The East Space is comprised of two pools. The exterior pool is quite large—sixty feet on a side. From this pool, you can look out to the surrounding country and experience the sunrise. There are actually two buttes visible from this space that the Sun rises between during the equinox seasons. This pool also has a *Skyspace* above part of it. Because of the opening to the east and the *Skyspace* directly overhead, I can take light from different portions of the sky and mix them. Through this simultaneous contrast, I can change your perception of the tangible light. Light inside the space from a red/orange sunrise in the east is going to totally change your perception of the color of the sky above through the *Skyspace*. The outdoor sky directly overhead at this time of day would appear as a completely different color.

The second pool is an interior space with no other opening but a very narrow slit in the east wall. I wanted to create a space to hold the heat by making a water seal. So to enter this space, you actually have to dive down into the exterior pool and come up inside the interior one. It is a very rarefied space, for the Sun images a

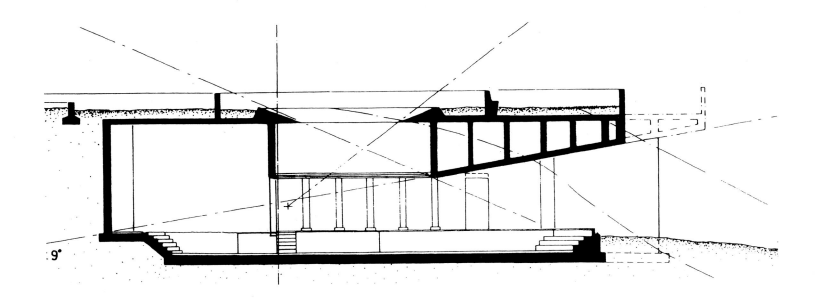

9°

plane of light across the space and into the water as well only at sunrise. The narrow slit in the east wall allows the light from every sunrise to enter the space, and the low angle of incidence of the rising Sun reflecting off the water extends the sunrise event for almost twice as long. The space will also create special light events on the days of the solstices and equinoxes along the west wall at the back of the pool.

The architecture of the East Space is defined by the movement of the Sun. In the plan view the two pools appear as intersecting triangles. The point of intersection is the narrow slit in the west wall of the exterior pool. From this vantage point, the north and south walls of the exterior pool align with the yearly extreme positions of the sunrises. The light of the Sun pivots through the slit in the wall separating the two pools, and enters the interior space. The west wall of the interior pool extends north and south only as far as the light reaches from the sunrises. In this way, the extreme positions of the Sun dictate the form of the space's interior.

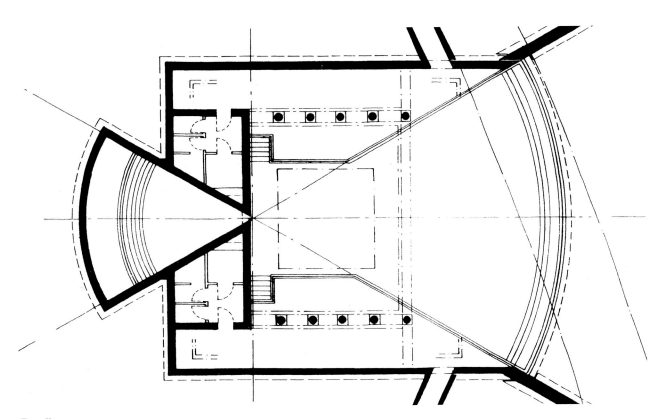

James Turrell

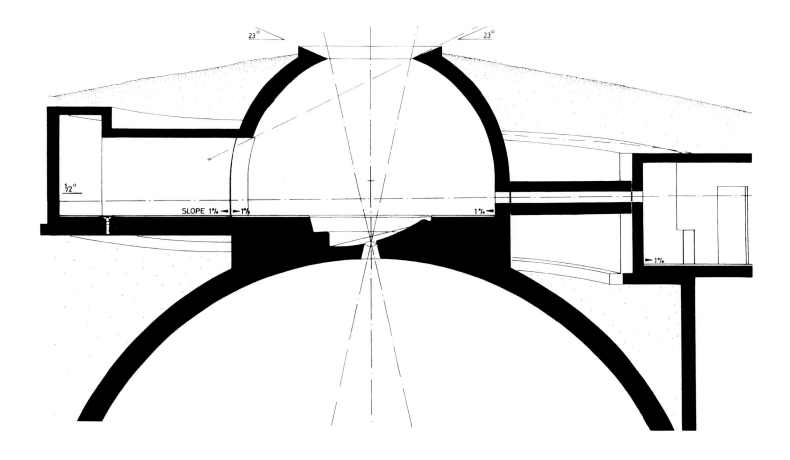

Bath Space

I wanted to create a space that would greatly magnify what was directly overhead twenty-four hours a day. I am not concerned with creating a structure with the accuracy of Palamor. A lens of quite a large diameter can be made very cheaply by using water instead of glass. Therefore, I designed a bath on top of the Fumarole Sphere that would also serve as a powerful telescope, focusing the light of the image on the sand covered floor of the sphere. The structure not only looks like an eye; the bath on top acts as the cornea. The sphere is 60 feet in diameter, and there will be a location at its midway point where you will be able to view the image from above. On a clear night, the floor will be covered with the image of stars or even the Moon, and someone relaxing in the bath will appear to you to be floating through the heavens.

The bath creates a ten-foot-diameter lens. The bottom of the bath is actually a tilted mirror with a hole in it. I wanted to tilt the mirror like this so the bath could also serve as a radio telescope. In this way, you will not only be able to view from the sphere below what is happening at zenith, but people reclining in the bath will also hear the objects that are currently at zenith. The pickup for the dish is up at the edge of the *Skyspace* above. Like the pickup on any satellite dish, it is an antenna. It sends its signal to an area in the floor, and like a crystal set, it requires no batteries—the radiation itself powers it. The signal is then sent through some narrow band filters to select things like the Sun, pulsars, planets, etc. From here the signal is put into a transducer that is in contact with the water. You will not hear anything until you put your head and ears under the water.

Now, the nice thing is that the bowl of the bath, which acts as the shell of the antenna, creates a lounge-like area to lie within since it is tipped up. So while looking up into the sky in the bath, if you have your ear in the water, you will hear the radio noise that the space is looking at through the opening. With our eyes we see only a very small portion of the electromagnetic spectrum released by celestial

Roden Crater
Bath Space

Elevation view
Atop the Fumarole Sphere
This space serves as an optical
and radio telescope
1994

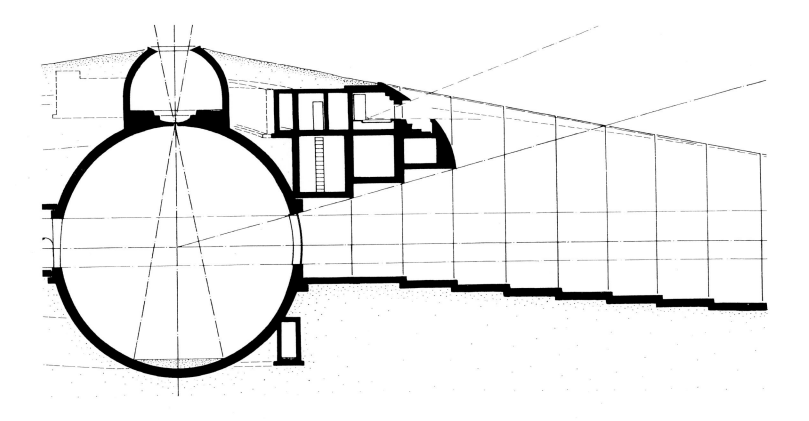

objects. The Bath Space is just extending part of that range into a range where most things are likely to happen. So the bath not only becomes a cornea for the eye but also an ear drum for the ear.

Fumarole Sphere

The Fumarole sphere is a sixty-foot-diameter sphere constructed of concrete and finished plaster. The ramp from the East Space enters the sphere at its midway point, and it is from this area that you can look down to the image projected from the Bath Space above. From the midpoint, you can continue up the ramp to the Bath Space or down the ramp to the bottom, where the focused image from the Bath Space appears.

The entry at the midpoint of the Fumarole Sphere also serves as a simple lens for the imaging of the Summer Solstice sunrise on the stone in the Sun and Moon Room. I need a crisp step coming up to the space so light is trapped and reflected out of the space. It is like walking through a camera. You need to have these bellows, or these ways of keeping light from reflecting and bouncing back to where the image is seen. Reflected light is unresolved and will degrade the image. So I need a series of baffles or edges to cut down the reflection and the knife edge refraction. They are steps, but they are different from steps because they have to be made precisely on the angle that is being protected. So sometimes the step has an off rise in relationship to the tread.

I have to be very careful with how the wheelchair ramps access this type of space. The type of light off the ramps is exactly what I am trying to avoid. So often the ramps approach at another angle or service another entrance.

There are two rooms adjacent to the Fumarole Sphere and two rooms closer to the South Space where people can stay overnight. The sleeping rooms above the Fumarole Sphere image the Sun at sunrise. This is done by closing a shutter or blind that has an opening in it that aligns the sunrise on the vertical wall over your head.

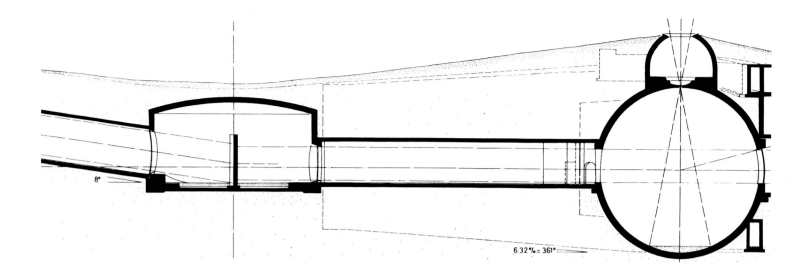

8°

6.32% = 361°

Sun and Moon Room

The furthest south moonset that happens every 18.61 years and the furthest north sunrise that occurs yearly on the Summer Solstice are imaged in Sun and Moon Room. They each appear on either side of a large stone in the center of this space, and each of their images is fourteen feet in diameter.

I have chosen the furthest south setting of the full Moon to image on the stone because the full Moon sets right before the Sun rises. This relationship produces a powerful light giving the most radiance and making the strongest image. The long tunnel that aligns with the furthest south moonset and images the Moon on the stone leads up into the crater. So it needs to be aimed over the far horizon of the crater bowl to capture the image of the Moon. This causes the tunnel to be aimed above the horizon of the place where the moonset would actually take place. So the image on the stone serves as a herald of the actual event on the horizon. You will have fifteen minutes from the time you see the effect inside the crater to walk up to the rim of crater and witness the actual moonset on the horizon.

The image of the Sun is brought into the Sun and Moon Room through three doorways and through the center of the Fumarole Sphere. The light of the Sun enters the room through a "pinhole" lens after passing through a hydrogen/alpha filter that reflects back everything except the hydrogen spectrum. This produces on the stone a fourteen foot image of the surface of the Sun with its sunspots and solar flares. The image of the Sun lasts four minutes, and then you can walk out and watch the actual sunrise.

Therefore, with both the Sun and the Moon event, you can experience this consciously formed way of looking at the phenomena. A heightened experience that is in some ways more real because you have removed all other ambient light.

Tso Kiva

Walking up the tunnel into the crater from the Sun and Moon Room, you will eventually come to a pool in the center of the crater, which is part of the drainage system. The space will last the longest because it is built on the basalt plug of the volcano. Many of the volcanos toward the southern end of Monument Valley are volcanic plugs—the cinder cones have eroded away. We are making the Tso Kiva on top of a plug that connects to the center of the Earth.

There are four places surrounding the space where you can lie down with your head below your feet. Your feet are pointed toward the crater center, and there is a neck role in stone that allows your head to drop down and direct your sight backwards toward the horizon of the crater. When you lie down, you see a shaping of sky that is more pronounced—a celestial vaulting.

**Roden Crater
Sun and Moon Room,
Fumarole Sphere**

Elevation view
To the right is the Sun and Moon Room.
The stone in the center of this room
will receive an image of the moonrise
of the furthest south lunar extreme and
the image of the sunrise of the
furthest north solar extreme.
1994

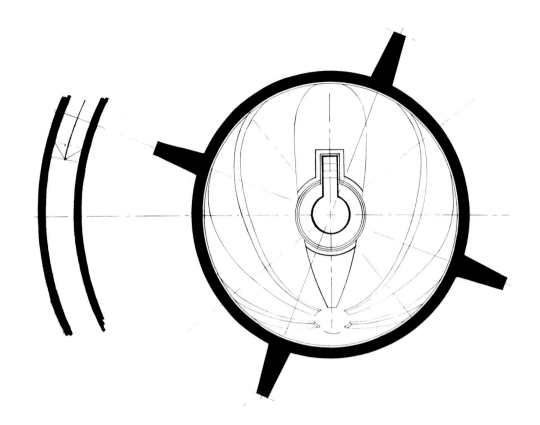

**Roden Crater
Tso Kiva**

Plan view
The pool is in the center of the drawing.
The four exterior points illustrate the
location of the markers upon which
one can lie to view the celestial
vaulting phenomena of the crater.
The arc on the left shows the ramp which
accesses the kiva from the floor of the crater
1994

**Roden Crater
Tso Kiva**

Elevation view
In the center,
steps can be seen
leading down into the pool.
Immediately below the pool is
the reservoir for the crater.
The opening in the kiva,
shown to the left, is aligned with
the Earth's axis and directs the
view of anyone looking through
the kiva to celestial north
1994

The Tso Kiva itself is a hemisphere, and these four seating situations are markers. The radius of the hemisphere is about 68 feet. The very bottom of the hemisphere meets the water, and is the highest level that the water in the reservoir can rise. Gores, or shapes cut into the hemisphere, cast displays of light onto and into the water. They also serve as entry ways into the interior pool.

The opening to the sky is not really a *Skyspace*. Instead, from the pool you look straight up through a ring that is held up by the four markers on which you lie to observe the horizon. The events imaged in the water look at the turning or tipping of the Earth through the year. This is why the ring is off center to the south. The ring is very high to emphasize the change in Sun angles throughout the year. The Tso Kiva doesn't create atmospheres like the other spaces do. It deals with shadow and light and patterns of shapes.

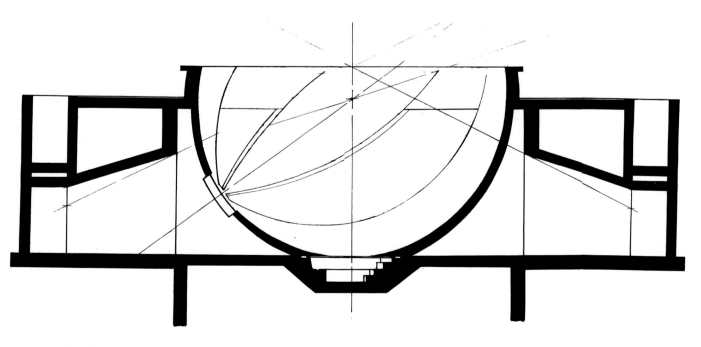

Photo: Jean-Luc Terradilos

Heavy Water

At Confort Moderne in Poitier, France, I designed a space in response to the baptistery in Poitier, the oldest in France. The installation is like Tso Kiva in the fact that it utilizes sky and water. You enter the space by submerging in water and actually swimming to the light. It is so much easier to image something in water than in air. When we see a swimming pool it looks as though the pool is filled with light—the light is contained in the volume of water. There was a complete coming together of water and light in this work: fiber optics turned the showers into a bath of light and the foot baths glowed. The work will be permanently installed in a ridge at le Crested near Vaisione Romaigne, northeast of Avignon.

South and West Space

I designed the South Space with Dick Walker, an astronomer with the Naval Observatory in Flagstaff. It will serve as a type of map, telling what is happening in each particular space during the day. It is the space that has been laid out with the most attention to celestial mechanics—a very magnificent sundial and moondial put together.

The West Space is primarily a sunset area. Both the east and west spaces deal with the pyrotechnics of sky color at the open and close of day. They draw our attention not only to sunrise and sunset, but also to the rising and setting of the night, which is marked by the projection of the Earth's shadow into the atmosphere. The phenomenon is called the

Photo: Jean-Luc Terradilos

Twilight Arch, and can be seen as a sliver blue band with pink above it, setting in the west prior to sunrise and rising in the east prior to sunset.

To some degree, a lot of my art is a "seeing aid." By calling attention to something, you attend to it, whereas you might not have otherwise. As one author once said, "It is not necessarily me that will stand up." A lot of what these spaces call attention to is already there.

There are ecologists that would challenge my art as being environmentally correct. They feel that we should do nothing to alter our environ. However, we don't protest the building of a coral reef, which is one of the biggest structures made by any being that is on the Earth. In the same way, we sort of excrete cities. I believe we make these concrete cities with as much forethought as the coral has in making the reef. Generally we are pretty much crustaceans. We build these houses and inhabit them, then we run outside and get into a moveable structure, and then go and get out of that into another shell—sort of musical hermit crab games. And yet these actions tend to close us off from the feeling of being involved with Nature. So that even though we make these structures just like coral or anything else that makes a barrier, we don't have knowledge of what we do. It's that feeling of being apart that estranges us from Nature. So I am interested in things that take away the estrangement. [6]

My desire is to set up a situation to which I can take you and let you see. It becomes your experience. I am doing that at *Roden Crater*. It's not taking from Nature but placing you in contact with it. *Roden Crater* has knowledge in it, and it does something with that knowledge. Environmental events occur; a space lights up. Something happens in there, for a moment, or for a time. It is an eye, something that is itself perceiving. It is a piece that does not end: it is changed by the action of the Sun, the Moon, the cloud cover, by the day and the season that you're there. When you're there, it has visions, qualities, and a universe of possibilities. [7]

Roden Crater

Northeast view
Sunset
1986

Above Left:
Heavy Water
Installation, Confort Moderne

Pool into Skyspace
Poitier, France
1991–92

Left:
Heavy Water
Installation, Confort Moderne

Skyspace into pool
Poitier, France
1991–92

James Turrell

1. Suzi Gablik, "Dream Space: James Turrell", *Art in America*, March, 1987, p. 135.
2. Julia Brown, *Occluded Front*, Interview with James Turrell, Lapis Press, 1986, pp. 42–43.
3. Excerpted from *James Turrell, Air Mass*, Interview with James Turrell, The South Bank Center, pp. 15–26.
4. Ibid p. 52.
5. Ibid p. 52.
6. Janet Saad Cooke, "Touching the Sky", *Archeoastronomy*, Jan/Dec, 1985, Vol. VIII, Nos. 1–4, p. 134.
7. Keith McDonald, "The Roden Crater Project", Interview with James Turrell, *Sedona Life*, Jan, 1979, p.47.

Robert Adzema

In the early 1970s, the world and I seemed to be running out of sync with each other. Technology was king, and profits were made at the expense of nature, the environment, and human well-being. I searched for and found a kind of time that was not full of anxiety and hurry, that respected nature. I wanted to give each task, person, and conversation the kind of time it rightly deserved. I also wanted to work with a sculptural form that was generated from its location on the Earth. Thus, I began the study of the kind of time and form spoken by sundials and gnomics.

From a sculptor's point of view, sundials provide a basic form and geometry on which to build. Solar time flows in a smooth movement of shadows from sunrise to sunset. This daily rhythm and the rhythmic changing light of the seasons became a powerful directive in my work. For the past twenty years, I have tried to make sunlight a more conscious matter, to give it a more tangible form.

The power of the Earth's meridian (north/south axis) in the positioning of a sundial is as generative a force as the sundial and sunlight itself. When I place a sundial sculpture, the north-south axis that develops on the ground or in the air gives the surrounding buildings, houses, even the shoreline where land and sea meet, a point of reference. This creates a strong sense of place which can be seen and felt. The spot becomes connected to the Earth and the heavens.

My work speaks of our collective relationship to the Earth, the heavens, the seasons, and the Sun. It strives to make people aware and physically awake to each specific place in time. The sundial sculptures are an invitation to pause and reflect and appreciate the moment.

Single Digital Sundial

This sundial sculpture was made with the support of the Forma Viva International Sculpture Symposium, conducted in 1986 in the city of Maribor, in the then Slovenia Republic of Yugoslavia, now Slovenia.

As a member of the concrete symposium, I was given a predetermined site, a concrete factory, and one month to produce the work. Each artist was specifically given the freedom to create a work of their own choosing in the then communist country.

Unique to the Maribor symposium was the fact that the sculptures were made in streets, squares, or parks, and not in isolated sculpture gardens. Working alongside concrete technicians, stress analysts, engineers, and contractors, artists were encouraged to exchange ideas and match and challenge one another with inventiveness. The idea of a cooperative art work was seen as an act of creative courage and a ray of hope, a victory of positive human values.

Throughout the ages, cultures around the world have studied the order of our solar system by creating light-and-shadow events. Robert Adzema's work revisits this ancient practice by making the science of sundials into a contemporary public art form.

≈

Single Digital Sundial
Maribor, Slovenia
1986

Single Digital Sundial
Maribor, Slovenia
1986

Single Digital Sundial
The hour of the day is projected
onto the ground by the Sun
passing through the sculpture

Forma Viva invited me to create a sundial in a somewhat formal setting in front of a local borough hall. The setting was accurately aligned for a dead-on south facing sundial. My project was technically challenging in terms of thin shell concrete construction. I had first developed the idea in my *Great Sundial Cutout Book* as a paper model. The sculpture was to use natural light to project the time in illuminated numbers on the ground. The time is told near the base in summer and further out in winter, where people actually walk through the illuminated time on the ground. I wanted to create a special place where people would pause in their day to reflect. At the edge of the large circular terrace I cast the phrase, "With the sun for this special place."

The Forma Viva Sculpture Symposium was started by two sculptors in 1960. It has now supported the creation of approximately 250 sculptures by artists from all over the world. Each symposium was held in towns and cities suited to each material or industry. Companies donated the money, time, and goods, while participating towns gave food and housing. Each artist was paid approximately $1,000 in Yugoslav currency. The generosity of these people amidst so much hardship and scarcity inspired a great deal of artistic generosity in me. I hope Slovenia will continue its tradition and example of inviting foreign artists to come and work.

Robert Adzima

Port Richmont High School Sundial

Following a screening/interview process, I was commissioned by the New York City Board of Education, New York City School Construction Authority, and New York City Department of Cultural Affairs Per Cent for Art Program to design a sundial sculpture for the front of the school's new addition and entrance. To my delight, the front of the school was off axis to the street line by 17 degrees, permitting me to develop a sundial visible when approaching the school from both the north and the south. This off axis north-south line also created a powerful tension to the front of the school, resulting in a notched and angled planter at the base and to the north of the sundial.

On a true north-south line, emphasizing the north-south axis of the site, I developed a noon mark solar calendar called an analemma. This is a brass strip

imbedded in a gray concrete pad, six feet wide by thirty-two feet long. A circular aperture near the top of the sundial casts a beam of light on the ground that crosses the north-south line, marking apparent high noon, solar time. The sunbeam is also an accurate solar calendar if noted at the same exact moment, standard time, each day of the year. It traces an elegant figure eight shape, the analemma, which describes the changing altitude, or seasonal declination of the Sun, and the equation of time. It also marks the Summer and Winter Solstices and the Fall and Spring Equinoxes.

The "equation of time" describes the difference between clock and solar time, which agree only four days a year. The difference results from the elliptical orbit of the Earth around the Sun, which causes the Sun to appear to move fastest in November and slowest in March. To reconcile sundials with clocks, it is necessary to add or subtract various numbers of minutes according to the declination of the Sun on that date. A line drawn through the length of the analemma intersects the four dates a year that solar and clock time agree. On dates when the sun falls farthest from the center line, more minutes must be added or subtracted to reconcile the two times.

The primary image of this sundial is that of a rudder, sail, or nautical instrument, which is encouraged by a wave form at the base of the dial. These images were developed as a result of interviews with a sensitive and involved school administrator who explained the town's nautical history.

Port Richmond High School Sundial

Each day of the year, the standard time noon shadow cast by the circular aperture near the top of the sculpture traces an analemma, a figure eight, solar calendar pattern on the ground. The image above shows the shadow's location at noon on the Winter Solstice.

A sundial sculpture seemed very appropriate to grace the entrance of a school. It demonstrates one of mankind's earliest scientific instruments, making visible the daily movements of the Earth in relation to the Sun and its daily rotation. The students or classes who choose to get involved have before them a ready study of the concepts of "even hours," of latitude and longitude, and of the specificity of any spot on Earth. If they try to work out their own sundials, they'll find themselves using geometry and geography and thinking about time as something more "real" and physical than clock time. I hope it gives them some sense of how their particular moment relates to the larger world of other places and other times.

If I have been successful, the project will affect the lives of the people who pass it daily, offering inspiration and perhaps an invitation to pause in their day, consider their place in relation to the world at large, notice sunlight and shadow, and try and understand its geometry. Maybe it will even suggest a direction, an idea to steer by.

Robert Adzema

Phyllis Yampolsky

It was never my decision to move the work I was doing as a painter to another dimension of art. It was a pursuit my conscience demanded whenever I came up with what I thought was a solution to a public or private problem that bothered me.

I began to design and produce events in the 1960s: the first Paint-In, multi-media town halls; art curriculums that grounded students in the basic creative process; a network of multi-media teen centers in ten upstate New York towns where teens hosted the whole town-at-issue forums; visual town hall systems for political campaigns; the youth pavilion at the San Antonio Expo in 1970; and an indefinite number of participation festivals.

The premise for all the events was the design of a physical or non-physical skeletal structure that people were invited to complete by some act of thought or expression. I enjoy best never knowing what it is the participants will create. The hope is that by structuring the invitation accurately, the people's activity will inscribe in them the idea, question, or discovery that I am trying to bring them. The potential of such events is in the shelter that a surround of festivity provides, making participation unscary.

Sun, Radiants and Shadow (S, R and S)

S, R and S [1] grew from a one time piece for the New Wilderness's 15th Annual Summer Solstice Festival in Central Park into its own series of festivals, because passersby, producers, and participants at each occasion insisted the event continue. By 1989 it had become North Brooklyn's major annual festival, and the organizing group had become the Solstice Company. [2]

The festival is a dawn to sunset event, designed to achieve by the end of the day, and through public participation of all ages, the construction of a sculpture that traces on the ground what the Sun is doing in the Summer Solstice sky.

The dates of most of our major holidays throughout the year are based upon the ancient practice of honoring the annual north to south journey of the Sun. Phyllis Yampolsky's yearly event, Sun, Radiants and Shadow, brings multicultural communities together from dawn until dusk to remember and celebrate the Summer Solstice Sun.

≈

Photo: Robert Adzema

Photo: Robert Adzema

Sun, Radiants and Shadows

Left: Raising of Sungate, dawn, Central Park
Above left: Marking of Shadow Line
Above right: Noon parade through Sungate
Central Park, New York City
Below: Decoration of Shadow Line
Loisaida, Brooklyn, New York

Phyllis Yampolsky

The piece first presents an astronomically calculated circular field, sixty feet in diameter. The first field was laid out by Russ Waugh, an astronomer at the Haydn Planetarium, and the succeeding fields by Robert Adzema, noted sundial sculptor.

The fulcrum of the piece is the Sun Gate, serving as a gnomon. It was designed each year by Adzema, and the last three years in collaboration with sculptors Mary Kay Coffin and Peggy Vail. Each gate is about sixteen feet high, and in keeping with the spirit of the rest of the structure, begins at dawn in skeletal form, later to be painted and festooned by the public.

The shadow line is created in a nonstop continuum by tracing the shadow of the Sun Gate gnomon as it moves across the field all day. The line is built by the public out of found objects, assuring that its character changes each year according to the site and the objects available. The first line was built from a truck load of golden bricks found on an old Brooklyn pier. The people played blocks with them, created miniature Stone Henges, and coated their segment with gold glitter, all in time to the moving shadow. In the late afternoon the Sun picked up the glitter, making the line look like a glistening archaeological find. The *S, R & S* site at Loisadia in New York City provided rubble that the children painted, glittered, flowered, and beribboned into objects so imbued with their innocence that the line and radiants became a genuine shrine.

In counterpoint to the rhythm of the elongating shadow line, sixteen radiants, each thirty feet long, are thrown out from the base of the Sun Gate in the direction of the Sun, once each hour from dawn to sunset. These indicate where the Sun is at that moment and which meridian of the globe is celebrating Solstice noon.

The radiant line is opened by throwing out a golden cord. It then becomes a platform for performance. Musicians, dancers, and other performance artists provide humorous, provocative, and meditative events throughout the day.

In Brooklyn, people of all ages participated and became reflections of the city's multi-cultural heritage. People from the Polish, Irish, Latino, Native-American, and African-American communities were magicians, puppeteers, singers, stilt walkers, storytellers, and dancers.

As the events grew, the performances expanded onto the adjoining field. Original games were added, such as the blindfold game, adapted from the Hopi Indian saying: "On the Summer Solstice one sees what one has heretofore been blinded to." In this game, a blindfolded person walks the radiant toward the Sun. At the periphery of the circle, the blindfold is removed and the person recites what it is he or she first sees. The vision is written down and hung on the vision tree. One child said, "I see God." For a while, there was a spate of children who saw God.

In the third year the town crier was initiated. As each radiant opened, and with bells ringing, the crier called out the hour and the countries celebrating Solstice noon at that time. The following year a painted clock that told the same story was hung from a pole at the foot of each radiant, adding to the crier's calls.

After each of the hourly performances and games, the radiant is closed by laying out strips of fabric 11 inches wide by 30 feet long. At first the strips were gradating hues of colored cloth that by the end of the day described the spectrum. By the third year the radiants had become canvas that the festival participants painted. At Loisaida the children painted and placed paper plates serving glittered and ribboned rocks up and down the radiants. It was their solution to a windy day.

The radiant is finally closed when one of the sixteen golden ribbons floating loose from the top of the gate is stretched out over each horizontal radiant and anchored at its foot. These diagonals were part of Adzema's Sun Gate design.

Sun, Radiants and Shadow creates a one day communal reality. Tasks done together with a field full of others, and in direct interplay with the demands of the Sun, exemplify the most satisfying definition of work, i.e. play, or vice versa. One time a mother called out to her son, "Come on . . . Let's go!" He was about ten, busy wrapping part of the Sun Gate with colored yarns, and he didn't answer. After her third call he called back, without looking up, "Can't you see I'm working?"

At the end of the day, the late shadow line overlaps the early radiants and the late radiants overlap the early shadow line. By sundown, the people have transformed the field into a giant sundial, the bands come out, and we dance.

1. Inspiration for *Sun, Radiants and Shadow*: Mimi Lobell, architect and expert on myths and symbols.
2. The Solstice Company consists of Robert Adzema, Nancy Buffum, Shawn Conlon, Beth Goldowitz, Susan Koch, Max Vasquez, and Phyllis Yampolsky.

Photo: Beth Goldowitz

Photo: Jackie Scesny

Photo: Jeffrey Schwartrz

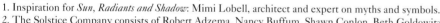

Sun, Radiants and Shadow

Top: The blindfold game
Left: Parading the radiant into place
Middle: Painting the radiants
McCarren Park, Brooklyn, New York
Bottom: Radiants at sunset
Loisaida, Brooklyn, New York
Above Right: Performance on the radiant path
Below Right: Sungate, radiant and shadow line at 10:30 A.M.
Central Park, New York, New York

Phyllis Yampolsky

Donna Henes

For more than twenty years I have served as an urban shaman, celebration artist, and unofficial "Commissioner of Public Spirit" for New York City. During these past two decades I have organized countless public participatory events and ceremonies in parks, plazas, museums, hospitals, institutions of learning, correctional facilities, and on the streets. I have also begun a monthly syndicated column, *From the Files of a Contemporary Ceremonialist*, that addresses cross-cultural ritual practice and the natural phenomena that inspire and inform it.

As shamans in every culture have always done, I create contemporary ritual for my community—which I consider to be all of humanity. My role is that of a catalyst: I initiate innovative, de-mystified systems for creative interaction, celebration, and communion. I work to facilitate transformative ways for people to interrelate. The spiritually charged atmosphere that I strive to establish provides the stimulation and safety wherein people can experience a sense of cosmic unity.

It is my special concern to offer significant and relevant ways for city people in modern times to observe and relate to the wondrous workings of the world. The vast majority of the planet's population now dwells in sprawling, paved, loud, and light-polluted megalopolises. We are disenfranchised from the natural world, which is itself in the process of disappearing. Despite what most of us learned as children about the Solar System, we find it hard to remember on a daily basis that we are at this moment upside down, rotating and revolving, and spinning through space at an incredible speed all at the same time. It is difficult to realize that we are part of, but painfully apart from, the plans and patterns of the Cosmos. I believe that the only thing that can save our planet from ourselves is for us to start thinking of ourselves as the planet.

Amulet Mandala

Amulet Mandala is a ritual of relationship: a ceremony of connectivity. It is a physical, gestalt illustration of the interlocking and interdependent nature of the Universe. It serves to establish contact and a sense of connection among the participants, as well as being a visceral reminder of the vaster and more complex interconnections between ourselves, other species, and the nonanimistic forces of Nature.

One orientation of healing which is both ancient and "new age" considers the possibility that much mental and physical illness is a manifestation of deep psychic "dis-ease": a break in the awareness of connection which holds us in proper alignment. *Amulet Mandala* was designed to remind us in actual and subliminal ways that we are indeed connected to each other, to our own inner selves, and to all the other elements that act together in the intricate network that is our Universe.

The format for *Amulet Mandala* is simple: it is patterned on the circle games that small children play. The participants sit on the floor in a circle. I sit in the center of the circle. I quietly unravel masses of knotted and tangled yarn. After a while, I begin to talk, spinning yarns. The theme of the ceremony is symbolized by the knot, the universal symbol for cosmic connectivity. I invite everyone to help unwind the yarn and put it into neat balls. All-the-while I talk and encourage others to talk about knots and all of the folkloric, etymological, religious, cross-cultural,

The beauty of Donna Henes's

work is that she motivates us

to get our bodies involved

in the process of learning.

The memory of an act, as simple

as standing an egg on end,

will stay with us

as a gentle reminder of

our vital balance within creation.

≈

Amulet Mandala

Indianapolis Museum of Art
Indianapolis, Indiana
1983

symbolic, and practical imagery of knots, weaving, and webs. The group shares myths, fairy tales, true stories, and reminiscences.

When the mass of yarn has been untangled and wound into balls, I tie a knot on each person and form a closed circle. While I am tying the knots I am saying softly:

Tying a knot is making a connection. Making a connection is making energy.
Making energy is making magic. Making magic is making love.
Making love is tying a knot.

Everyone joins in the saying/singing/chanting, all the while throwing the balls of yarn at one another across the circle, making more knots and creating a visual web out of the yarn. By the time we run out of yarn, we are all connected. Our interconnectedness becomes very obvious because each person's movements cause the web to quiver. Movement can be felt as well as seen by every person.

We continue to chant and play, eventually getting tangled together in this web which symbolizes the network of the Universe. It can become very silly and funny, and usually everybody ends up laughing together.

When each person leaves, he or she takes one knot as a reminder of the relationship of the group and to retain a sense of strength based on that memory. The yarn is left in its original tangled state, ready to be taken and used elsewhere. Thousands of people from schools, hospitals, convention centers, and museums in fifty cities and nine countries have added to and taken from the accumulated energy in the highly charged yarn.

Donna Henes

Eggs on End: Standing on Ceremony

The Solstices and Equinoxes, the four cross-quarter days that divide each season in half, the full and new Moons, eclipses, and other sky phenomena are what I call "Celestially Auspicious Occasions." They are milestones that enable us to recognize ourselves as participants in the planetary cycles of our Solar System—the seasons of the year and the seasons of our lives.

Soon after I started celebrating the seasons, a friend of mine returned from the Orient with an odd bit of equinoctial information. Apparently, in pre-revolutionary China it was customary to stand eggs on end on the first day of Spring in order to guarantee good luck for the entire year. What an intriguing idea! I immediately set out to prove its validity on American soil.

Saturday at 6:50 A.M. a group of us celebrated the 1976 Vernal Equinox in the park in the manner of Chinese peasants. The egg feels discernibly heavier, and you can feel the yolk moving around on the inside seeking its balance in the Universe. We stood eggs on end in the park and at least one on everybody's kitchen counter for the good luck that observing such a phenomenon can bring.[1]

The following Equinox I mustered all of my trust in cosmic continuity and advertised a public gathering to stand eggs. I fervently believed that the eggs would stand again. Still, the tiniest thrill of terror seized me—"Please, please let it work." What a primal prayer! If the eggs had not stood, the Earth would have to have been sorely off orbit, and I wouldn't have a worry in the world!

Of course, they did stand. The event itself was and has remained utterly simple. The site, some megalith urban Stonehenge, is decorated with a circle cast, marked in Day-Glo orange ribbons, transforming a secular public place into a sacred ground. Scientific/mythic information sheets are distributed along with jelly eggs. Flares are lit to denote the number of days, weeks, and months in the year. An orange laundry basket containing 360 eggs is passed around the crowd. We hold the eggs up in the air together, pledging to walk on the Earth as if we were walking on eggs, promising in honor of the season to protect our fragile yet resilient planet home. We count down the minutes to the Equinox, and when the time is right, stand our eggs on end in unison, in salute to Spring.

Eggs on End: Standing on Ceremony
Vernal Equinox Celebration
World Trade Center
New York, New York
1984

Eggs on End: Standing on Ceremony
Vernal Equinox Celebration
World Trade Center
New York, New York
1986

The next morning a photograph of the eggs standing on end against a brilliantly lit skyscraper background appeared in the New York Times, and the rest is history. *Eggs on End: Standing on Ceremony* has, from the first, captured the imagination of the press as well as the general public. Over the years, the egg events have been covered by every major television, radio, and wire service network in the world. The phenomenon sparks a zestful curiosity and appreciation for the mysteries of Nature. It is impossible to calculate how many millions of people have been exposed to and inspired by this delightful demonstration of astronomical wonder.

There is something powerful in the image and experience of an egg standing upright that touches people deeply and elicits extremely old and rarely accessed emotions. Standing an egg on its end, feeling the yolk shift inside, finding its perfect point of balance, is like holding the entire Universe in the palm of your hand. The feeling of excitement is profound and permanent.

An upright egg on the first moment of Spring becomes the symbol of a new season, the birth of new life. *Eggs on End: Standing on Ceremony* is every bit a traditional vernal fertility rite, a popular, contemporary celebration of the return of green and growth and light after the dark winter. It is immaterial whether or not an egg will stand at other times of the year, as some critics have tried to say. The important thing is recognizing the symbol, the season, the kindred souls that surround us. Cynicism magically disappears amidst sincere participation. Like the buds and birds of early spring, we are renewed, refreshed, and energetic. We can then turn with optimistic resolve back to what we have come to believe is the real world.

Eggs On End: Standing on Ceremony
Vernal Equinox Celebration
Battery Park

New York, New York
1982

---

1. Donna Henes © 1976. Published in *Heresies*, a feminist publication on art and politics. Spring, 1978.

Photo: Kathy Kennedy

Donna Henes

Fern Shaffer
Othello Anderson

Othello Anderson

I began my career as an artist with a strong sense of environmental awareness. As far back as I can remember, the idea of a spiritual essence has always been present in my life. When I was a child, my grandmother read and told stories that had spiritual and humanitarian underpinnings. The stories' themes of integrity, sensitivity, and responsibility played a major role in the shaping of my interests and perspective on the world.

Having learned of past and present peoples who embraced their relationship with Nature, it disturbs me to see our current society disregarding this close inter-dependency. The reality of our world has given me the necessary ingredients to create environmental art.

Currently I am working on paintings that manifest my concerns about the impact of environmental devastation on our forests. I have concentrated specifically on forests that have been depleted as a result of acid rain and fog. Through my paintings, I've tried to show the paradox of how rain, which is meant to be life-sustaining, can lead to the destruction of life. My paintings convey a sense of urgency with respect to the developing crisis.

Fern Shaffer

My interest in science has always directed me to information about the environment. By recognizing how everything is interconnected, our society can avoid mistakes that will only come back to haunt it. It makes no sense to poison the water

The team of Fern Shaffer and Othello Anderson strive to bring a sense of balance into our modern lives through the ancient practice of prayer and ritual. They hope that the images they produce through documenting these events can help to inspire others to bring ritual and prayer for the Earth into their own lives.

≈

when we will ultimately be the ones to consume it. The pattern is repeated over and over again revealing the crisis potential of our culture's desire for immediate gratification. Living in an increasingly dangerous, toxic, and stagnant environment led me to investigate the dilemma through my art.

Green is one of the main colors of the Earth. Because it is the color of foliage, it represents the life-sustaining process of photosynthesis. However, this life-sustaining green has also recently been associated with the theory of the Greenhouse Effect. The images that came to me when thinking about the Greenhouse Effect were so devastating that I was compelled to paint them to show the world what it might look like someday. The color of the atmosphere I painted is chromium oxide green, which in itself is toxic. To show the various stages of the Greenhouse Effect, I completed four large canvases to fill an entire room. The earth is blackened, scorched, and barren, and the sky is heavy and thick with a toxic green atmosphere.

When physicists started paying serious attention to nonlinear systems in their own domain, they began to recognize the complex power of Nature's interconnectedness. The equations that governed the flow of wind and moisture, for example, looked simple enough until researchers realized that the flap of a butterfly's wings a millimeter to the left could deflect a hurricane in a totally different direction. In example after example the message was the same: everything is connected, often with incredible sensitivity.

A unique organization called Spindrift, written about by Larry Dossey, M.D. in *Recovering the Soul: A Scientific and Spiritual Search*, explores the relationship between prayer and Nature. The organization designed an imperical study with rye seeds to measure the effects of prayer on the growth of plants. The seeds were divided into two groups of equal number and placed in a shallow container filled with vermiculite. A string was placed down the middle of the container dividing the seeds into A and B. The seeds on one side were prayed for and those on the other side were not. After the seeds had grown, it was found that there were significantly more rye shoots in the treated (prayed for) side than the control side. This simple test, repeated many times with numerous practitioners, indicated that the effect of thought on living organisms outside the human body was significant, quantifiable, and reproducible. We can employ these same concepts using the power of thought to re-energize areas of the planet.

Winter Solstice

We create a sacred space to execute our work of ritual and prayer. Our prayers consist of energy and thought centered on the equal balance and harmony between Nature, science, and spirit. We view the Earth as a living entity which has energy points that can be activated through ritual, prayer, and touch. Acupuncture works in a similar manner by unblocking the energy in the human body.

The washing of crystals in Lake Michigan was a clearing away of imperfections—a purification, a ritual as old as religion itself. To clean is to sanctify. Our rituals create a mythology, a new story, or repeat an old story in order to keep the information alive. The process manifests itself through images. Rituals are actions that speak to the heart and soul, and don't necessarily make sense in a literal way. People respond to the mystery, the unknowing, but deep down they understand on a nonlinguistic level.

To endure the bitter chill of lake water, freezing mist, and biting winds during a private ceremonial ritual epitomizes the spirituality of existence and the delicate balance that must be maintained. It was about 5 A.M. during the Winter Solstice, with a wind chill of -85 degrees. The purity of the crystal was symbolic of our prayer and healing gestures for the waters of the Great Lakes.

The vestment was made of all natural materials, raffia, canvas, and assorted fetishes. The color green was used to symbolize the coming of Spring. Incased in the ice was the reflection of man, a frozen, helpless image causing us to lament the magnitude of Nature's power. To believe that mankind can control and manipulate Nature in mechanistic ways is to be out of touch, since in fact we do not possess such power. We must work as a team to respect and honor Nature, and to restore the balance of Nature, science, and spirit.

We believe these rituals help transform our lives. By becoming aware of environmental concerns, recognizing the need to join forces with Nature, and incorporating the spiritual aspects of our existence, we can help direct a healing process and reverse the destruction of our environment. As artists, we strive to communicate these concepts through visual images and experiences.

Winter Solstice
Lake Michigan
1985

Urban Series

December of 1990 was a month that brought us a Blue Moon, the presence of two full Moons within the same calendar month. It is a rare occurrence that symbolizes to us a time of high universal energy. Therefore, we chose the event of the Blue Moon to perform our *Urban Series* ritual. To get to the art studio, we had to travel through an open space that was being used as a dumping ground. This area kept drawing our attention to the waste of resources, the abuse of the land, and the dissipation of life.

The *Urban Series* was the first time we brought our rituals to an urban landscape. This site was juxtaposed with a thriving, vibrant, beautiful city skyline. Transparent plastic materials were used to access the light and energy which was necessary for this healing ceremony. These materials also represented the presence of nonbiodegradable waste which threatens our environment.

The *Urban Series* was the most difficult ritual to do since there were so many distractions. The local crowds and the stench from the rat-infested garbage were problems, but when the police came we really became self-conscious. It was a very hot and humid day. Fern was standing at the top of a garbage dump and Othello was at the bottom of the dump shooting up. A policeman got out of his car and proceeded to climb up the hill to get a closer look, thus invading the sacred space. His lack of respect and sensitivity made us feel vulnerable. The rhythm was broken and a deep sense of sadness came over us. It was symbolic of the Philistines making their presence felt once again—modern times clashing with the ancient.

The essence of evolution lies in the journey. Over the years, our various works record our journey. We perform rituals to bring spirituality back into the community and the world at large. Our use of symbols, dance, and drumming may appear primitive, but through the practice of ritual we realize the interconnectedness of everything. Our society is starved for the spiritual content that has dissipated over the last few centuries. We as artists living in a technological age respond to the spiritual need. Using today's scientific methods, such as the camera, we document the ancient practice of prayer, which is our contribution towards an equal balance between Nature, science, and spirit.

Urban Series
Chicago, Illinois
1990

Fern Shaffer and Othello Anderson

Juan Geuer

Eye Growing

The sand scorpion *Paruroctonus masaensis* of the Mojave Desert does not see or hear the insects it feeds on. Its only contact with the outside world is through minute receptors in its legs that are sensitive to the most subtle disturbances in the sand. These receptors serve it well to sense and catch its prey. The *Paruroctonus masaensis* reminds me of our human condition. The few windows that the human has into the known energy spectra are also extremely small. They too are designed to help us find our prey and survive. However, at the impasse humanity has now reached, such egocentric strategies have become detrimental. And then as soon as a window opens up to shed some light, we tend to plug it up with interpretations and assumptions, for we hate uncertainty.

Many of our sacred plugs are part of our cultural heritage, of our rational and mystical systems of science, philosophy, and art. We all know about that metaphysical itch to have all the answers in our heads. I too hate to leave the provocative mumblings in the jungles and deserts unanswered, for I live with the frustrating awareness that we depend on this same jungle.

How can you make the blind scorpion see the Mojave Desert? If the situation in the desert should drastically change, would eyes grow on the scorpion in a time of need? If so, "eye growing" ought to be the ultimate art form: a revitalization of our sensorium. I believe it would require a perceptive type of creativity, because at every step of the way, we won't know where we are going, and we ought not pretend.

In my youth, I spent many years in the Bolivian Jungle. One time I tramped with my native Aymara friend through the deep valleys and the forests towards the Rio Beni, a tributary of the Amazon River. My friend and I knew each other in our humanity of terrified beings. We both sensed the threat of annihilation in the call of birds. Yet we laughed about each other's antics, and we had to, because we both lived in different universes. Our friendship was based on the flexibility of humor. Our nerves were tuned to particular but different needs.

Linear coordinates were meaningless to my friend. He did not map his environment in these abstractions. He had a great acuity linked to a very complex and sophisticated system by which he interpreted smell and sound, the type of undergrowth, the behavior of animals, wind direction, shadows, and whatever was part of the multi-dimensional space he lived in. He made charms to ward off evil, placing bits of poisonous plants or bones of dangerous animals into a decaying mass of an animal embryo—a ritual to protect his passage between unborn and death, a strategy to foil time. There was a great deal of intelligence and cunning in this man, but it was based on utterly different premises than my own. Both of us were inclined to deceive and circumvent the overwhelming power manifested all around us. We were both biased by our cultural restrictions. Is this an unavoidable human condition?

My family and I came to Bolivia to escape the Europe of the Second World War. As a teenager in 1933, I witnessed the collapse of the humanist culture of Hitler's Europe. I was born in Holland, into an artist's family and into the world of Rilke, Rudolf Steiner, and Nietzsche. What was it that so disempowered the European, and specifically, the German intelligentsia so that it could not stand up

Juan Geuer uses his work

to increase the information that we

can comprehend through our senses

His Loom Drum *presents to us*

a twenty-nine-year history of

North America's major earthquakes

and Karonhia *brings the*

art of the sky into the

National Gallery of Canada

≈

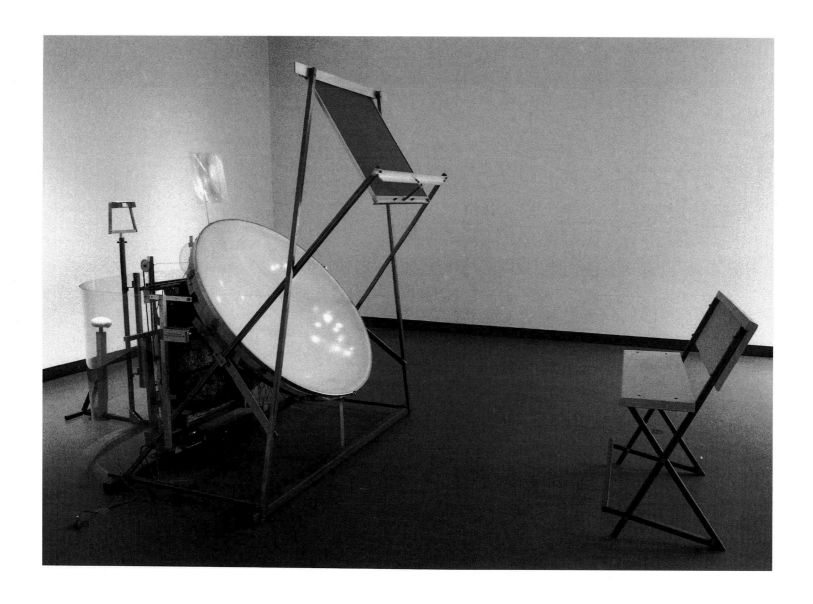

The Loom Drum

Visualizes the seismic activity recorded for the 5,500 earthquakes, measuring 4.0 or more on the Richter scale, that occurred on the North American continent between January 1960 and January 1989. (Time Exposure)
1986–1990

Juan Geuer

to the rise of totalitarian brutality? Remembering discussions my parents had with their friends, I placed much of the blame on the glib cynicism of Nietzsche's famous mirror paradox. This paradox was at the heart of the all pervasive assumption that there is no verification possible, that the fruits of our speculations cannot be checked. These intellectuals severed their lifeline with reality, and caused a failure of the heart. I relay this to show how easy it is to find an excuse to duck our social responsibilities in the face of a major historical challenge. The challenge today is to grow with all of humanity into a larger understanding of our world.

If Nietzsche and his epigones had ever bothered to investigate how our perceptional system actually works, their conclusions may not have been as disempowering. When thoughtful people these days clamor for a paradigm change in our way of living, it may be helpful to understand more about the inherent flexibility of our perceptional system, and the way we interface with the deserts and jungles out there.

In 1954, I moved to Canada, now with my own family, and took a job in a scientific institute. It turned out to be as fascinating as the wilderness I left behind. With my artist's mind and eyes, I was plunged in with geophysicists. I distrust science, as many artists do, and hate man's pretended dominance over the natural world. However, new windows opened to me while studying the physique of our planet: the way she trembles, the way she builds her mountain ranges as her drifting continents clash, and how her magnetic aura pulsates and wanders through the ages. Watching a seismograph drawing—its wiggly line on a drum—I started wondering what on earth would be impelled to dance in these strange, chaotic, jerking

The Loom Drum
Wiring and switching points that activate
over 800 light bulbs embedded behind
a round, concave, featureless screen

motions. It has been always my belief that understanding is some kind of bodily sense, a type of miming. I started dreaming of making an apparatus by which I could establish a clear sensual contact, some kind of an all embracing impact on my senses, between the innermost awareness ability of a person and the Earth. Scientific method had made its impact on me.

The Loom Drum

This sculpture was one of my experiments to find a connection between geophysical events and the perceptional capabilities of our gut feelings. I intended *The Loom Drum* to make us more familiar with the dynamics of the "heat engine" we live on. After all, this engine's chaotic turmoil helped shape the life in which we have our being, though as humans we see only a frozen instant of its geological processes.

The Loom Drum presents the seismic activity recorded for the 5,500 earthquakes, measuring 4.0 or more on the Richter scale, that occurred on the North American continent between January 1960 and January 1989. A drum-like structure, with a myriad of switching points and complex wiring, activates over 800 light bulbs embedded behind a round, concave, featureless screen. The data is concentrated geographically, sequentially, and by intensity into a 15 minute, repeating cycle of flashing lights, accompanied by the soft drumming sound of the switches. A contracting of the time scale by a factor of one million by going from 29 years to 15 minutes!

The viewer can experience information in two distinct formats. From the rear, the flashes representing earthquakes are referenced scientifically to their geographical location and their moment in time. The flashing lights are seen superimposed on a geologic tectonic map of the North American continent, appearing in the precise locations of each earthquake. The map is painted in transparent colors on a mirror above the concave screen. To a viewer sitting on a small stool, it appears as a virtual image, almost like a hologram between the lens and the viewer.

Sitting on the bench in front of *The Loom Drum*, a viewer appreciates the flashing lights in the featureless, concave, translucent Plexiglas screen as patterns in space and time, without apparent reference to anything else. They are the sparks that fly when rigidity opposes dynamic forces. My hope was that the image of a pattern might reveal a minute instant of meaning.

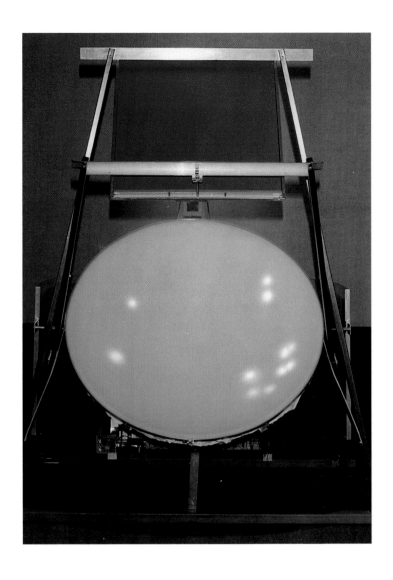

The Loom Drum

Above: Featureless screen behind which
flashing light bulbs are imbedded
(Time exposure)
Above Right: From the rear of the work
the location of the earthquakes are projected
onto a mirror above the concave screen

The Loom Drum

Flashing lights are seen superimposed
on a geologic tectonic map of the
North American continent, appearing in the
precise locations of each earthquake.
The map is painted in transparent colors
on a mirror above the concave screen.

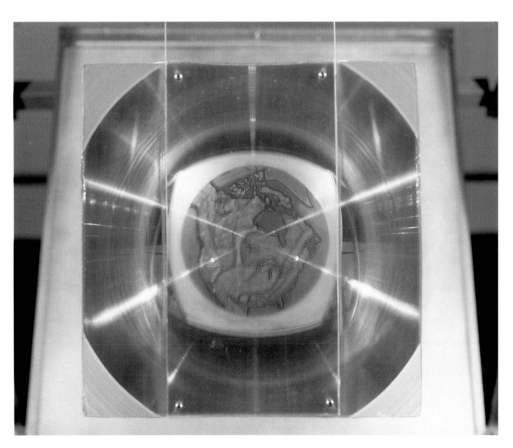

Juan Geuer

Karonhia

The tenet that a work of art ought to be autonomous, made for art's sake, has always struck me as impossible and inappropriate, because in reality, nothing is self-referential. A determining factor for *Karonhia* ("Sky" in the Mohawk language) was my encounter with a place. Built in Ottawa in 1989, the National Gallery of Canada is girded and intersected by a few halls that are regarded as public spaces devoid of "art." In the mind of the architect, these spaces were required for people to prepare themselves before entering into the sacred realm of human culture.

Karonhia consists of four pairs of large mirrors anchored to the rotunda balcony and angled upward so that they reflect the sky through the glass cupola above. The mirrors in each pair are also angled toward different cardinal points so that the varying tones and intensities of eastern and southern light, for example, are reflected side by side. The viewer can move around the balcony of the rotunda to view the sky in all different directions. He or she may challenge time or simply stare at the light. I suggested this work to the Gallery because, as I put it, "Now that we know what we have done to this planet, no art gallery should be without an observatory."

The architect's idea of the sacred domain of our human culture is a long, outmoded concept. There is a thin line between "revelations of our innermost being" and the sucking aura of our narcissistic culture. All we do owes its presence to something else. There can be no visual art without light. Studio artists used to deliberate about the differences in the quality of light from the different quadrants of the sky. *Karonhia* has the demythologizing quality of a scientific test. We ask whether some of our assumptions are right or wrong, and we humbly accept the answer. Through the mirrors, the rotunda has attained a sense of verticality to detect the critical realism in the soaring clouds or the polluted sky.

Karonhia
National Gallery of Canada
One of four sets of mirrors that reflect the sky
above the rotunda of the museum
Ottawa, Canada
1989

Karonhia
National Gallery of Canada

Four pairs of large mirrors,
each angled toward different cardinal points,
are anchored to the rotunda balcony and
angled upward so that they reflect the
sky through the glass cupola above.
Ottawa, Canada
1989

Certainly, refinement of our aesthetic sensitivity is a prime condition for "eye growing." And our technological sophistications will expand our senses and warm our wits to the things that are. But there is more. The scorpion stings its prey with a venom to make it digestible. We humans tend to do the same, but we inject precast concepts, thereby frustrating absorption. Anybody ever involved with pattern recognition knows how true this is, and yet our ability to recognize patterns such as a face in a crowd exemplifies an amazing capacity. We have to study these paradoxes, and we have to study the physiology of our perceptional system. We must consider, for example, the chaotic motions of the scanning eye, which are so small and fast that they cannot be observed by that same naked eye. Where and how does this chaos meet the unpredictable and the rest of the chaos of creation? How flexible are we in our basic make-up? Can we absorb the dynamics of the totally unexpected?

Patrick Zentz

Patrick Zentz use the mechanical vocabulary of technology to draw us into a heightened awareness of our world's natural systems.

≈

I grew up on a dry land farm in south central Montana. Dry farming is an occupation of hope—hoping it will rain. In this environment one learns, early on, that watching the sky is as integral an activity as tending the ground and the crops it supports. Every single thing makes a difference, and it is the astute observer with good intuition who will most likely be the one to coax sustenance out of the situation.

I began my undergraduate work in biology because of a fascination with living systems and their interactions with one another. As I approached graduation, I began to realize that my interest in system interaction was more closely aligned with investigations going on in the arts than in the sciences, although there were and still are parallels. The inquiries of the Minimalists and Conceptualists of the late '60s and early '70s intrigued me greatly. These artists dealt with analytical processes in a manner very different from what I was accustomed to in scientific methodology. The processes of their inquiries were often end products in themselves. Much of what they were investigating involved human emotion and thought, not just abstract theorems. I switched my study from the sciences to the arts.

In graduate school I felt an affinity for the earthworks that were gaining recognition in the art world. Most of this work used the surface of the Earth as a space upon which to make a mark or gesture. But the most important development of the movement for me was the opening up of the confines of the museum and gallery to include a space which had not been used in the Americas since prehistory. The natural environment became a viable place to investigate and present ideas.

My work over the last twenty years has been an evolving attempt to comprehend how we understand our environments and ourselves within them, and since the mid-1970s it has been concerned with investigating environmental perception. Keeping in mind that I did not want to leave permanent marks on the environment, I developed a series of works that were based on various forms of instrumentation. Much like transits and other survey instruments, these pieces of sculpture could be set up in an environment and then removed without changing the site in any way. Their purpose was to translate dynamic information occurring at a specific site into another kind of information. The first series, called *Terregraphy Instruments*, was designed to draw the wind, create color from soil, draw the horizon, and record the movements of plants and the three dimensional information from a square meter of soil. The inquiries were site dependent and were an attempt to comprehend the feel of a specific place.

Creek Translator

The next series of works attempted to translate elements of a specific place into sound. Sound was of interest as a formal element because through it the work would be time specific, and thus tied directly to the presence of a viewer. Entitled *Day*, the piece was powered by wind. It utilized three instrumentation systems to translate specific components of a particular site—horizon line, temperature change, and flow of creek water—into sound. The *Creek Translator* consisted of a framework that suspended a dulcimer-like instrument over a lever system. The levers were connected, via floats, to the water of a small creek that flowed beneath

Photo: Frederick R. Longan

Creek Translator

The currents of the wind and
the flow of the creek
play the song of the day
Big Spring Ranch, Montana
1985

Creek Translator

Detail

the piece. When the ripples in the creek caused the five floats to rise and fall verti-
cally, the levers converted this fluctuation into a horizontal fretting motion on the five
strings of the instrument. Windmills connected to rotary picks provided the system
with a potential for making sound. The creek produced a score that the wind activated through the interface of the *Creek Translator* system. The two other instruments
for *Day* converted temperature change into drumbeats and the horizon line into flute-
like tones. The three environmentally interactive systems were recorded for a
twenty-four-hour period in the fall of 1985. An edited recording of the translations
was produced as an encapsulation of this particular environment at a specific time.

In addition to translating information into different forms, I am also interested
in the linguistic content of mechanisms.
Mechanical systems are, themselves, a
kind of visual language that yields information about function in both their static
and kinetic states. The sculptural use of
such systems further provides a means for
clarifying the intent or concept of an
object in a nonlinear manner. Just as
mechanism implies movement, which is
another time specific element, the kinetic
and sound elements of *Day* were attempts
to both tie viewer presence to the work
and make that presence the element that
formally completed the work. Time,
place, and presence are, it seems, the concrete elements that define experience.

Patrick Zentz

Heliotrope

I have also been interested in working within interior spaces, for they can provide a kind of "petri dish" environment for controlled experiments. Essentially, architectural structures are machines that modify environments to meet human needs, making spaces more comfortable and more manageable.

A work done in the Nevada desert introduced components of the natural environment into a building that had excluded them when it was built. The work, titled *Heliotrope*, is in the Richard Tam Alumni Center at the University of Nevada, Las Vegas. The transit of the Sun across the Vegas Valley, the temperature change, and the wind are elements of the desert ecosystem utilized in this piece. Three massive wood and aluminum rings, with diameters of twelve, ten, and eight feet respectively, track the apparent movement of the Sun throughout the day. The movement of the rings guides a laser beam that is projected onto the floor of the atrium. A line corresponding to the southern horizon of Las Vegas is engraved into the marble floor. Throughout the day, a two-inch circle of laser light occupies a position over the engraved horizon line on the floor, which mirrors the real Sun's transit above the actual horizon of the desert. Daily and seasonal changes of the Sun's ascension and declination are consequently apparent inside the building.

Arranged around this central sculptural element are eight small log drums which form a circumferential array. Each drum has a striker that is electronically activated by external temperatures. The first drum begins beating when the temperature reaches fifty degrees Fahrenheit. The second starts at sixty degrees, the third at seventy, and so forth. Thus, each temperature increment from fifty to one hundred and twenty degrees creates a different rhythm that is audible in the atrium.

A circular configuration of lights forms an eighteen-foot diameter ring at the base of *Heliotrope*. This ring is responsive to the wind direction, and different segments of it light up as the wind direction shifts. Directly overhead, and mounted on the skylight that caps the building, a large rotor turns at a rate relative to the speed of the wind. The Sun casts the shadow of the revolving rotor onto the circular balcony walls of the second floor. In doing so, it provides an additional indication of external environmental activity to those who find themselves, by choice or necessity, within the building.

Heliotrope
Richard Tam Alumni Center
University of Nevada
Las Vegas, Nevada
1991

Patrick Zentz

Snake River System

An installation completed in 1993 further develops the idea of the viewer as a necessary presence, a formal component in the completion of a work. *Snake River System* is an environmentally interactive system designed to translate wind activity into kinetic actions: light patterns and sound. The polished surfaces of three rotors reflect sunlight as the wind turns them. The flashing semaphore-like pattern that is created relates directly to wind speed and the angle of the Sun. A large sail orients the display in response to wind direction. As it does so, it causes a circular array of tonal bars beneath to be struck by small mallets. The tonal bars are cut to lengths proportional to the height of the corresponding horizon segments toward which they are pointed. As the wind vane moves, it translates the visual phenomenon of the horizon line into sound. Its aluminum mainframe grid structure is intended to mimic, visually, the indigenous metric agricultural forms, sprinkler systems, hay bales, row crops, and the reflective rectilinear components of the Snake River Correctional Institution. When people move around the system, their presence is defined by the sound of gravel on the walkway, and then that sound is inculcated into the work. The sound of their treading literally and conceptually completes the piece. In order to hear the subtle tonal-bar translation of the horizon, viewers must interrupt their own progress on the walk. The entire work is seeded with crested wheatgrass which, when mature, will provide an additional organic response to wind activity both visually and aurally. The project offers an opportunity to apprehend a "whole" system environmentally responsive, and is completed only by the presence of the viewer/participant.

Currently, I continue to ranch in south central Montana. There is no separation between so-called art activities and agricultural work. Both are joined by daily experience. What might happen on horseback or on a tractor easily influences work in the studio. Much of agriculture is involved with tasks that are, at first glance, monotonous and fatiguing. Driving tractor, fixing fence, or moving cattle consists of endless hours of doing the same thing over and over. A kind of trance-like state often results, and is a fertile source of many unpredictable ideas. Conversely, intense involvement with definition, pattern, form, space, and relativity in the studio affects agricultural plans and the production of food. I view the natural environment as a threshold between those ideas we know (science) and those things we feel (art). It seems that the synergy gained in passing back and forth over that threshold is now critical to us, as we define our niche in the last days of the twentieth century.

Photo: Christopher Autio

Photo: Christopher Autio

Photo: Christopher Autio

Patrick Zentz

Douglas Hollis

Sky Soundings

I was once asked how I became interested in working with natural forces, and I suggested to the person that he "go fly a kite." This was not as flippant a response as it sounds. For me, the experience of building and flying kites in the mid-seventies was very profound, and inspired many of the ideas I've worked with since. The physical connection created by the kite between the hand and the sky, the line becoming a vocal cord of the wind both heard and felt, and the sense of being inside a place made of sound, all first occurred to me during this time. I organized several nighttime celebrations called *Sky Soundings* to share my discoveries. The events took place on several evenings in a large field on the edge of San Francisco Bay.

People began to arrive in the late twilight and stood in small groups talking quietly. The six-foot, winged box kites lay on their backs, holding small, glowing light sticks, like fallen knights lying in state. The evenings were dark, cool, and often foggy. Edible hand warmers (baked potatoes) and mulled wine were provided to help stave off the chill while we waited for the wind to rise. Light breezes punctuated by small gusts gradually gave way to a steady wind. The six kites were walked out to the launching place, faced into the wind, and with a gentle push launched into the sky. The lights looked like a moving constellation overhead, and the lines of different materials created an ensemble of choir-like sound. It felt as if we were within an invisible cathedral. These events taught me that people were not just an audience, but participants as well.

I continued learning about the nature of sound during my two year residency with the Exploratorium in San Francisco, a place where art, science, and human perception all come together. I built my first aeolian harp during this time. My investigations since then have focused on the quality of public places, on encouraging people to experience and understand natural phenomena, and on helping people recognize themselves and others as an integral part of those phenomena. The use of sensory instruments to provoke interaction has evolved as a central idea in my work from my earliest experiments with wind and water to my current interest in making places that people will want to inhabit and that will age well and increase in meaning as time flows over them.

My general interest in waves, and my specific interest in sound as a vehicle for exchange and communication, has to do with a desire to bring all of the senses into a more dynamically balanced relationship. I intentionally try to downplay the tyranny of the eye and intellect, and amplify our sensual and intuitive involve-

Douglas Hollis uses his work to heighten the awareness of our senses to the natural surround. Many of the following projects pay particular attention to our perception of sound and wind currents.

≈

Below and Right:
**Sky Soundings
An Acoustic Kite Performance**
San Francisco, California
1975

Field of Vision
Winter Olympics

900 Windvanes
Lake Placid, New York
1980

ment with the world. Although I have made many structures and places that produce sound when in contact with moving air or water, my work is really more concerned with learning to listen, and in so doing, shifting the way we attend to the world. I believe that we need to shift our attitude from one of imposition and dominance to one of regard, interdependence, and conversation.

Field of Vision

I did *Field of Vision* for the 1980 Winter Olympics in Lake Placid, New York. It manifested my phenomena drawings, linear structures that defined surfaces and spaces activated by wind, and explored the choreography between windscape and landscape, two entities that influence each other's form. Composed of a field of 900 simple wind vane elements—a plane of red dashes against sky and snow, the work became a ghost contour, echoing the contour of land lying below it. As the snow fell and drifted, a second harmonic wave of snow formed. Flowing through the field in streams and currents, the wind was a visible medium, as in a field of tall grass.

Many of the projects I did in the 1970s and early 1980s, including *Field of Vision*, were temporary works, built with minimal means and within short periods of time. These projects were opportunities for mutual education. My natural hesitancy to jump to conclusions resulted in works that "walked" lightly and waited patiently. They were essays that asked questions about how to create physical, interactive connections between people and their environments, and how to weaken the perceived boundary between the "I" inside and the "It" out there. These works also established a very good foundation for later long term works. Because these works were built in public, non-art sites, frequently with the verbal, and sometimes physical, help of residents, I learned to pay attention to the language of location, which conveys the preexisting dynamics of place.

Douglas Hollis

A Sound Garden

In 1982 the National Oceanic and Atmospheric Administration (NOAA) constructed a new N.W. Regional Research Center on Lake Washington, in Seattle,
Washington. Artists Siah Armajani, Scott Burton, Martin Puryear, George Trakas,
and I were all invited to propose works along the one mile shoreline. We did not set
out to work collaboratively, but because of conversations amongst ourselves and
with the people of NOAA and the local community, our works did take on a sequen-
tial harmony with one another and with the landscape. *A Sound Garden* is the
orchestral culmination of a decade of small works that aim to articulate and celebrate the movements of wind, water, and landscape through a medium of sound.

Walking the path along the shoreline of Lake Washington, one encounters a
side path paved with triangular brick and crushed rock. The path meanders up a rise
of land, and takes one on a journey of sensory experience. This journey of hearing,
sight, and movement is really what the work is about. Clustered at the top of the
wave of land, a grove of simple towers support pairs of aluminum wind-organ pipes.

A Sound Garden
National Oceanic and
Atmospheric Administration

Wind-organ Towers
Seattle, Washington
1983

These pipes are attached to pivoting flames that move like windvanes, directing the pipes into the wind and producing a warbling, whale-like sound. The sound varies as the speed of the winds rises and falls. The pipes are a brushed silver color, creating lines of light that float in the air. The towers are gray, and at times disappear against the Seattle sky. The overall experience is one of being within the wind and a resonant dome of sound.

Listening Vessels

Someone once referred to my work in general, and I think this work in particular, as a "hearing-aid." It's a good description of what I want my work to do: extend our ability to listen. The *Listening Vessels* series extends the activity of listening in a wonderful way. The works utilize another phenomena of Nature: a particular curved surface and the way sound waves are focused to and reflected by this surface. More importantly for me, they are truly a "conversation piece"; unlike some of my other projects, they are not activated by wind or water, but rather by people. Situated a hundred feet apart, two people can have a whispering conversation, immersed in a pool of ambient sound.

I have had many opportunities to work in collaboration with other artists, architects, and landscape architects. Just as I have approached working in collaboration with natural forces in the past, I view working with other artists as a challenge. By blending and weaving my perceptions and knowledge with others, I am driven to think in new ways. Issues of use and usefulness extend the process of making places into one that is deliberately inclusive of the communities being served. The extended process creates a forum for exploring sustainable environments which begin to change and even heal past transgressions and oversights.

Carnegie/Armory Park Design Plan

One of the projects that best exemplifies the extended process is the *Carnegie/Armory Park Design Plan*, underway in Tucson, Arizona. The team that created the work includes landscape architects George Hargreaves and Mary Margaret Jones, artists Anna Valentina Murch and myself, and Martin Yoklic, a consulting designer with the University of Arizona's Environmental Research Laboratory. We devised a plan to reconstruct the historic landscape that surrounds the 1901 Carnegie Library (now a children's discovery center) and rehabilitate the adjacent Armory Park (now partially occupied by a senior center). The two-fold project will result in an outdoor performance area, resonant with the surrounding Arts and Theater District.

Douglas Hollis

Our extended research process involved many public forums in which the community was able to share its memories, knowledge, and desires with us. We also spent a lot of time learning about the special qualities of the desert environment and how living in the desert might be expressed in our work. The resulting design incorporates history, art, landscape, and resource conservation such as water harvesting, photo voltaic lighting, and evaporative cooling structures.

The central element of the design is a stage flanked by grass and stone terraces. A wing-shaped ramada floats above this stepped platform made of slats that are angled to limit the Sun's rays during the summer and to let the sunlight through in the cooler months of the year. The ramada is supported by branching treelike columns. During performances, these columns can provide an armature for lights, back drops, or other effects. The columns also have a water mist element that will help cool the terraces for more casual daytime use.

Below the stage is a cistern, a basin that collects rainwater harvested from the roof of the senior center. Low-velocity fans pull air in from behind the stage and move it across the surface of the water. The air cools as it passes, and then flows through a grill at the front of the stage into the depressed lawn area, collecting in a pool of coolness where the audience sits. Trees planted on the sitting slope are situated to provide both shade and good sight lines.

The various elements of the design will combine to make a place that speaks to the mind and the spirit, as well as to the body. Our design will provide both psychological and physical comfort, and revitalize the historic center for wider community use. What we have proposed is both a literal performance space and a metaphor for theater—a passive stage for the ongoing theater of everyday life.

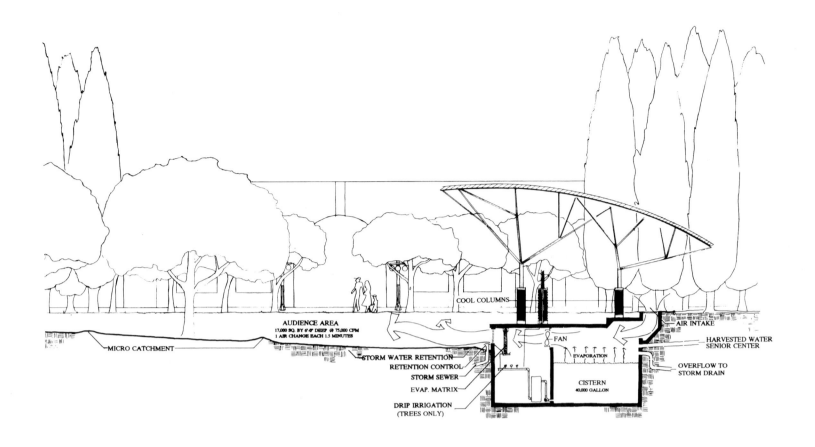

AUDIENCE AREA
17,000 SQ. BY 6'-8" DEEP @ 75,000 CFM
1 AIR CHANGE EACH 1.5 MINUTES

COOL COLUMNS

AIR INTAKE

MICRO CATCHMENT

HARVESTED WATER
SENIOR CENTER

STORM WATER RETENTION
RETENTION CONTROL
STORM SEWER
EVAP. MATRIX

FAN

EVAPORATION

OVERFLOW TO
STORM DRAIN

DRIP IRRIGATION
(TREES ONLY)

CISTERN
40,000 GALLON

Douglas Hollis

Peter Richards

Public Art is a contemporary term used to describe a very old practice: expressing in a creative act the relationship between people and the place where they live. With the ever increasing heterogeneity of our country and the attendant richness of differences in tradition, language, personal histories, and religion, it often seems as if the one thing we have in common is the place where we live. [1]

The process of making public art, like any creative process, is best served by simple ideas. It is a process that requires the artist to serve as a social interpreter, aesthetician, and the clear articulator of ways to respond to the relationship between things, people, and places. This process invites people to think creatively and critically, and it may ask people to respond to a particular place and circumstances in ways they may not have done before. It provides an opportunity for people to recover the history of the place where they live, to influence the appearance of their neighborhoods and cities, and to participate in the public and political sphere. It is a process of civic virtue; it deepens the liveliness and sophistication of social discourse; and it ultimately increases a community's feeling of ownership and investment in the public domain. [2]

Over the past twelve to fifteen years I have used water as an avenue for investigating how different aspects of Nature and human nature are interrelated. Water is a fundamental ingredient whose varied forms and characteristics shape the world and our existence. The study of natural and imposed time systems and their fluctuation between harmony and dissonance has been a common and related thread throughout most of my work from that time forward. My working relationship with The Exploratorium, a museum of science, art, and human perception, has provided a foundation for my interest in how people behave in public and how their behavior reflects and affects their surroundings.

In the process of developing works at a number of outdoor public sites, I have realized that landforms and land events no longer have the influence that they once had for many of us. Naturalist Barry Lopez observed that "the perceptions of any people wash over the land like a flood, leaving ideas hung up in the brush like pieces of damp paper to be collected and deciphered." Much of my work reflects an attempt to gather some of those ideas before they blow away, to encourage others to gather their own, and to use the land as a base for the creation of new ideas.

The characteristics of the works that I am going to describe certainly fall within conventional criteria of public art, informed by the understanding that meaningful works are linked with a deep need for connection, not only to one another but also to our surroundings.

Wave Organ

Wave Organ is located on a jetty, a constructed spit of land that reaches a couple hundred yards out from San Francisco's north waterfront. Harbor seals and sea lions cavort and feed here, and they are often joined by sea gulls, pelicans, cormorants, and coots. The site for the *Wave Organ* is situated between the two

The work of Peter Richards

brings our attention to the beauty

and nurturing quality of water.

His Wave Organ *uses the*

relationship of the Sun to the

Earth and Moon to drive this

symphony of the elements,

while The Spring *uses*

history as context for

returning the life of a spring

to a community.

≈

Wave Organ

City view
San Francisco, California
1986

extremes, the raw Nature of the bay on one side and the dense urban landscape on the other. It's a nice place to pause, a neutral zone where you can escape and think cosmological thoughts or just watch and listen as the fog moves in under the Golden Gate Bridge.

The inspiration for the *Wave Organ* came from an audio tape made by Bill Fontana, who recorded the sound of a floating concrete dock in Sydney, Australia. The sound that he captured from a vented flotation chamber had both a watery quality and a surprisingly deep, sonorous aspect with a slight electronic edge. At the time I was working on temporary light sculptures that addressed the interconnectivity between wind conditions, wave action, and tides. Intuitively, I knew that sound could add a whole new dimension to this work. I came to understand how the sound was being made while explaining an exhibit on sound resonance to a friend at The Exploratorium. This discovery, and my finding an avenue for understanding the physics involved, spawned a period of experimentation and tinkering, and eventually led to the installation of *Wave Organ* in 1986.

I installed a prototype version for New Music America '81 on the site. I miked the piece and sent wave music over to the Exploratorium on a telephone line so people could hear it there. Frank Oppenheimer, the founding director of The Exploratorium, really loved the sound that it made and decided that we should raise some money to have it done permanently.

Peter Richards

Photo: Susan Schwartzenberg

In thinking about all the things that one considers when planning an installation, I was particularly taken by a small rock garden that was built by a retired merchant seaman on the south-facing side of the jetty. The builder had carefully incorporated pieces of carved granite that were dumped out there when the jetty was built. Used as riprap, the stone had come from an old cemetery in Laurel Heights which was being bulldozed to make way for more housing. The material was quite wonderful: exotic chunks of Carrera marble from Italy, beautifully carved architectural pieces of Sierra granite, and numerous pieces of red sandstone from Arizona.

George Gonzalez, a sculptor and stonemason who had learned his craft in France and had completed a number of projects in Europe and in the States, became my collaborator. He uses traditional stone-building techniques, which include dry, mortarless joints. By cutting each stone precisely, gravity and the density of the stones themselves become the glue for holding the structures together. George's responsibility was the stonework and mine was the overall project management and the building of the pipes. We assembled a crew of masons, an equipment operator, and a crew of apprentices provided by the California Conservation Corps. We started in September of 1985 and finished in May of 1986. We did not work to a blueprint; we allowed the site and the stone material that we had found dictate the form of the listening areas and the organ pipes.

Photo: Susan Schwartzenberg

Wave Organ

View of Alcatraz
San Francisco, California
1986

Jack Russell, a marine engineer, provided engineering oversight, ensuring that our foundations were sound and that our installation would strengthen rather than weaken the jetty. Collectively, we created something that will endure for a long time and that has come to be a regular destination for people who need to step away from their daily pace for brief periods of time.

The *Wave Organ* is an instrument played by the tidal forces, a sort of marine aeolian harp. Waves resonate captive columns of air inside a series of concrete pipes up to fifteen feet long that rise from sea level and vent through the stone. The sound emitted ultimately depends on the position of Sun and Moon and the weather conditions. It ranges from mute at low tide, to the gargle of drainwater, to mysterious, harmonic soughing when the long Pacific swells run in from the Gate—the vocalized rustle of currents in a giant kelp forest.

—GREY BRECHIN, *Architectural Historian*

The *Wave Organ* provides a place that enduces a frame of mind that allows one to become sensitive to the total acoustic landscape of the site; its music becomes part of a much grander concert. Many times while sitting quietly, I have noticed my sensitivity to the ambient sounds sharpen so rapidly it was as though someone had turned up the volume. It is times like this when the interplay of the wave music with the fog horns, sea gulls, sailboats, airplanes, and children becomes a spontaneous symphony, one whose personality is cyclical in nature as it reflects the rise and fall of the tides, the evolving weather patterns, and the activities of the city. The basic nature of this symphony is based on the relationships of the Moon to the Earth and the Earth to the Sun.

The *Wave Organ* is not about hearing. It is really about listening. It is about paying attention to one's surroundings and to interrelationships.

Peter Richards

The Spring

Springs, or wells, have always played a special role in the human psyche, offering images of sustenance, refuge, and well being. They have been, and still are in many areas of the world, places where people meet, joke, gossip, flirt, and exchange important information. I speculated that the spring on New York State's Artpark property near Lewiston might play host to similar exchanges, a speculation that provided a point of focus for my work between 1988 and 1990.

The spring on the Artpark property once played a vital role in the area. Centuries of spring runoff had cut into the side of the gorge, creating the only convenient access to its upper shores for several miles up or down river. Fresh spring water, river accessibility, and protection from the elements were probably very inviting to the area's early inhabitants. This speculation is supported by the remains of an indigenous village in the adjacent grove of woods and by the location of the area's first trading post and the subsequent economic and strategic growth of the surrounding village and township.

In the early 1960s the area became the receptacle for thousands of yards of material excavated from a nearby hydroelectric project. Artpark, a place where people come to experience and get involved in the process of art making, was offered as remediation. As a park, the area had again become an inviting place, but the spring no longer had a role. The flow of the spring emerged from a brush-infested and trash-ladened drainage and fed a small cattail marsh. The drainage of this marsh was then relegated to a series of pipes that led to the river.

Even though Artpark attracts lots of people during its summer season, the amenities provided do not suggest a harmonious union between Nature and human nature.

The Spring
Artpark
Lewiston, New York
1987–88

The architecture of the place successfully provides various spaces for people to work and mix with artists and crafts people. It is utilitarian, and provides no buffers between the intense and exciting work and play that goes on and the sometimes harsh yet spectacular setting on the Niagara River Gorge. Many of the artists who have come to work there over the years have addressed the nature of the site and its relationship to the area and community, but all of their experimental projects are temporary and are removed after their respective summer sessions are over.

The first phase of the project, executed during a two-week period in July of 1988, consisted of clearing the site of underbrush and debris, and making a detailed site plan complete with contour lines, tree location, prominent stones, direction of prevailing breezes, shaded areas, sound levels, water flow, and pedestrian traffic. I also consulted with local plant specialists, and mined long time residents for stories and anecdotes about the site. Through this conversation with the land itself and the people who lived on it, I hoped to be able to create a visual language that would communicate and inspire a reflective and respectful attitude towards what has and what would hopefully continue to transpire at the site. In this same vein, I hoped to create a place where visitors to the park and members of the community could go, either individually or in groups, to escape the summer heat and refresh themselves.

The visual language for the installation relied on forms constructed with building techniques and materials used by the various peoples who have lived in the area from the earliest of times. Foundation stone from the nearby Schovill Mansion (built in the mid-19th century) was used to construct several terrace and retaining walls. Another retaining wall was built using 150-year-old barn timbers;

Peter Richards

116 / 117

Photo: Vonda Longin Banon

Photo: Vonda Longin Banon

Above and Right:
The Spring
Artpark
Lewiston, New York
1987–88

yet another wall was built from stone quarried from cliffs that form the edge of the gorge. A springhouse was also built from stone slabs from the river gorge and framed by two prominent earth mounds, suggesting that the bounty of this spring is an offering from Mother Earth. These mounds quote nearby burial mounds built by ancient peoples.

Cold and pure water flows from the springhouse downstream to an area that is defined by a canopy of foliage provided by oak, mulberry, hickory, and maple trees. The water entering the upper end of this outdoor room flows through a channel, forming a double helix cut into a large, flat stone. It then spills into a bowl carved into a glacial boulder found in a nearby glacial moraine. The water from the bowl feeds a small pond defined by a stone curb. Some aquatic plants were present and others, along with a variety of aquatic animals, were introduced. Because the site is shaded and lies in a slight depression, the air is chilled and held captive by the coolness of the pond, providing a resting place that is ten to fifteen degrees cooler than the surrounding park lands. The overall site was planted with food bearing plants which would encourage a greater population of animal life and be available to all other visitors as well. I was happy to see birds and animals return to the site once the construction activities were completed.

The Spring was a personal vision that was realized by a community of people working together. In its eighteen-year history, Artpark had never approved a permanent installation. In this case I believe they agreed to support this project because they recognized a need for such a place, and because Ed Pers, Project Manager for all artist projects, took a personal interest in the idea. His suggestions for ways of getting community members involved was important because with their interest and support came a greater likelihood that the installation would be properly maintained and enhanced over time. To garner initial involvement, George Gonzalez agreed to hold a two-week stone mason's workshop at the site, where he trained seven people from the surrounding area. Four of these people continued to work on the project for the duration, contributing much more than just their labor on the stone retaining walls. One was a photographer who documented the whole project. She was also a botanist, and developed the overall planting schedule. The other volunteers were all avid gardeners, and continued taking care of the place after I had gone.

As I reflect upon the differences and similarities of the *Wave Organ* project and *The Spring*, it is clear to me that what joins them is the careful consideration of the human spirit inherent in their designs. Each is a celebration of the human potential for living in concert with the rhythms of Nature. This is a condition that some of us have had and lost, and a condition that is still attainable for most of us.

1. "Art Along the Waterfront: A Guide to Opportunities for Public Artists and Public Art on the Embarcadero of San Francisco." A planning study conducted by Tim Collins, Laura Farabough, Michael Oppenheimer, and Peter Richards. 1991.
2. Ibid.

Peter Richards

Buster Simpson

The following projects share in a common discussion. The prospect of trying to balance a wheel already set in motion exemplifies the task before us and the exasperating dilemma these works confront. The *Seattle George Monument* exists in an artificially sustained sylvan landscape. It speaks of historical assertion upon the landscape. Fittingly, this monument sits upon the site, not with it. *Host Analog* and *Exchanger Fountain* both bring environmental issues to the urban context: natural phenomena which city populations are detached from and often indifferent to yet dependent upon. The complexities and balance become the poetic politic.

Host Analog

This sculpture is part of the Oregon State Convention Center. The intent of the piece is to introduce into the urban landscape an indigenous natural phenomenon known as a host, or nursing log. The piece is about real time, accommodating landscape that hosts the notion of metaphorical history and the measurement of time with concurrent events affecting the host log's regeneration. *Host Analog* illustrates the complexities of entropy, bringing what at first appears to be disorder into an ordered urban cityscape. It is an exclamation of the discord between the systems of interdependence and those of convenience. *Host Analog* eludes to two icons, the cliché of the fallen column and the large logs, often dated, at the entry of logging communities.

An old growth Douglas Fir windfall from the 1950s was located for the installation in the Bull Run watershed adjacent to Mt. Hood. Eight segments, measuring eight feet by eight feet, were trucked to the recipient of Bull Run's water—the city of Portland. Sited on a thirty by ninety-foot terraced landscape at the Oregon Convention Center, the log's raw expression contrasts with the existing formal landscape.

Joining with the citizens of Portland, the *Host Analog* continues to drink from the same waters that nurtured it for over 1500 years. To encourage a nitrogen fixing mycorrhizal environment conducive to plant growth, the host log must be kept moist, so that complex decomposing processes may be encouraged. A water feature/irrigation system is installed over the segmented host log to mist water vapor periodically and keep the log wet. The misting is accomplished with water jets (similar to the ones used in the produce department at a food store) spaced approximately three feet apart and tapped into a stainless steel supply pipe three inches in diameter and sixty feet long. The arch struck by this pipe spine echoes the architectural entrance of the convention center.

Seed and seedlings of cedar, fir, and hemlock were gathered from Bull Run. Seeds were broadcast on the nurse log to germinate by chance, and seedlings were planted at intervals employing a scientific methodology. As new growth develops, their root structure will hug the outer skin of the host log, eventually becoming an arched colonnade of roots as the host rots away and the tree structure endures.

The success of this piece is dependent on its continuance. Future developments need to accommodate themselves to the *Host Analog*, just as the regenerated forest landscape has accommodated itself atop the host log. It requires the patience of a thousand years.

Parables are woven throughout the work of Buster Simpson. Look closely and you will hear the story of the forests, the first settlers of the North American continent, and the life force of our planet home sprouting in the concrete of our cities.

≈

Host Analog
One of four porcelain enamel signs
adjacent Host Analog

Host Analog

Eight-foot by eight-foot class two logs with
stainless steel misting irrigation system
Portland, Oregon

Buster Simpson

The Timber Summit held in 1993 at the Convention Center adjacent to the
Host Analog begged the questions, "Are we in balance as the host and parasite? Are
we eating ourselves out of house and home?"

Seattle George Monument

In a poetic attempt to consolidate concerns of assertion and assimilation, *Seattle George Monument* simultaneously portrays Chief Seattle (originally Chief Sealth) and George Washington. The monument's base is a trellis, an open cube with a grid functioning as a curtain wall and a gazebo. A tripod supports a cone torso and the monument's head, twenty-four aluminum profiles of Chief Seattle fanned out to create an armature for English Ivy growing out of a Boeing 707 nose cone planter. A sharpened template will act as a wind vane, trimming the ivy overgrowth into a 360-degree evergreen bust of George. Eventually, as the vines cover the head, Chief Seattle will become a memory. The indigenous culture is figuratively a foundation upon which the present is an overlay. The cone and tripod suggest an inverted lodge, and at the same time refer to George Washington's work as a surveyor, with the cone becoming his plumb bob. The silhouettes were appropriated from their namesakes on the city and state logos.

The use of the term monument in this piece is a reference to the subtle survey markings as much as it is to monumental sculpture. Sandblasted into the plaza adjacent to the monument are references to two historical events in 1855. On the north/south axis is a reproduction of the first survey map connecting Seattle to the national rectilinear survey grid. This system facilitated the establishment of land ownership disregarding land forms and natural boundaries. The survey team embarked on the survey shortly after the signing of the treaty of 1855. Chief Sealth was one of the cosigners of the treaty. On the east/west axis is a sandblasted portion of Chief Sealth's famous speech given at the time of the signing. The text is in Lushootseed, the written language of the Salish. The gazebo is aligned parallel with the north/south Willamette Prime Meridian, although the adjacent built environment is askew. The interface of the vines growing on the grid of the gazebo suggest reconciliation of the surveyed grid with the landscape.

As a monument to man's manipulation of Nature, the sculpture in itself attempts the same. The impending topiary shearing of George Washington's bust is not assured. Failure to manipulate the English Ivy does not prevent this piece's success. Nature inevitably does not do what we plan or predict. The topiary realization of George's head is only a transition or a fluke in an artificially sustained sylvan landscape atop Interstate 5. A mechanical watering system meters out water like clockwork onto the sculpture and the adjacent landscape. If this man-made landscape is interrupted by disease, neglect, or change of aesthetic sensibility, the armature, Chief Seattle, will be re-revealed, reaffirming Chief Sealth's quote:

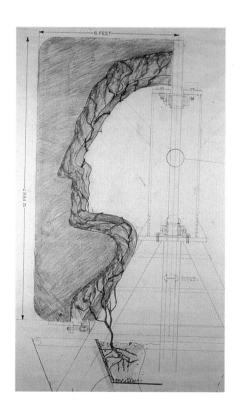

Seattle George
Washington State Convention Center

Elevation drawing
Seattle, Washington
1988

Seattle George
Washington State Convention Center
Seattle, Washington
1989

Buster Simpson

122 / 123

At night when the streets of your cities and villages
will be silent
and you think them deserted,
they will throng with the returning hosts
that once filled and still
love this beautiful land.
The white man will never be alone.
Let him be just
and deal kindly with my people
for the dead are not powerless.
Dead did I say?
There is no death.
Only the change of worlds.

Exchanger Fountain

Santa Ana your water nurtures and your hot winds cool.
The water kissing your lips is an offering.

The above text condenses issues exemplified in the *Exchanger Fountain*, a drinking fountain adjacent to a willow and embraced by an ovular fence. The fountain's gray water nurtures the willow tree and naturally cools the drinking fountain, illustrating the interconnectedness of humans and Nature. The design for the fountain was inspired by historical accounts of the city and antigray water sentiments. It also incorporates the need for wheelchair accessibility.

The fountain's dish, inscribed with the text and mounted with a drinking bubbler, mimics the shape of the farm disc which was used to till the once predominant agrarian economy that relied directly on the Santa Ana River. The disc is mounted on a leaning tufa column, one foot in diameter, which is set into a tree pit and extends two and a half feet above the ground. The stone is scored by a deep groove to accept the cooper water supply line and to channel gray water. The line spirals up the stone and the gray water spirals down, resembling an Archimedes' screw.

After the patron drinks, the "spent" water (gray water) spills through the disc and saturates the highly absorbent tufa stone. Evaporation, resulting from southern California's dry, warm climate, cools the stone mass and consequently the drinking water supply line. The remaining gray water then saturates the tree pit which the fountain shares with the willow tree. The sprouting willow tree post, cut from the banks of the Santa Ana River in 1993, refers to Anaheim's first fence—a living fence of willow posts that encircled the community in 1856. This willow tree, once part of the indigenous landscape, is now an anomaly among the large planted palms in the city's formalized streetscape.

A steel fence encloses the fountain. It rises from the square pit and evolves into an elliptical fence with an orbit of recycled redwood. The fence embraces the fountain's precarious angle which accommodates the disabled. The recycled redwood cladding mimics the granite veneer of the adjacent office towers.

I trust people are conscious of the offering they make: cooling the next person's drink and nurturing the willow. Reflected in the fountain is the water "kissing your lips," and the interdependence of us all.

Exchanger Drinking Fountain
Accessible "watering hole"
Anaheim, California
1993

Source of the willow pole, Santa Ana River

Planting of willow pole

Sprouting of willow pole, three months later

Michele Oka Doner

I am concerned with process, interested in how things are born, how they grow ripe and how they decay. In the years before I was five, we lived in a small house with a huge mango tree that filled up the backyard. When the mangos ripened, we could not eat all the fruit that fell into the yard. The mangos would lie on the ground and slowly rot. I used to watch the ants crawl in them and the yellow jackets come. The whole cycle of that tree was so vivid.

I also grew up within walking distance from the ocean. I discovered the same sense of process in the tides, the interaction of the Moon and the water, how each affected the other. I was constantly aware of the growth and change and the season for algaes and grasses floating up on the beach. My interest in working with accretion technology comes from this experience of childhood. I wanted to find a material that spoke of its process of creation. Mineral accretion, the process by which marine animals synthesize their shells, and by which coral reefs form, has been envisioned as an ideal underwater building process for many years. Attempts have been made since the 1940s to harness this process for man-made use. Efforts have centered on mineral deposition: the use of an electric current to distill and solidify calcium carbonate and other abundant minerals from the sea water and to deposit them on a cathode.

The sculptures that use this process are literally grown in water in the same way our bones grow. All life came from the placenta of the ocean waters. The dissolved minerals in water are the same minerals that are in our bodies. Our blood is primarily salt water. I realize that our bodies generate bone material in the same way the ocean makes coral reefs, with electrical current.

Medical professionals have recently begun healing broken bones with electricity. They understand that if you break a bone, electric current will help make it grow faster and heal. I am using electricity to extract the calcium from the salt water.

Accreting minerals for the use of man has a rich history. It begins with the idea of Second Nature, the human modification of the natural, original landscape as Cicero described it in *The Nature of the Gods* in the first century B.C.

> We sow corn and plant trees. We fertilize the soil by irrigation. We dam the rivers to guide them where we will. One might say that we seek with our human hands to create a second nature in the natural world. [1]

In sixteenth century Italy, during the Renaissance, the notion of a Third Nature arose. It was first expressed by the writer Jacopo Bonfadio in a letter describing the gardens on the shores of Lake Garda in 1541.

> nature incorporated with art is made the creator and connatural of art, and from both is made a third nature, which I would not know how to name. [2]

The mingling of art and Nature produced neither pure art nor pure Nature, but qualities that are altogether unique to the combination. Third Nature introduced the visual poetry of art and design to Cicero's vision of the original modification of Nature.

Michele Doner has been studying the mineral accretion process the Earth uses to build many of its structures, including the bones in our bodies. Her work in Santa Monica creates a physical and poetic gateway to the life of the ocean and her experiments in Venice, Italy hold promise for applying accretion technology to save the architectural foundations of this city.

≈

**Grotto of the Animals
Villa Medici, Castello**

Castello, Italy
1546

Bringing naturally occurring mineral formations together with man-made architectural constructions was a typical manifestation of Third Nature. It led to the practice of covering walls and grottos with accreted minerals. The Romans used the technique at an ancient grotto discovered among the ruins of the Villa of Vopisco at Tivoli.

The ruin was described by architect, humanist, and mathematician, Leon Battista Alberti in his mid-fifteenth-century treatise on architecture. Alberti recommended the revival of this intriguing, encrusted art form, and among those whose interest he sparked was Cosimo De' Medici, who then commissioned the building of the *Grotto of the Animals*, Villa Medici, Castello. The De' Medici grotto was created in 1546 by taking stalactites and a porous material called spugna from the caves in which they were growing and transplanting them into the grotto. The tissue-like quality of the spugna and the muscle-like contours of stalactites, as well as their ability to grow through the constant condensation of water, led to mineral formations, which they called "living rock." Once the spugna and stalactites were in place in the grotto, water from nearby reservoirs was drawn to flow gently among them, resuscitating the living rock within an architectural framework.

Just as the idea of the Third Nature in Renaissance Italy was seen as a marriage between Nature and art, accretion technology in this century is the union between Nature, art, and technology.

During the 1960s, the United States Naval Civil Engineering Laboratory in Port Hueneme, California, experimented with mineral accretion by applying a modest current to such porous, fibrous materials as wood pilings. The Navy hoped the resulting cathodic action could be used to strengthen and protect their shoreline installations against erosion and attack by boring organisms. Accretion petrifies the wood by drawing minerals in and creating limestone, improving the wood's structural characteristics.

Michele Oka Doner

Santa Monica Obelisk

In the mid-1980s I began to work with the Marine Resources Development Foundation in Key Largo, Florida, to explore and help realize the potential of accretion technology. Commissioned by the city of Santa Monica, California, in 1986 to create a site-specific sculpture for Ocean Park Beach overlooking the Pacific Ocean, I constructed a pair of vertical armatures at the Foundation's Key Largo site and immersed them in their saltwater lagoon in 1987. The armatures appear wrapped by a continuous wave-like spiral and twisted like the interior caverns of a univalve shell. They measure thirteen feet and six inches each in length. They speak visually of the ocean before them, its life and texture, ebb and flow. The use of minerals from the salt water for an ocean site fulfilled the city's requirement for "appropriateness," and met the requirement for durability against the elements of ocean and beach, especially the salt air. The sculptures took three years to accrete several inches of thickness, and I installed the accreted columns in January, 1992.

By using sculpture to explore accretion technology, the result was neither sculpture in the traditional sense, nor a pure scientific experiment designed to replicate a biological process. Instead, the interaction between biological, technological, and artistic practice assumed larger dimensions of their own: a Third Nature.

This project is the first note in something that I think will be a song. It was an experiment. The larger project that will prove this technology's worth has yet to materialize.

Above left:
Santa Monica Obelisks
Armature for one of a pair of sculptures
ready for immersion into salt water
Key Largo, Florida
1987

Above right:
Santa Monica Obelisks
Accreting in salt water
Key Largo, Florida
1991

Right:
Santa Monica Obelisks
Accretion Process Details
Development from
Wire Mesh to Marine Habitat
Mesh Armature 1987
October 1988
June 1990
May 1991
August 1991
November 1991
Key Largo, Florida

Michelle Oka Doner

**Santa Monica Obelisks
Ocean Park Beach**

Mineral accreted columns
Santa Monica, California
1986–1992

Photo: Ed Goldstein

The Venice Accretion Project

The Venice Accretion Project was conceived at the same time and grew out of the commission for the ocean front site in Santa Monica. The purpose for the initial project was to demonstrate the possible applications of mineral accretion technology on the lagoons and canals of Venice. The choice of Venice served a dual purpose. Venice has an established tradition of combining art with Nature, dating at least to the Renaissance. The architecture of the Ca d'Oro survives as a poignant example of Bonfadio's Third Nature at work:

> Its rippling patterns, ideally designed to be seen against their own reflection in the water of the Grand Canal, have the same fairy-tale quality we recall from the exterior of St. Mark's. [3]

In addition, Venice faces an environmental challenge for which modern accretion technology is uniquely equipped. Perched in the shallow waters of the Adriatic Sea,

The Venice Accretion Project

Rendering by Jordan Doner
Proposal to use accreted minerals to fortify
the foundations of the buildings in
Venice, Italy
1991

Venice's base is eroding due to a combination of man-made pollutants and natural forces. The historic building facades are being corroded and eaten away at their foundations. The cement-like hardness achieved through accretion technology may be used to fortify building structures exposed to water at a relatively low cost, eventually securing the foundation of the city itself.

Several tests conducted in the northern part of the Venetian lagoon were quite successful. We used five suspended sculptures, submerged them for several months, and found that the Adriatic was indeed amenable to accretion.

The initial results of *The Venice Accretion Project* confirmed the belief that electro-deposition of minerals can be instrumental in fortifying Venice's past and preserving her future. Also, the unexpectedly rapid rate of accretion in the cooler waters of the Venetian lagoon established the viability of accretion outside of tropical climates.

In the near future, I envision a pilot project that will combine art and environmental protection: wave-like configurations of accreted minerals fortifying the selected waterway in Venice. These gradually undulating configurations of living rock will visually mimic the movement of water, evoking the essence of tidal rhythm and motion. Since Venice has large tidal changes, the work will be visible at low tide. The wave motif recalls the Renaissance idea of the "endless water chain," an echo of Third Nature. Both the sixteenth-century water chain and the envisioned accreted waves visually abstract the flow of water. With accretion, possibly for the first time in Venice, aesthetics may combine with a healing or medicinal function to protect and preserve art and architecture.

Venice was founded in the fifth century by people fleeing persecution in the cities of Italy. In their pursuit of protection, they traded stone walls for the isolation of water. It is ironic that sixteen centuries later mineral accretion may, in effect, turn water back into stone, to help protect Venice and assure its survival for centuries to come.

1. Claudia Lazzaro, *The Italian Renaissance Garden*, pg.9, Yale U. Press, 1990.
2. Ibid.
3. Janson, *History of Art*, Prentice-Hall, 1964.

Michele Oka Doner

Reiko Goto

Why butterflies?

> Because they are messengers from the insect to the human world. Not because they are here for us, but because they are among the only insects to which we feel any positive response, when we notice them—and most people don't.
> —ROBERT MICHAEL PILE, *Butterfly Conservationist*

In 1988, I collaborated with Jeff Brown, a landscape architect, on a temporary public art installation using fennel as a major element of the design. Jeff suggested using fennel because it is a non-native invasive plant found everywhere in the bay area, including rocky hills, vacant lots, sidewalks, and old railroad tracks.

One day after our installation, I noticed a big green and black striped caterpillar on a fennel leaf. When I touched the caterpillar, orange horns emerged from its head and a strong aroma of fennel was emitted. This moment brought me back to my childhood in Japan. My parents' yard had an orange tree that was home to large, beautiful bright green caterpillars. They had artificial eyes on their backs, and when I scared them, orange horns came out of their heads and they emitted a strong odor. Sometimes I saw large yellow and black swallowtail butterflies near the tree, and every year they would return.

I have been in America since 1981, and didn't realize how much I used to love viewing the butterfly cycle until I saw the caterpillar on the fennel leaf. The discovery made me very happy, for I realized that something familiar to me was always nearby. I found myself wanting to be closer to butterflies. I started collecting caterpillars and rearing them. I called the San Francisco Insect Zoo to learn more about this type of butterfly. Its name is anise swallowtail, and the female butterfly is believed to come back to her birthplace to lay her eggs.

My husband Tim and I live in a place that used to house a community arts center called Crossroads Community/The Farm. The Farm was on five and a half acres, under and within a freeway system. Even though much of the Farm's area has been converted to other uses, there are still some surviving plants, including fennel. I was able to find many anise swallowtail caterpillars close to home.

In 1988, I was an artist in residence at the Headlands Center for the Arts in Marin, California. I presented two installations, *Haru* and *Natsu*, involving the metamorphosis of the anise swallowtail butterfly. An essential component of both of these installations involved the release of the butterflies. I never detained the butterflies in the exhibition space unless they had broken wings or would have had to be released into bad weather.

The Yerba Buena Garden Project

In 1991 the San Francisco Redevelopment Agency sought artists to implement a site-response to a garden area of the expanded Moscone Convention Center. One of the initial requests of the artists was to "contribute to the project's overall sense of place and to one's sense of orientation within the place."

We all need to learn to create our homes and cities with respect for the habitat needs of other species with whom we share our planet. Reiko Goto has begun part of this process by creating a garden that provides larva and nectar plants for the nurturance of butterflies within downtown San Francisco.

≈

Photo: Richard Barnes

Haru
Headlands Center for the Arts
Fennel, Butterfly Chrysalisides
Marin County, California
1989

**Butterfly Garden
Yerba Buena Gardens**

Butterfly Garden in lower left
San Francisco, California
1993

Photo: Barry Deutsch

Anise Swallowtail
Papilio Zelicaon

Reiko Goto

The redevelopment agency became interested in the idea of a butterfly garden after they saw a slide show of mine which included the two Headlands butterfly installations. However, I felt that inviting butterflies into the downtown roof garden would not be an easy job for either the butterflies or myself. I decided that even though the probability of creating a quality habitat experience in the Yerba Buena Gardens Meadow was nearly impossible due to location constraints, I could promote my ideals by introducing the type of plant materials that would nurture insects and animals.

I spent a year submitting different possibilities for the project to the redevelopment agency. During this period, I began an extensive study of local butterflies and their habitat needs. I met Leslie Saul, director of the San Francisco Insect Zoo, and asked her about common butterflies in San Francisco. She gave me lists of butterflies and their host plants, and also brought me to the Nature Trail in Golden Gate Park. There I met Donald Mahoney, Ph.D., who works as nursery coordinator and Nature Trail supervisor for the Strybing Arboretum. Don suggested my meeting with Barbara Deutsch, who had been rearing butterflies and creating a butterfly garden on a slice of what is left of wild hillside on Potrero Hill. She has been developing her garden, a small trail, since 1984.

I will never forget my first meeting with Barbara. She showed me a few kinds of larva plants that looked like weeds, and explained what kinds of butterflies use them. After returning from Barbara's house, I found many of these plants and different kinds of caterpillars near my home. They were always near me—I just hadn't noticed! Leslie, Don, and Barbara truly introduced me to the world of butterflies. Their knowledge is based on active experimentation and observation, rather than on books.

Photo: Cesar Rubio

Top: **West Coast Lady**
Vanessa Annabella

Middle: **French Lavender**
Lavandula Dentata

Bottom: **Virginia Lady**
Vanessa Virginiensis

Photo: Barry Deutsch

Finding the right plants for the garden was not a simple task. Books were of little use, since many of the plants that the butterflies traditionally used have been lost to development. Decreasing the habitat of native plants threatens wildlife, and butterflies are no exception. Some of the species have had to find other food sources: red admiral found pellitory; anise swallowtail use fennel rather than cow parsnip; painted lady, west coast lady, and gray hair streak use malva.

I felt the garden design needed to be reviewed by an entomologist and a botanist to give it a firm footing in reality. Also, there was concern that the concept of the urban reintroduction of butterflies would get lost in the stronger visual element of the garden design. I talked the dilemma over with Barbara, and she offered to help with the project. She also suggested that I work with Leslie and Don before giving my final proposal to the redevelopment agency.

My final proposal for the Yerba Buena Garden involved creating an urban garden for butterflies. The garden provides a convenient and well-stocked rest stop for butterflies as they traverse the urban landscape of the Bay Area. To accomplish this, I introduced larva and nectar plants as hosts for the butterflies. In addition, I devised a system to protect the vulnerable larvae, and established a program of nurturing maintenance.

I have developed a maintenance plan to train garden workers in proper butterfly garden care. They need to be aware that the plants and composition of the butterfly garden are in some cases directly at odds with traditional areas in the garden. Many of the larva plants are considered weeds, and their appearance seems somewhat unkempt to those more familiar with the controlled techniques of the classic garden. In addition, the garden workers need to develop an awareness concerning the life cycle of the butterfly, and adapt gardening methods to accommodate the creatures' habitat. Finding alternatives to pesticides will be an important issue, since herbicides and pesticides will be prohibited in order to protect all life throughout the garden—both insect and human. The maintenance plan explores these important issues.

Photo: Barry Deutsch

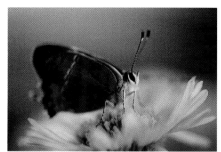

Photo: Barry Deutsch

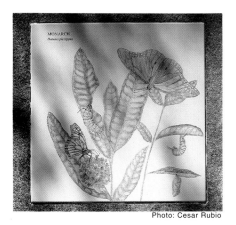

Photo: Cesar Rubio

Reiko Goto

Photo: Cesar Rubio

In addition to creating a welcoming environment for butterflies, the garden provides an opportunity for audience awareness and education. Rather than focusing solely on the end product, the garden directs attention toward all aspects of the butterfly life cycle. To further educate the public, four plaques were installed, each illustrating the stages of metamorphosis for a different butterfly species.

The butterfly garden must be viewed as an ongoing project. That is, the site will need to settle in for a year or so, giving the plants time to get established. Following this, continuous study will be necessary to determine which butterfly species are attracted to the site and how the garden may be adjusted to accommodate their needs.

Recently, while visiting my favorite butterfly garden with a group of grade school teachers, one of the major questions I heard asked was, "What are we supposed to be looking at?" It is a good question, indicative of our cultural need for immediate gratification, as well as our impatience with all things natural. But the most telling part of the question is the notion of looking at something. Standing away, we see things based on our intellectual and aesthetic training. We compare, contrast, criticize, and appreciate a display. I hope this butterfly garden becomes something more, an oddly kept amalgam of weeds and plants, piles of clippings stacked near their source, an obvious sense of unmanicured chaos, which under close inspection is filled with life and purpose. A place where the inquiring mind can search and discover, where careful and present awareness is rewarded by the flash of a caterpillar's colorful coat, or the camouflage of a chrysalis.

By briefly introducing simple concepts like larvae plants and nectar plants, the garden will whet the appetite of the curious. A tour of the undergrowth, "belly down and nose-in-the-dirt," may nurture a visitor long after he or she has left. The garden is meant to be experienced, not just looked at.

My partners and I envision for the future a wildlife corridor of interconnecting green spaces designed with habitat needs in mind. It will promote the propagation and movement of wild creatures, and encourage awareness of Nature's wonders, even within the heart of the city.

Lynne Hull

My primary focus is on trans-species art: sculptures that are usable by wildlife or enhance wildlife habitat. After years of making studio art about my concerns for nurturance and endangered life cycles, I wanted to make a direct, positive gesture toward the Earth. I live in Wyoming where Nature, not man, is still the dominant force. If there are more antelope than people, why not make art for wildlife?

Except in a very few instances, all humankind's activities are aimed at benefiting itself as a species if not as individuals. So much of what we do in our lives has had a detrimental effect on the species with whom we share the planet. As an artist I had spent years objecting to our harmful effects on the environment. Could I instead make art to counteract them? Surely centuries of civilization would enable us to act on behalf of other species. If art is a leading edge of civilization, as we hope, is it not possible that trans-species actions can be done as art? Can art atone for some of the losses we have caused?

Desert Hydroglyphs

Since I was raised in New Mexico the first action that occurred to me was connected to the magic of finding water in the desert. Even a few ounces of water can mean survival for wildlife if water is scarce. With hand tools, I carved the first *Desert Hydroglyphs*, cutting channels a few inches deep into horizontal rock surfaces to hold water from runoff rain and snowmelt. The symbols, functional and contemporary versions of ancient petroglyphs, are in shapes abstracted from animal body parts and tracks.

I avoided working in places that already had ancient rock carvings or other unique features. I wondered as I carved whether a deer would recognize an abstract, enlarged deer track or bone shape, or what the shapes would mean to an antelope.

Lynne Hull's art speaks of our interaction with the rest of the animal kingdom. Her works are an offering of nutrance, protection, and habitat.

≈

Desert Hydroglyph
A carving to capture water for wildlife
Moab, Utah
1986

Desert Hydroglyph
A carving to capture water for wildlife
Near Canyon Lands National Park
Utah
1993

Lynne Hull

Trans-species art must be attractive in the most basic sense of the word: the species it is designed for must be attracted into using the sculpture.

I was intrigued with the idea of creating artwork appropriate to other ecosystems. In pine-forested mountains, marten havens could improve the marginal pine marten habitat by providing a winter den. These enable marten, who depend on old growth forest, to survive in younger forests and the edges of clearcuts. For ponds and marshes, I launched the first of a series of sculptural floating islands for waterfowl nesting. For the high plains near my home raptor roosts provide safe resting places for hawks and eagles. On the plains where there are few trees, these large birds of prey are vulnerable on the ground and sometimes electrocuted on power poles.

All my works are researched and designed with the help of wildlife biologists and zoologists, as well as monitored for wildlife use whenever possible. A zoologist recently saw two young golden eagles on one of the raptor roosts, and a researcher photographed marten tracks on snow leading into several marten havens last winter.

Next I thought about sculpture as part of whole site design. Recently I finished a design collaboration at Pine Bluffs, Wyoming, with wildlife biologists and landscape architects, funded jointly by the NEA and the Wyoming Game and Fish Department. We designed the area for wildlife habitat enhancement, environmental interpretation, and art that functions in both these areas. Applying what I learned on this project to several other sites, I've worked with school children to build a bird and small animal garden on the Navajo reservation, worked on a pond in England, and along rivers in Massachusetts and Montana. Often these projects involve a wide variety of people and agencies in odd collaborations.

Lightning Raptor Roosts

In 1990 I received a New Forms: Regional Initiatives Grant from the Colorado Dance Festival and the Helena Film Society, a regrant from NEA, Rockefeller Foundation, and Apache Corporation funds. I had proposed to do a pair of *Raptor Roosts*, one with a nesting platform, somewhere along I-80. With the help of Wyoming's "Wildlife Worth Watching" program and the Bureau of Land Management (BLM), a site was selected adjacent to a small parking pull-out, in a bare, windy section of the Red Desert. Only the bright yellow rabbit brush blooms and the summer lightning storms moving through the area offered inspiration.

Other site visits and agency meetings followed. Pacific Power and Light Company (PP&L), which has done extensive work toward raptor safety on its power lines and has helped on my previous roosts, agreed to donate poles and install the sculptures. My work process is to design and rough out large sculptures,

then reassemble them on site. With Mark Ritchie, my carpenter friend, I wrapped yellow wood lightning shapes around power poles, topped them with perching elements, added wagon wheel hoop clouds, and prebuilt the sculptures in a BLM garage in Rawlins. As these forms developed, Mark felt the sculptures might be too elaborate, too fussy. It's awkward to work on a huge pole angled up on a crane when I'm standing on the ground or on the piece. I never really see the whole roost until it's up, when it's really too late to make many changes. Then site interaction affects them profoundly.

On a cold, sunny November morning we moved the pieces to the site. Wind was coming up, clouds were moving in, a few snowflakes blew around us as we shivered and tried to get cold, gloved hands to work tools and refit boards. The BLM raptor specialist adjusted the wire mesh on the nesting platform to make sure bird claws couldn't get caught. Game and Fish personnel observed, photographed, and videotaped. The PP&L crew, with their massive line truck and crane, drilled the prairie and raised the roosts. Far from looking too elaborate, as Mark had feared, the nesting roost now looked skimpy and a little awkward in the overpowering landscape.

We installed the other roost close enough to the parking area for travelers to observe hawks and perhaps a few wandering eagles perched on it. Raised, the sculptures looked as I had hoped. Sun breaking through the cloud cover made the yellow "lightning" leap out in the now dull tan landscape. Enjoying their break from power pole installation and repair, the crew discussed problems Pacific Power is having with eagles trying to nest on big power poles. Clearly we needed to do more of these sculptures.

Lightning Raptor Roost
Safe perching and nesting sites
for birds of prey
Red Desert, Wyoming
1990

Lightning Raptor Roost
Ferruginous hawk nest
1993

As we drove away from the site, Mark said, "Now they don't look too busy. The scale of the landscape compared to the scale of the garage changes them completely." I hoped the hawks would find them attractive.

Edward Abbey has said, "Artists have two jobs: to make art, and to be subversive." Because I work in collaboration with the "establishment"—Pacific Power, the Bureau of Land Management, and other groups—I felt I was not being subversive. Later, thinking back on that morning, I realized I'd kept all these agencies, personnel, resources, and equipment tied up for the better part of a day. They made art for wildlife in a sweet collaborative subversion—a successful art project by Ed Abbey's definition after all.

Two years later I saw Tom Rinkes, the BLM raptor specialist who had worked on the project. He mentioned that Ferruginous hawks have been proposed for listing as a threatened species. He had just banded a young hawk on our nest. It had been the second successful summer of raising young Ferruginous hawks on the sculpture, thereby making the project a success on his terms. The following fall I went out to look at the nest. It is beautifully constructed out of twisting sagebrush twigs. With this additional volume, the sculpture no longer looks skimpy but rather balanced and complete. The art is now a success on my terms.

Recently I saw in the morning paper that over forty eagles have been found dead in the past few months near outdated power lines and open oil pits in the Little Buffalo Basin. More mitigation, atonements, and grief. Time to make more art.

Lynne Hull

Constance DeJong

It is only to us that the animal exists in time.
The antelope and the monkey, the wild cat and the squirrel appear,
disappear in a world where there is nothing but the present. *

The real starting point for my project was my interest in the relations between humans and animals. Initially, around 1988, I was developing ideas for a novel on the subject. When I was discussing the work, I was informed of a public art competition for the Woodland Park Zoo in Seattle and encouraged to apply. I put together a proposal, and eventually, was awarded the commission. So by chance, one unexpected conversation played an important role in redirecting me from writing a novel to creating an outdoor work, a private to a public experience.

My original proposal was simply to create an audio work for the zoo which would include spoken language, natural sounds, and animal voices. These three elements comprise the final recordings I made. But the writing of my texts was profoundly affected by my one month residency in Seattle and my access to all parts of the zoo grounds and activities. During this period, I saw how the zoo used language and to what ends and purposes. Nearly all the zoo's signage presents what might be called information: facts and figures about the animals. Such information represents only one kind of knowledge. It may increase what we know, but in another sense it reduces our understanding by objectifying the animals. The elephant or the lemur of the zoo, for example, becomes a symbolic animal, defined and rendered static, frozen out of time.

Animal space and visitor space are visually unified in this place where we are too,
the humans and the other animals of the zoo. Gone is the privileged position
we once erected for ourselves, our imaginary elevation. Across unseen barriers
we now view the other animals at eye level or from below or from some awkward angle.
This way of seeing says: our only privileged position is to be in the company of animals
and to catch a glimpse of them . . . the privilege of seeing them at all.

I decided that I wanted to bring a reflective mode to the zoo since it really did not offer one. I wanted to create a quiet alcove, a place the visitor could discover. The alcove would contain a plain park bench, and someone sitting on the bench would activate a recording of sounds and language that might stimulate him or her to reflect on the moment, on the complex topic of relations between animals and humans.

Humans are the talking animals, the world is ours to name. Perhaps in
animals we see silent stretches of space, time—even of familiar land where in the field,

Through the following project,

Constance DeJong has brought

a fresh voice to the zoo

which explores our relationship to the

rest of the animal kingdom.

≈

---

*This is one of the spoken texts that have been recorded and play at audio-equipped benches at the Seattle Zoo. (They are hereafter indicated by italics.) The recordings are 35–50 seconds in length and delivered by people of different ages, cultural backgrounds, and nationalities, a mix of female and male speakers. The human voice is always in duet with an animal voice.

Bengal Tiger

India
Southeast Asia
Endangered

the plain and, lest I forget, in the darkness of night animals are
seeing me long before I notice them. And under animal eyes one
feels oneself becoming visible, if only for an instant.

I once came upon a Canadian lynx in a forest in Cape Breton, Nova Scotia. Perhaps this encounter was the real starting point for my project. Without warning I found myself in the path of a wild animal, a fairly large animal, and the lynx was looking straight at me. The eyes, I can see them now—a long unblinking gaze. The lynx decided the moment; he (I think he) walked into the woods with his back to me, stopped, and over his shoulder, looked around at me once more. I realized that the encounter, which I'd never had before, was unlikely to happen again. Our crossing of paths made me feel utterly isolated in the woods. In the long-lasting aftermath, I was aware of the isolation of humans living only among humans.

We define accented moments as those that contain external happenings
which mobilize our resources . . . as when, without warning,
human beings and animals encounter each other. It is then that the sight,
the smell, the sound of them takes hold of us in an instant. Time enough
to feel the cloth against our back, the blood against the vein. And our
quickening pulse taps out how long it's been since animals were with
humans at the center of a world.

Constance DeJong

140 / 141

That experience in the forest took me into a room, a kind of mental space for dwelling on the great separation that has occurred for many of us: Culture has become nearly everything and Nature is far away. Our distance from animals is not only physical, but metaphorical. So, not only do the spoken texts give voice to relations with captive and noncaptive animals, but with animals of the imagination.

The animals have been feeding us. Oh, not as meat but as some
other form of nourishment that fuels a very old desire to forge
imaginary links with other members of the food chain. Thus the deer
and elk have been close family members, frequent husbands and wives
revered for their loyal ways. And beyond the family circle, the cow has been
mother to the whole world, the Earth forever replenished with her milk.
Before we cooked the goose, humans rode on the ganders' backs,
harnessing their freedom to be at home on water, on earth, or in the air.
And long before the rabbit was the cuddly character we nuzzle in our cribs,
the great white hare stole light from the heavens and set the world on fire.

Indifference to animals has meant a loss of habitats and often an additional loss when land cleared in the name of food production can no longer sustain plantings and herds. Indifference to animals has meant harvesting and torturing "laboratory specimens" so that humans can prosper as the apex of life forms (or can have a better soap product). A change in how we think of and view animals can precipitate a change in how we treat animals. I don't mean we will become animal lovers in some trivial or sentimental way, but that we can affect policy in important areas such as city planning, agriculture, and food and pharmaceutical production. Does policy begin with a day at the zoo? It can, yes, it can. I contributed a work there to be part of that process.

Merely standing, merely eating, sleeping, or performing countless
other natural functions—the animals remind us:
they are not performing at all. Their life runs parallel to our
clock driven days and has the uncommon virtue of serving
no function in the schedule of useful activities.

Ideas about Nature reflect the dominant beliefs of a particular era. Ideas about Nature change over time, determined or at least influenced by considerations such as economics, religion, and gender, to name a few. In writing this project, I came to view Nature as the environment where we exist. This is it. Nature is not far away; it is not a place to which one goes on a vacation. In grappling with the zoo as an institution, I sometimes believed my writing was paying respect to the animals in the terrible confines they endure and will not escape from. Captive animals are a blatant display of our indifference toward them, our dominion over them, our view of Nature as a separate place out there somewhere—rather than in our backyards.

Ten, nine, eight, seven, six, five, for two million years
animals and humans have shared the Earth's environment.
Time enough to recognize all the days are numbered

All animal portraits courtesy Gerry Ellis Nature Photography, Portland, Oregon ©

Spotted Owl
Northwest Coast North America
Endangered

Blue Poison Dart Frog
Surinam
Endangered

Ring Tailed Lemur
Madagascar
Endangered

Opposite: **Asian Elephant**
Southeast Asia
Endangered

William Jackson Maxwell

My work has focused on site specific, environmental issues for the past twelve years. What led me in this direction was a re-exploration of my own history. The rediscovery occurred shortly after graduate school in 1976, when I returned to my hometown in Auburn, California, and started exploring my old haunts. The memories that emerged from my early childhood experiences, living and playing in the woods of northern California and digging holes to that ever elusive China, are the cornerstone of my current work.

My father's family was in the logging business, and in the late Spring of each year we would pack up and move from Auburn to the new logging camp for that year. For me it was a great adventure, since each new logging site offered a distinctly different experience in the woods. In one camp, located in Forbes town, I attended a one room school. My classmates and I spent considerable time exploring the woods. We collected salamanders, butterflies, and other insects, but more importantly, we used our imaginations to turn ourselves into human dump trucks, steam shovels, and logging rigs.

My experiences in the majestic forests contained mysteries that still inspire me today. Once, while I was adventuring in the forest with some friends, I wondered off on my own and noticed two turtles. Nothing unusual about this, except that the turtles were luminous, the larger one being a florescent red and the smaller one a florescent orange. They were midway up a dirt ramp that connected two ponds. I stood there mesmerized by their presence, and realized that I had to share this discovery with my buddies. I ran as fast as I could to get my friends, but when we returned, the turtles were gone. I have since returned to the site on many occasions, hoping to find them. They never reappeared there, but they reappear continually in my work. When I think about the destruction of the rain forest, I not only think about biodiversity or global warming. I think also of the loss of not being able to imaginatively explore the forest and experience its nature, to create our own stories which become part of our own personal history and essence.

Brazilian Stump

These works were interactive pieces that I completed on the campus of the University of Colorado in Boulder. The campus had lost many of its elm trees to disease, and I used the stumps to focus attention on the loss of life of the rain forest. It took many months to carve images into the stumps, and as people became aware of me, I would engage in a

William Maxwell uses his work

to foster communication

and understanding

around ecological issues.

He brings the dialogue of rainforest

habitat and species loss to a college,

the issues of threatened

and endangered species

to a fine arts facility, and creates

a public forum at a civic center on

implications of the atomic age.

≈

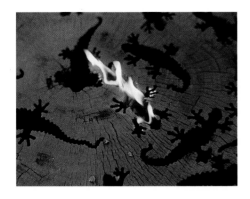

dialogue concerning the issues of the rain forest. After the carving was finished, I began the burning. This also took several months to complete, and sometimes the burns were large enough to garner attention and considerable dialogue.

All the images I worked with represent the mysteries of life or the loss of species. The salamander is associated with a power to extinguish fire, and has considerable mythological significance in many cultures. The Carolina parakeet was the only indigenous parakeet in the United States, ranging as far north as Maine and as far west as Colorado. It came into conflict with fruit farming and was hunted into extinction because of its vulnerablity.

The *Forest Stories* stump is related to the story of the two turtles. After finishing the carving and burning of the stump, I coated the book with blackboard paint. I then wrote the story of the two turtles directly on the stump. I left the pencil there in the hopes that other people would relate their own personal stories or experiences in the forest. The piece was located on the lawn in front of the university's Norlin Library. On many occasions I would walk by and observe people leaning against the stump while reading the text on the book. The particular site was selected because of its close proximity to a memorial bench made of wood from the rain forest. I never saw the bench used, and it seemed lonely and abandoned, in stark contrast to the number of students who used the lawn in front of the library.

Brazilian Stump
University of Colorado

Carved and burned stumps of blighted elm trees on the university's campus
Boulder, Colorado
1990–1991

William Jackson Maxwell

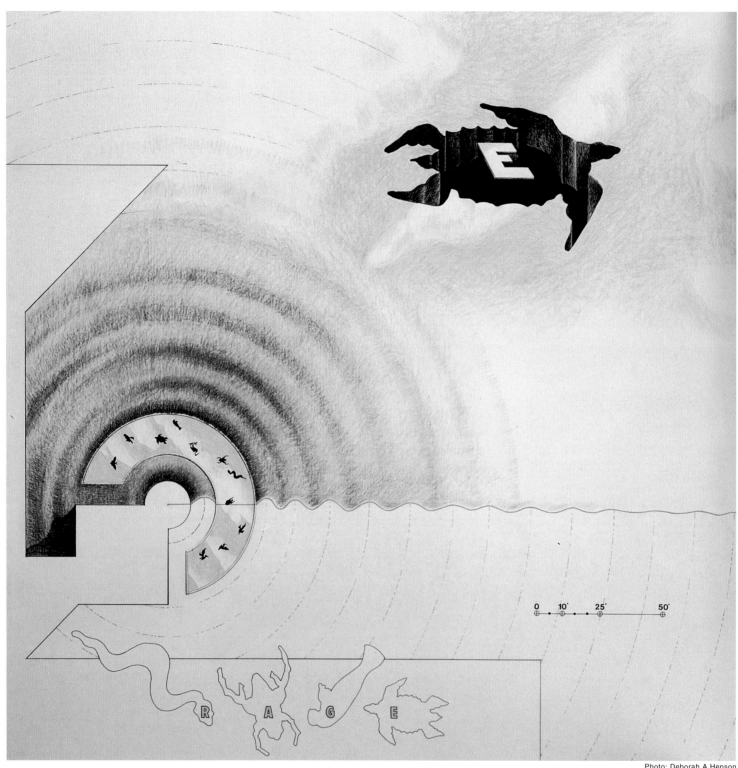

Endangered

This piece occupies the landscape directly in front of the Center for Fine and Performing Arts at the University of West Florida in Pensacola. In the center of the site, the art gallery connects the two wings of the new building. It acts as a bridge or connection between the fine and performing arts. I used the central position of the gallery as my reference point for the water and landscape site work. A small round building attached to the central corner of the gallery became the generating spot for the landscape genesis. I conceived of it as a seismic beacon sending out signals through the Earth as pulses. The generating pulses manifest themselves as waves in the lawn, large concentric berms that decrease in size and frequency as they fan out from the round house.

Endangered
Center for Fine and Performing Arts
University of West Florida
Pensacola, Florida
1994

Plan Drawing by Cristopher Melton, Architect

Around the base of the round house is the first wave, or berm. This wave gives way to a water mote that surrounds the round house. On the other side of the water mote, the concentric waves begin again. Within the moat are images of animals that are extinct, such as the Carolina parakeet; or endangered, such as the manatee or hawks beak turtle; or not yet endangered, but potentially threatened if we do not heed what is happening with the environment and the species with whom we share this planet home.

The images first appear magical and unexplainable as a negative space within the water. The space then fills with mist and is mysteriously illuminated from within, giving it a life-like appearance. A single letter floats in the center of each image, combining to spell the word "ENDANGERED." During the day, the letters appear as suspended pools of water reflecting the sky, and in the evenings, they appear as black letters floating in a volume of light and mist.

The water feature is controlled by a computer that allows me the flexibility to give the piece fuller meaning by spelling out other words such as anger, danger, enraged, degrade, denigrade, genera, end, etc.

The landscaped area outside the water feature is designed with several functions and meanings. First, it functions as the conveyor or medium environment for the principle message of endangerment expressed in the moat. Also, the berms are graded in a manner that allows the rainwater to collect and reflect the sky. As the water drains, it recedes toward the center like silver fingers, very subtly supporting the overall notion of disappearance and loss. The berms closest to the water are designed to support people. A person can very comfortably lean back on a particular berm and reflect on the meaning of this environment.

Ground Zero

When I was invited to design a public artwork for the Las Vegas City Hall Complex, it brought back memories of growing up during the 1950s. At that time, the world lived in constant fear of the atomic bomb and complete awe of the phenomenon of a potentially disastrous chain reaction. In my work for the Las Vegas project, I wanted to integrate these early feelings and realities in the artwork, and show how my feelings about the nuclear threat have evolved. I wanted to create a dialogue with viewers, and elicit their responses to the issue, as well as express an overall concern for the local desert environment.

The artwork's site is the southern facing wall of city hall and adjacent reflecting pool. I chose to focus on issues of civic responsibility, nuclear testing, local history, and the environment. I wanted to create a work that would get people's attention and cause them to stop and consider their responsibility to the health of the environment. The overall design responds to the visual impact of the Vegas Strip. The building's circular structure reminded me of a target, and was the starting point for my idea to simulate a nuclear detonation. The target continues into the water, but transforms from Plexiglass into kinetic lines on the surface of the water. Jets just below the surface create small pixels, or raised dots, on the water. This is the point at which the nuclear detonation occurs. Images that relate to the local flora, historical events, and nuclear testing appear to radiate out from the center of the target. During the detonation, as each ring section of the target appears on the water, all the images in that zone disappear, as though destroyed in a nuclear blast. This happens in seven radiating zones until the last image is gone; then everything disappears and becomes still.

In the evening, the wall is washed with color to represent the afterglow from detonation. Images projected into the center section of the target migrate across the wall, joining other previously projected images. They disappear and reappear, while their reflections interact with the detonation sequence in the water.

I wanted the piece to stimulate dialogue, and at times I've gotten more than I bargained for. Some people are horrified by the image of a simulated nuclear detonation, while others accept it as a symbol of one of the truths of Las Vegas, Nevada. The images both on the water's surface and on the wall represent ghosts of the endangered environment. They call attention to how the desert environment is fast

Ground Zero
Las Vegas City Hall
Las Vegas, Nevada
1993

Photo: Charles Morgan

Above:
Ground Zero

Detonation after image of amphibian
Agitated pattern from jets
below the surface of the water
Right:
Target Lines
Agitated water simulates the
shock waves of a nuclear detonation

Ground Zero
Las Vegas City Hall

Details of wall illumination
Las Vegas, Nevada
1993

Photo: Charles Morgan

William Jackson Maxwell

148 / 149

being destroyed in order to simulate a fantasy world totally out of context with its site. The images are in some cases symbolic. For example, a red feather refers to Wovoka, a northern Paiute who introduced the ghost dance and its consequences to many of the Plains Indians. Another image is the coyote, depicted emitting a nuclear howl. The coyote is one of a few animals who expand their territory as man takes over more land and resources. It stands in defiance to the encroachment, and adapts to survive. I view the coyote as a symbol of hope.

The images should not only be taken in a negative context. I see a need to face the nuclear age with sanity and civic responsibility, and to revere our coexistence with the beautiful world of the infinitely small. Science working in balance with the world's natural order can be very majestic, but is disastrous when perceived short term needs destroy the harmony. This sculpture will be successful in my terms if it helps the community to reconsider its rapid expansion at the expense to the environment. I hope it fosters an exploration of ways to live in harmony with the rest of the inhabitants of this region.

It is like the hundredth monkey. If we get enough people thinking and acting in a way that contributes to transformation, it becomes something mysterious, moving through the culture unseen—as if genetic. My work is part of this philosophy; it is only a particle in the immense world, but it begins to open people up to other ideas, and as it does so, it gains strength untill finally we wake up one day and we are doing it. It happens through example, symbol, and image. As it washes over our psyches, we begin to accept a new way of thinking without realizing the process has been working on us. It naturally takes over.

Patricia Johanson

A major theme in my work from the beginning has been to reconnect city dwellers with Nature, and ensure the survival of plant and animal populations. I envision a new kind of public landscape that balances the needs of human beings with those of the living world. My designs often combine restored ecologies with public access, and transform our traditional image of parks into "ecology gardens."

In 1960 I began writing about designing the world as a work of art. My drawings transformed both functional infrastructure and living Nature into art. I devised specific proposals that would restore fertile land, natural waterways, swamps, and wildlife corridors to major urban centers. Other drawings combined aesthetic images with parks and habitat, or used art to address environmental concerns such as erosion, sedimentation, flooding, water conservation, sewage treatment, and garbage mounds. Design strategies such as *Line Gardens* envisioned the continuity necessary for the survival of large populations, while *Vanishing-Point Gardens* proposed networks of related forms essential to migrating animals. My art projects became incorporated into daily life, and were interwoven with natural ecosystems. The hallmark of my work became to incorporate everything, and to harm nothing.

Fair Park Lagoon

For the next twelve years I worked at putting these ideas forward by exhibiting project drawings in museums and art galleries and by building sculptures that became part of the living landscape. In 1981 I got a call from Harry Parker, then director of the Dallas Museum of Art. He had seen an exhibition of mine that used plant forms as the basis for large-scale buildable projects combining art with infrastructure. Harry asked if I would be willing to come to Dallas to look at "their old mud hole in Fair Park," and see if I could do anything with it in time for the Texas Sesquicentennial. At this point there was no money and no community interest, but Harry felt that if I produced a splendid new design for the lagoon, the Dallas Museum could exhibit the drawings and raise the money. When I asked about the program and budget, he was blissfully casual: "Just do whatever you think needs to be done. This is Dallas. If they like it, they'll build it."

On my first visit to Fair Park it was apparent that the lagoon was environmentally degraded. The shoreline was eroded and the water was murky. Fertilizer from the lawn washed into the lagoon every time it rained, causing algal bloom. There were few birds, no waterfowl, and hardly any plants, animals, or fish.

I began by developing my own list of concerns which included creating a functioning ecosystem, providing living exhibits for the Dallas Museum of Natural History, controlling bank erosion, and creating paths over water so people could become immersed in the life of the lagoon. I also began to research what different animals eat, because food plants and nesting materials attract wildlife.

Eventually, two Texas plants were chosen as models for the sculptures because their forms coincided with the strategy of the design. The delta duck-potato, *Saggitaria platyphylla*, had a mass of twisted roots that I arranged to prevent water from eroding the shoreline. The spaces between the roots became microhabitats for plants, fish, turtles, and birds. The roots were built as five-foot wide paths for visi-

Patricia Johanson's sculptures bring her concern for species habitat to the forefront of public work. She has been able to address the need of the environment and endangered species while providing the public opportunities for access and education.

≈

Saggitaria Platyphylla
Fair Park Lagoon
Paths and microhabitats
Dallas, Texas
1981–86

Patricia Johanson

tors, while thinner stems rose above the water to serve as perches for birds. Leaf forms further out in the lagoon became islands for animals, while other leaves along the shore formed step seating and overlooks. All the sculptural elements were deployed as lines of defense to break up wave action and prevent further erosion of the shoreline, which was being eaten away at the rate of eight inches a year.

A second sculpture was based on a Texas fern, *Pteris multifida*. The spine and leaflets of the plant were twisted to create bridges, causeways, and islands, while cut-out shapes between the walkways became small-scale water landscapes—flower basins and fish ponds. Pond cypress trees will provide a shady canopy over the entire sculpture when they reach maturity.

Biological restoration was a key element in the design of Fair Park Lagoon. Snails, clams, freshwater sponges and shrimp, fish, reptiles, and waterfowl are both visually attractive and serve as members of the food chain. Landscaping was chosen not only as a design element, but also for its food and habitat value. A littoral zone of plants that root in shallow water was created around the edge of the lagoon to stabilize the banks, reduce turbidity, and provide nesting sites for insects, birds, and small mammals. The amount of nutrients available to algae was reduced; water quality was improved; and various species of fish were introduced into the food chain.

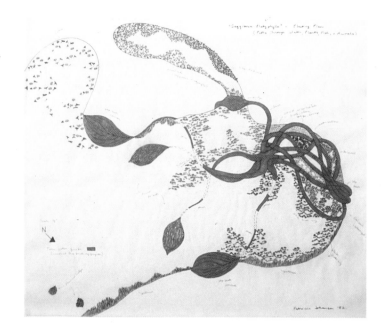

Saggitaria Platyphylla
Fair Park Lagoon
Planting Plan
1982

Fair Park Lagoon
Providing access for children
to explore habitats

**Peteris Multifidia
Fair Park Lagoon
1981–86**

Photo: William Pankey

Flocks of wild birds started to arrive, and today the lagoon teems with life. Few would suspect that the landscape is a functional flood basin and a recreated swamp with an educational agenda. The sculpture provides access to a functioning ecosystem.

Ultimately my design took five years to construct, cost more than two million dollars, and suffered numerous agonizing design changes. *Pteris multifida*, for example, designed as a series of long span arch bridges, was mostly built as flat pathways and reduced in size by one-third when funding ran short. Since I had no role in the construction phase, I cannot claim total satisfaction with the aesthetic results. Nevertheless, the lagoon is an unqualified success because people love it and are learning to develop more respectful attitudes toward the plants and animals that have chosen to make Dallas their home. Fair Park Lagoon clearly combines the ideal world of aesthetics with the profuse phenomena of Nature, and represents the kinds of compromises artists have to make in order to succeed in the real world.

Patricia Johanson

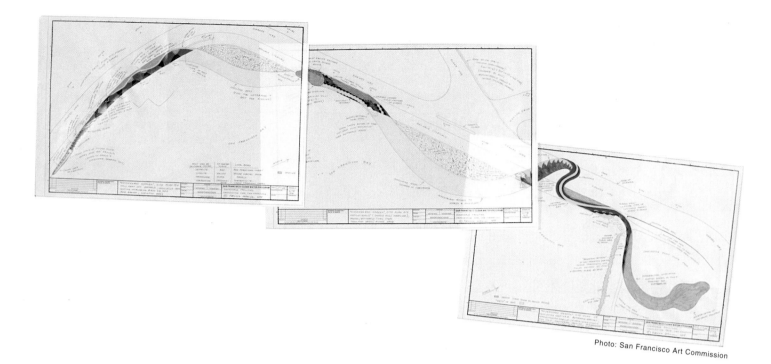

Photo: San Francisco Art Commission

Endangered Garden

In 1987 I received a call from Jill Manton of the San Francisco Arts Commission. Jill had seen an exhibition of my drawings for *Tidal Landscapes* in 1984, and thought the concept of a sculpture that transformed with rising and falling water would be perfect for a project along the San Francisco Bay. Specifically, the project involved a new thirty-million-dollar sewer that was mandated by the Environmental Protection Agency because the city was dumping raw sewage into the bay. The Department of Public Works (DPW) had suggested a standard sewage facility for the site, and was immediately attacked by local citizen groups protesting the visual degradation of this sensitive bay front property.

Using the guidelines of the Percent for Art Program, the Arts Commission of San Francisco approached the DPW with the idea of incorporating an artist into the design team. Initially there was considerable opposition within the department to this idea, especially since I was made codesigner of the entire project. It seemed obvious, to me at least, that decorating a sewer would make no sense, and that my creative role was to turn it into something lovable, beneficial, and useful—something beyond its basic function. Eventually I was accepted when it became apparent that my aesthetic and environmental program would help the DPW obtain permits which they desperately needed to realize their project.

After months of research on the site, I discovered that the environs hosted a large number of endangered species, and that formerly it had been an environment rich in native plants, butterflies, birds, waterfowl, intertidal life, fish, and shellfish. By providing appropriate food and habitat it might be possible to aid species that were struggling for survival, and involve people in the issue of extinction. Since the site was adjacent to a new California State Recreation Area, it seemed logical to make the sewer structure an extension of the park. By burying the sewer, its roof could become a baywalk, thirty feet wide and one-third of a mile long, increasing public access to Candlestick Cove.

The image selected for the project was the endangered San Francisco garter snake, with its colors and patterns translated into a series of gardens which would provide sustenance for locally threatened species. The head of the serpent, an undulating sculptural earth mound, rises up to twenty feet high out of a meadow of native food plants. The mound is covered with flowers that provide nectar for adult butterflies and host plants for their larvae, and is sculpted into microhabitats: windbreaks, sunning platforms, and shelter from predators.

Endangered Garden
Original site plans
San Francisco, California
1988

As the snake curves around a small beach, *Ribbon Worm Tidal Steps* provide access to the bay. The *Worm* also serves as a ramp for the handicapped, and at high tide its lower loops fill with water, creating habitat for vertically-zoned intertidal communities. The sculpture will become encrusted with barnacles and marine growth, and populated by shrimp, worms, crabs, hydrozoa, sponges, and algae. Thus, the *Ribbon Worm* becomes a living sculpture—simultaneously aesthetic, functional, and nurturing.

The paving along the baywalk mimics the red, yellow, and black patterns of the San Francisco garter snake. The greenish blue scales of the snake's underbelly are echoed overhead by a sculptural arbor. Cavities, crevices, and nesting shelves for birds are incorporated within the arbor, as are wildlife food plants and native vines. Petroglyph depressions in the pavement fill with rainwater, and become birdbaths.

My original design for *Endangered Garden* contained many other unique features, including tidal staircases—images that would transform from flowers to snakes and from mussel shells to butterflies. A forty-foot wide band of shellfish substrate would have provided an edible, walkable path where the body of the snake curved through the mud flats. This textured mixture of sand, gravel, and shells would have attracted littleneck clams, the fish and crabs that eat them, and a whole range of new shorebirds. I also planned a ramp based on the serpent's tail. Unfortunately, the opportunity to construct these elements was lost due to political maneuvering and subsequent budget cuts. The built serpent will end in a purely decorative-coiled overlook that lacks the life-sustaining value of the original features.

The project lost much of its habitat value because once the construction permits for the sewer were issued I was not in a strong position to defend all of the original features. Public artists are always vulnerable, and many projects don't even get built. *Endangered Garden* is a beginning, but we still have a long way to go toward realizing that public works can make a major contribution to both ecology and public recreational space.

Endangered Garden
Coiled Overlook and Cantilevered Tail
Revised Design
1989

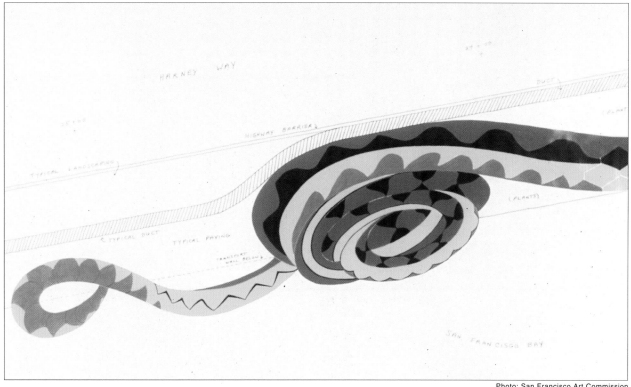

Patricia Johanson

Park For A Rainforest

Both *Fair Park Lagoon* and *Endangered Garden* recreate ecosystems within the context of environmental sculpture. *Park for a Rainforest* (1992) is a huge organic sculpture based on a Brazilian aerial plant that is interwoven with the drama and potential danger of the Amazon jungle. The project is meant to bring people into direct contact with untamed Nature—a world where humans can experience and learn, but not reign supreme.

Leaves, flower stalk, and aerial roots of the bromeliad *Tillandsia streptocarpa* are translated into slender ramps, seating, and viewing platforms, which provide public access to every level of the rainforest. People can view everything from the ants and ferns and debris of the forest floor, to the dense screen of foliage at around thirty feet that cuts off sunlight below, and blocks the view of the upper stories, to the bird, butterfly, and flower-filled levels of the canopy, to above the treetops. As paths thread through the trees up to the height of a fifteen-story building, the vertical garden is revealed with its unique communities of life at every level: orchids, mazes of lianas, chattering monkeys, bats, iguanas, tree frogs, sloths, toucans, king vultures, and harpy eagles.

The Brazilian project is camouflaged, designed to blend into the Amazon rainforest both in color and construction. The supports resemble tree-trunks, and the ramps and overlooks are interwoven with the forest, yet structurally independent, so as not to alter or damage the existing ecosystem. The project is meant to reveal the forest; thus it will grow in an organic manner from the existing conditions of the site. Surveying, engineering, and aesthetic decisions are fluid and subject to change.

The park focuses on the complexity and minutiae of Nature, allowing scientific research, exploration, and discovery in a zone where humans and Nature coexist. At the same time it points out the fundamental rift between ecology and art. The hallmark of living things—growth and transformation—is difficult to reconcile with the unchanging perfection of ideal form. *Park for a Rainforest* will become encrusted, and possibly subsumed, by tropical vegetation. The project offers both spiritual renewal and a harsh grounding in reality. The culmination of true ecological art may well be its own demise.

Park for a Rainforest was commissioned for Projecto Omame, and exhibited in Brazil during the Earth Summit in 1992. Its construction was seriously discussed by both the Brazilian Minister of the Environment and the Director of Brazil's National Parks. Because they saw the project as related to tourism, funding was not considered a problem. The subsequent impeachment of President Collor de Mello, and a host of political problems, has led to the inevitable delays that seem to accompany all large projects.

During the Summer of 1993 *Park for a Rainforest* was exhibited at the National Museum of Fine Arts in Rio de Janeiro. Two weeks in the Amazon and renewed ties with current government officials has brought new cause for optimism. The rainforest project is unquestionably loved and wanted, and that long sequence of practical steps that must be taken before a project can be constructed is again underway.

**Tillandsia Streptocarpa
Park For A Rain Forest
The Vertical Garden**
Model
Amazonas, Brazil
1992–ongoing

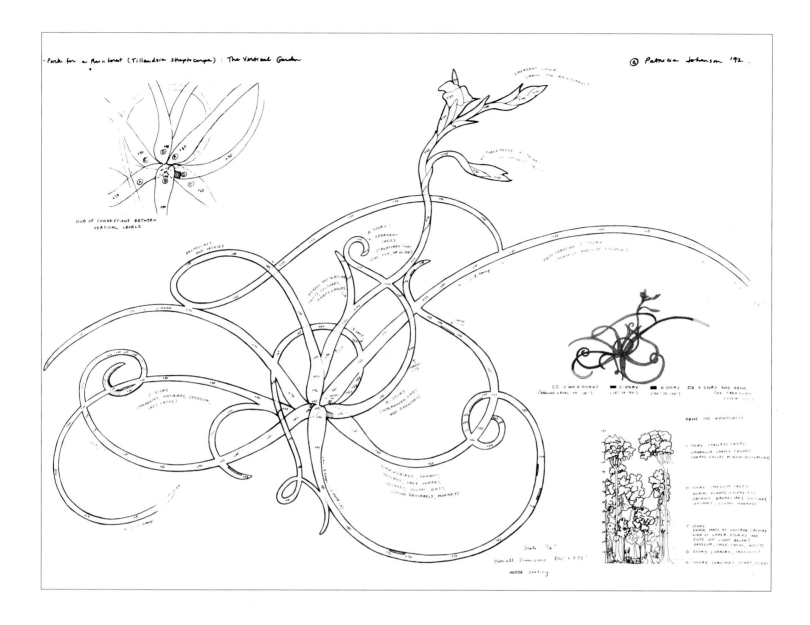

**Tillandsia Streptocarpa
Park For A Rain Forest
The Vertical Garden**

Site plan
Amazonas, Brazil
1992–ongoing

Some of the aims of my work are to recreate ecological communities, support wildlife, and introduce urban dwellers to intricate webs of life within the context of art projects and public parks. While it is obvious that such tiny sites cannot ultimately affect the survival of populations, a major purpose of my work is to show how human activity can be incorporated into natural ecosystems. Many people are unaware that a diversity of life forms, including obscure invertebrates and microbes, is essential to creating soils, regulating climate, cleansing water, and maintaining planetary health.

I believe it is critical for us to develop an intuitive understanding of the fact that we not only affect our environment, but are in turn biologically formed by it. The forest, swamp, and plant and animal communities have been removed from our daily consciousness and replaced by an endless stream of man-made products. We need to become reacquainted with the intricate workings of raw Nature in order to understand that our environment is not merely decorative. It is a major force in determining who we are, and ultimately whether or not we will survive. By creating nurturing, life-supporting public places, artists can help reestablish the bonds between people and the living world.

Patricia Johanson

156 / 157

Alan Sonfist

In the twentieth century we have totally separated ourselves from our natural environment: We have become Nature-haters. We use television to witness our natural surroundings. People drive to the beach where they watch the sunset in their cars with the windows rolled up and the air conditioner on. Around our dwellings we put trees in boxes and try to grow them in geometric shapes. We have forgotten what it is like to walk through an asymmetrical young forest filled with the sounds of animals, or walk on the beach, smelling the salt water and feeling the wind blow on our faces. Since my career began in 1965 I have made art that recaptures these unique natural events for urban and suburban dwellers.

My life began in the teeming jungles of the South Bronx. On the way to school, I passed smoldering fires and packs of dogs eating garbage. There were no trees anywhere—the few that had existed were long dead. There were only concrete streets and brick buildings. The streets were divided into local gangs, and each gang controlled a section. Each day, my walk to school was a passage through terror, and my survival counted on it. The South Bronx was my first experience with Nature.

Several blocks away there was an isolated forest where no one played. It was a deep ravine of the Bronx River near an abandoned ice-house where they used to make ice from the Bronx River water. There were cliffs and a bridge across the river, so I played on both sides of the ravine. The smells of the freshness of the earth were in direct contrast with the smells of overcrowding and urban decay. Instead of gang members, there were turtles and snakes. Instead of the wild dogs who could sense my fear and would attack if I entered their territory, there were deer and fox who were curious and gentle and would let me enter their world. This forest became my sanctuary.

As I grew older, more people from the neighborhood spent time in the forest. Little by little, the undergrowth was trampled down, garbage was strewn everywhere, and fires were set. Later, when someone drowned in the river, the city decided that the forest was a dangerous place, so it cut down the trees and poured concrete over the roots. The bedrock cliff was buried under the gray monotonous carpet of our city. My forest disappeared.

Through my artworks, I recreate the forest of my childhood. I know from my own experience that the forest saved me as a child. It gave a very basic dimension to my life. I want to share that basic dimension with other people.

Time Landscape

My earliest environmental narrative landscapes were reclamation projects such as *Time Landscape*, started in 1965 at Houston and La Guardia Place in New York City. It is important to plant indigenous forests because the city is losing its heritage. In New York City, people do not witness a normal fall. The leaves don't change into vibrant colors because of the heat retention of the concrete. Outside of the city, gradual moisture retention in the soil enables gradations of color changes in the leaves. In the city, people don't get a sense of this cycle, except maybe in areas of Central Park.

Our culture has traditionally built monuments to glorify humankind's achievements or to remember great people and events. Alan Sonfist works to create monuments to Earth's natural processes, particularly as they pertain to native flora.

≈

Time Landscape

A park comprised of the native flora
that existed at this site in Manhattan
before European settlement
New York, New York
1965–present

The site I chose to work with was an urban wasteland: a vacant lot covered with rubble, cement, broken glass, and steel. In designing the landscape, I researched the botany and geology of the indigenous forests of Manhattan, and was able to re-create the soil and rock formations that existed there before human intervention. I planned for the future so that the sculpture would continue to evolve.

For the city dweller, *Time Landscape* is the only place where one can find the indigenous forests of Manhattan which existed before colonial settlement. It stands as a testament to why the Native Americans and later the Europeans settled there. They didn't come because of the concrete walkways. Nestled in a canyon of towering, anonymous apartment buildings, the once-vacant lot now offers the viewer three natural terrains: an open field of grasses and flowers, a pioneer forest of birch, cedars, and flowering brush, and a mature oak forest. Migrating birds and other small animals make *Time Landscape* their home within the city.

Ed Koch was an early supporter before he was mayor because he lived close to the site. While he was mayor, he supported my proposal, which I originally presented in 1969, for fifty sites throughout the city. Years after the completion of *Time Landscape*, the city received a grant of six million dollars to pursue some of these projects, and I will help them with the development of the program. Two of the projects are presently in the planning stages: a site on Roosevelt Island where we are going to create an island-type marshland, and another site in the Bronx where we are reclaiming a stream and wetland.

We honor our human architectural heritage, but we have obliterated our natural heritage in the cities. We have to honor both in order to create a continuous city fabric. In addition to bringing up a forest, we should honor and reconstruct streams, marshland, and all the natural events that have occurred on the sites of cities. People must understand that the city is not just concrete, and when they look at a landscaped park, they should know that it is not indigenous to the original landscape.

Alan Sonfist

Photo: Courtesy the Kansas City Art Institute

Circles of Life

In the environmental sculpture in Kansas City, *Circles of Life* , I combined the recla-mation of a natural forest with a metaphoric statement of human intervention. The sculpture was created for the Centennial of the Art Institute, with the help of the Contemporary Art Society, the National Prairie Association, and a local developer.

I thought it would be a poetic parallel to create a sculpture that would repre-sent the next hundred years, so I choose for its site a grove of ornamental shrubbery planted over a hundred years ago. In the center of the grove I made a thirty-foot column of bronze castings of tree fragments that were native to the site and had been removed when the ornamental shrubbery was planted. It is the column of knowledge of the area's ecological history. Surrounding this column, I planted a native prairie. The prairie was then enclosed by young tree saplings that represent a cross-section of all the trees native to Missouri.

In the early years of the piece, the prairie dominated the trees, but then as the trees matured, they began the natural progression of taking back the prairie by their shade. My goal is for the prairie to evolve into a forest and for the trees to dominate the bronze sculpture of remembrance to the ancient forest. As the sculpture grows, the native trees will intertwine with the bronze castings, so that human created and natural branches become inseparable. This sculpture is a symbol of the growth of the community as well as a record of its past. My hope is that people will respond to the distinctive contrast between the ornamental landscape of the site and the rebirth of a natural system.

Circles of Life
Kansas City Art Institute
Detail
Tree fragment sculpture before and after
the growth of the surrounding trees
Kansas City Missouri
1985-2085

Circles of Life
Kansas City Art Institute
Top Right: Summer 1986,
two seasons after installation/planting
Bottom Right: Autumn 1987
two years after installation/planting

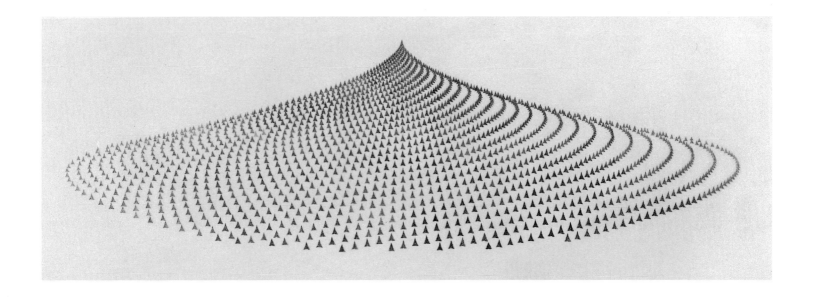

Tree Mountain—A Living Time Capsule

In 1982 I began work on *Tree Mountain* which is a collaborative, environmental project that touches on global, ecological, social, and cultural issues. It tests our finitude and transcendence, individuality versus teamwork, and measures the value and evolution of a work of art after it has entered the environment. *Tree mountain* is designed to unite the human intellect with the majesty of Nature.

Ten thousand trees were planted by the same number of people according to an intricate pattern derived from a mathematical formula. The mathematical expansion changes with one's view and movement around and above the mountain, thus revealing hidden curves and spirals in the design. If seen from space, the human intellect at work over natural formation becomes evident, though the trees blend harmoniously.

Tree Mountain is 1.5 miles in length, .15 miles in width, and elliptical. Height is site-specific and depends on the incline. Both shape and size are adaptable to areas of land reclamation and the preservation of forests. For the model I chose silver fir because these trees are dying out and it is important that we preserve them. Otherwise, any tree could make up the forest as long as it could live three to four hundred years. The trees must outlive the present era, and by surviving, carry our concepts into an unknown time in the future. If our civilization as we know it ends, or as changes occur, there will be a reminder in the form of a strange forest for our descendants to ponder.

Tree Mountain is a collaborative work, from its intricate landscaping and forestry to the funding and contractual agreements for its strange, unheard of land use of three to four centuries. The collaboration expands as ten thousand people come together from around the world to plant the trees that will bear their names and remain their property through succeeding generations. People can leave their tree to their heirs, be buried under it, or sell it at auction or by other means. The trees can change ownership, but *Tree Mountain* itself can never be owned or sold, nor can the trees be moved from the forest. *Tree Mountain* represents the concept, the soul of the art, while the trees are a manifestation of it. Though they may be salable, collectible, and inheritable commodities—gaining stature, fame, and value as they grow and age as trees—ultimately neither can be truly owned. One can only become a custodian and assume the moral obligation it implies.

In the meanwhile, the trees remain part of a larger whole, the forest. Individual segments of a single, limited edition, the trees are unique patterns in the design of their Universe. They live on through the centuries—stable and majestic, outliving their owners who created the patterns and the philosophy but not the tree. There is a strange paradox in this.

Tree Mountain—A Living Time Capsule
Plan for Realization
Ylörjärvi Sand Pits
10,000 trees, 10,000 people, 400 years
1.5 miles x .15 miles
Ylöjärvi, Finland
1992–94

Wheatfield—A Confrontation
Battery Park Landfill
1.8 acres of wheat
New York
Summer, 1982

Early in the morning on the first of May 1982 we began to plant a two-acre wheat field in lower Manhattan. The planting consisted of digging 285 furrows by hand, clearing off rocks and garbage, then placing the seed by hand and covering the furrows with soil. Each furrow took two to three hours.

Since March, over two hundred truckloads of dirty landfill had been dumped on the site, consisting of rubble, dirt, rusty pipes, and other garbage. Tractors flattened the area, and eighty more truckloads of dirt were dumped and spread to constitute one inch of topsoil needed for planting.

We maintained the field for four months, set up an irrigation system, weeded, and cleared out wheat smut (a disease that had affected the entire country that year). We put down fertilizers, cleared off rocks, boulders, and wires by hand, and sprayed against mildew fungus. "We" refers to my two faithful assistants and a varying number of volunteers, ranging from one or two to six or seven on a good day.

We harvested the crop on August 16 on a hot, muggy Sunday. The air was stifling and the city stood still. All those Manhattenites who had been watching the field grow from green to golden amber, and gotten attached to it, the stockbrokers and the economists, office workers, tourists, and others attracted by the media coverage, stood around in sad silence. Many cried. TV crews were everywhere, but they too spoke little and then in hushed voices.

We harvested almost one thousand pounds of healthy, golden wheat.

Wheatfield affected many lives, and the ripples are extending. Reactions ranged from astonishment to tears. A lot of people wrote to thank me for creating *Wheatfield* and asked that I keep it going. After my harvest, the four-acre area facing New York Harbor was returned to construction to make room for a billion-dollar luxury complex. Manhattan closed itself once again to become a fortress, corrupt yet vulnerable. But I think this magnificent metropolis will remember a majestic, amber field. Vulnerability and staying power, the power of the paradox. [2]

Agnes Denes

Wheatfield—A Confrontation

My decision to plant a wheat field in Manhattan instead of designing just another public sculpture grew out of a long-standing concern and need to call attention to our misplaced priorities and deteriorating human values.

Manhattan is the richest, most professional, most congested, and without a doubt, most fascinating island in the world. To attempt to plant, sustain, and harvest two acres of wheat here, wasting valuable real estate, obstructing the machinery by going against the system, was an effrontery that made it the powerful paradox I had sought for the calling to account.

It was insane. It was impossible. But it would make people rethink their priorities and realize that unless human values are reassessed, the quality of life, even life itself, was in danger. Placing the wheat field at the foot of the World Trade Center, a block from Wall Street, facing the Statue of Liberty, also had symbolic import. My work usually reaches beyond the boundaries of art to deal with controversial global issues.

Wheatfield was a symbol, a universal concept. It represented food, energy, commerce, world trade, and economics. It referred to mismanagement, waste, world hunger, and ecological concerns. It was an intrusion into the citadel, a confrontation of high civilization. Then again, it was also Shangri-la, a small paradise, one's childhood, a hot summer afternoon in the country, peace, forgotten values, simple pleasures.

What was different about this wheat field was that the soil was not rich loam but dirty landfill full of rusty metals, boulders, old tires, and overcoats. It was not farmland but an extension of the congested downtown of a metropolis where dangerous crosswinds blew, traffic snarled, and every inch was precious realty. The absurdity of it all, the risks we took, and the hardships we endured were all part of the basic concept. Digging deep is what art is all about.

Wheatfield—A Confrontation
The Harvest
New York, New York
Summer, 1982

**Wheatfield—A Confrontation
Battery Park Landfill
Financial Center**

1.8 acres of wheat planted
and harvested by the artist
New York, New York
Summer, 1982

awareness, and forming new insights and new methods of reasoning. This is the essence I often refer to in my writings, the sum of an analytical process that has the potential to reach beyond itself and become the thermometer or gauge of its time—the summing up or perspective needed for the missing overview.

In a time when meaningful global communication and intelligent restructuring of our environment is imperative, art in the public sphere can assume an important role. It can affect intelligent collaboration and the integration of disciplines, and it can offer benign solutions to problems. It can bring people together in meaningful and provocative ways, while it enhances and rebuilds environments.

Humanity is at a turning point, facing major decisions in order to survive on the planet while it strives to maintain its moral values and the quality of life. A well-conceived work can have a profound impact on human values. I created my first ecological site work in 1968 with these concerns in mind, and have been developing these concepts ever since. Artistic vision, image, and metaphor are powerful tools of communication. Artists can motivate people and influence how things are perceived. The type of art I am discussing here can become a great moving force, not only enhancing the present but shaping the future. The artists' vocabulary is limited only by the depth and clarity of their vision and their ability to create true syntheses well expressed. [1]

Agnes Denes

Agnes Denes

Notes on Eco-Logic: A Visual Philosophy and Global Perspective

All my philosophical concepts seem to culminate and come to life in my environmental/sculptural works. They are meant to begin their existence in the world when completed as works of art, and come to full realization as they grow and evolve with the changing needs and perspectives of humanity.

The issues touched on in my work range between individual creation and social consciousness. We have entered an age of alienation brought on by specialization, a by-product of the Information Age. This is an age of complexity, when knowledge and ideas are coming in faster than can be assimilated, while disciplines become progressively alienated from each other through specialization. The hard-won knowledge accumulates undigested, blocking meaningful communication. Clearly defined direction for humanity is lacking. The turn of the century and the next millennium will usher in a troubled environment and a troubled psyche.

For the first time in human history, the whole Earth is becoming one interdependent society with our interests, needs, and problems intertwined and interfering. The threads of existence have become so tightly interwoven that one pull in any direction can distort the whole fabric, affecting millions of threads. A new type of analytical attitude is called for, a clear overview, or a summing up. Making art today is synonymous with assuming responsibility for our fellow humans.

I believe that the new role of the artist is to create an art that is more than decoration, commodity, or political tool—an art that questions the status quo and the direction life has taken, the endless contradictions we accept and approve of. It elicits and initiates thinking processes. My concern is with the creation of a language of perception that allows the flow of information among alien systems and disciplines, eliminating the boundaries of art in order to make new associations and valid analogies possible. My ideas are unorthodox compared to those usually dealt with in the art arena. I incorporate science and philosophy into my work, and allow the concept to dictate the mode of realization. The materials I work with are as diverse as the concepts that dictate them. By allowing this flow of information to infiltrate the art arena, art can be more than just another self-styled, elitist system busy with its own functions. Art is a specialization that need not feed upon itself. It is capable of imbibing key elements from other systems and unifying them into a unique, coherent vision. Art need not be restricted by the limitations inherent in the other systems or disciplines.

An art dealing with these issues has the power to make statements with universal validity through the assessment of a world whose issues it reflects and analyzes—and thus benefit humanity. When the creative mind is aimed at global communication and concerns, the door is open to a new form of art that goes beyond the self and the ego, without being selfless. This art must assume the difficult task of maintaining a delicate balance between thinking globally and acting independently. For the ego must remain intact in order for the self to act fearlessly, with certainty and confidence, and it must be relinquished in order to think universally.

In this sense I see the importance of art emerging beyond a personal style, trend, or region, pointing to new ways of seeing and knowing that enhance perception and

In the following projects,

Agnes Denes works with

the organic process of our world

to bring attention to our

use of the Earth's resources.

In the process

she challenges us to

rethink our priorities in life.

≈

ing as soldiers. The cultural garden would unify cultural symbols. The heart of the sculpture, the forests, are the only place where Nature is allowed to be free.

The goal of *The Natural/Cultural History of Paris* is to show the evolution of the land from the time prior to human intervention through the building of the cultural capital of Paris. Each park can exist on its own merit with its own unique vegetation.

Like public monuments commemorating historic events, my artworks record forgotten forests, the movements of the Sun and hidden geological formations, and our interaction with our environment. My environmental landscapes recapture the history of the natural environment specific to each different site. They are civic monuments that honor and celebrate the life and death of the land. As in all my artworks, I am looking for fixed moments in time, and using them to show how time evolves.

At the end of the twentieth century, we are starting to become aware that we are interdependent with our natural environment, not in battle with it. My artworks create an awareness of this interdependency. Our survival depends on this awareness. In becoming disassociated from Nature, we are losing ourselves. Just as the churches in the Renaissance created a spiritual understanding of ourselves, I am creating a greater awareness of our place within this Universe.

I see my art as being almost like an archeological digging up of ruins. Except I am not dealing only with human archeology: I am dealing with natural events that have disappeared from our cities, and I am trying to reveal these events so that people can witness them again. By understanding our history, we can protect our future. It is only by people in suburban and urban areas understanding our natural heritage that they will have an interest in protecting the Redwoods in California or the Amazon Rain Forest. It is only by understanding what is in our own backyard that we gain a greater sense of protecting the rest of the Earth.

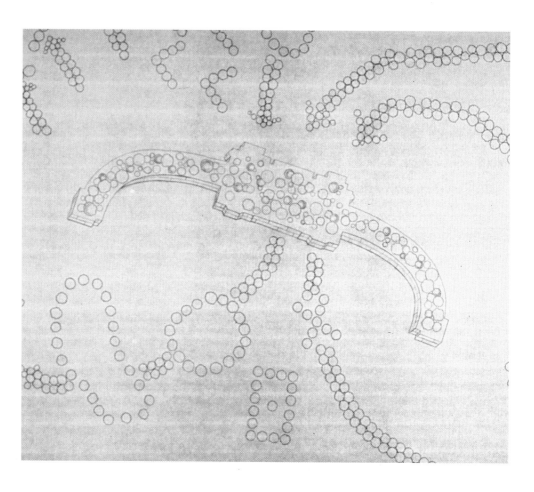

Natural / Cultural History of Paris
A Narrative Environmental
Landscape Sculpture
Detail
Paris, France
1991–

Alan Sonfist

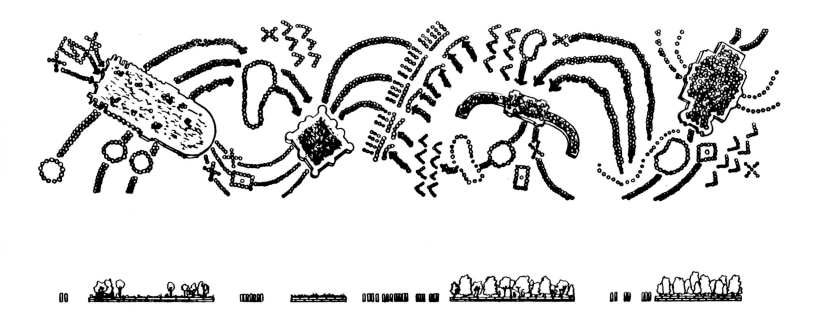

The Natural/Cultural History of Paris

The Natural/Cultural History of Paris is now in progress in France. My concept of a narrative environmental landscape sculpture refers to Rousseau's "Lettre a d'Alembert," which helped develop my theory about the fundamental antithesis between society and man. Rousseau discusses the artificial uniformity imposed on people by civilization, which causes them to ignore "the needs of Nature." Consequently, as culture appears to attain an ever-increasing splendor, humankind is more and more alienated from its original nature and prevented from being its real self.

I am creating a series of narrative parks for a new section of Paris, La Defense, representing the natural history of Paris in relation to its cultural development. Each separate park will be shaped in the contour of one of Paris' well-known cultural monuments, such as the Louvre, Notre Dame, the Arc de Triomphe, the Eiffel Tower, the Bastille, the Madeleine, Place du Trocadero, or Les Invalides. Each park will be atop a pedestal made of the same materials as the cultural monument that it represents. The park will be planted with the vegetation indigenous to the region, from a mature forest to a marshland to open wildflower grasslands. The landscape planted in the pedestal will show how the city looked before human intervention. There will be steps leading up into the historical landscape and pathways that replicate the actual pathways within the cultural monument itself. There will be a plaque describing the cultural significance of each monument in each narrative park.

For Notre Dame, which is on an island that was once wetlands, I will reconstruct the historic wetlands and the existing steps that lead into the church. The pathways through the wetlands will be the same as those through the church. The Arc De Triomphe will be planted as a pure beech forest, indigenous to the city before human intervention. The center walkway will open up into the circular movement of an arch. The Eiffel Tower, because of a slightly higher elevation, will be a mixed oak-beech forest. People will be able to walk around both the perimeter and pathways through the park.

As a secondary concept of the environmental narrative landscape, I plan to connect the separate parks by a grand formal garden with circles, squares, and lines of hedges that would mimic the battle plans of Napoleon in the form of an abstract painting. This concept addresses the inhumanity of war, with hedges ironically pos-

Natural / Cultural History of Paris
A Narrative Environmental Landscape
Sculpture

The sculpture visualizes the
historic monuments of Paris
such as Notre Dame and the Louvre,
and shows the historic vegetation that existed
within the original perimeter of the building
before that monument existed.
Paris, France
1991–

Circles of Time
Villa Celle

Left: View within the olive grove
Above: Detail evoking Roman Road
Florence, Italy
1985–1987

Circles of Time
Villa Celle

Detail of ancient tree limb monument

Circles of Time

Circles of Time incorporates the metaphor of human intervention within the reclamation of the original land. Built at Villa Celle, an estate near Florence, Italy, the sculpture traces the use of the land from the primeval forest to the present. I chose a hillside in the olive groves, visible as a picture plane from the surrounding hills and presently used as pasture for sheep. I researched the area thoroughly, and did a series of drawings of the site to find a plan that would best harmonize with the surrounding hills.

Circles of Time was planned to represent the history of that part of Tuscany in an archaeological layering, reminiscent of the growth rings in trees. The center ring, built on raised ground, is a primeval forest, the land before the advent of man. The next ring represents the first settlers, the Etruscans, who cultivated herbs for cooking and medicinal use. The next ring represents the influence of the Greeks, with godlike sculptures using bronze branches cast from endangered trees. Thus, even as the Greeks used gods to represent Nature, I would have Nature represent gods.

The next ring is the Greek symbol of victory: a nine-foot tall laurel hedge, pierced with low passageways for entry. The next layer is a Roman road around the circle, built of stones in the interlocking Roman fashion. This road is recessed to align itself with the contours of the surrounding hills. The stones used are indigenous rocks that represent the geological history of Tuscany. The outermost ring of the circle fully integrates the sculpture with the current agricultural uses of the land. The grid of olive trees in which the sculpture was set was transplanted into a circle so that local farmers can collect the fruits of the trees, and the original grasses were replanted so that sheep can still graze beneath them.

Alan Sonfist

Photo: Courtesy the Kansas City Art Institute

Photo: Courtesy the Kansas City Art Institute

Alan Sonfist

Tree Mountain begins its existence when it is completed as a work of art. As the trees grow and wildlife takes over, as decades and centuries pass, it becomes a fascinating study of how the passing of time affects a work of art. It can become a thermometer of the evolution of art. Through changing fashions and beliefs, *Tree Mountain* can pass from being a curiosity to being a shrine, from being the possible remnants of a decadent era to being one of the monuments of a great civilization— a monument not built to the human ego but to benefit future generations. *Tree Mountain* is a living time capsule. [3]

On July 5, 1992, World Environment Day, at the Earth Summit in Rio de Janeiro, the Government of Finland announced that its Ministry of the Environment and the United Nations Environment Program were sponsoring *Tree Mountain* as Finland's contribution to help alleviate the world's environmental stress. This will be the first time that an artist has been commissioned to restore environmental damage with an artwork that is global in scale, international in scope, and unsurpassed in duration. *Tree Mountain* will be realized on a full scale in the Pinziö gravel pits, Ylöjärvi, Finland, in 1994.

1. *Notes on Eco-Logic: A Visual Philosophy and Global Perspective*, © Copyright 1990, Agnes Denes.
2. *Wheatfield—A Confrontation*, © Copyright 1982, Agnes Denes.
3. *Tree Mountain—A Living Time Capsule*, © Copyright 1983, Agnes Denes.

Tree Mountain—A Living Time Capsule
Detail

Agnes Denes

Sherry Wiggins

The relationship that human beings share with their environment has come to lack physical and spiritual intimacy. I work to create site specific sculpture that corresponds to specific histories, physical experiences, and natural landscapes. These environments have taken form in benches, bridges, channels, fences, gateways, walkways, and waterways—all structures that invite people to participate…to walk, to sit, to think, or simply to be. I hope that these contemplative places offer opportunities for people to connect with the natural world.

Lost Borders

Lost Borders is a landscape art project that explores the edges and boundaries that frame urban life and natural systems. The piece is part of a large-scale transportation project for the city of Denver, called the "Speer/6th/Lincoln Reconstruction Project." Speer Boulevard is a historic parkway that runs through the center of Denver. When the project is completed, two blocks of this boulevard will be put underground, and a park will be built on top of the tunnel. Rampways from the new park will lead down into Cherry Creek, which is a small sandy creek that runs parallel to Speer Boulevard. *Lost Borders* will be constructed on the northern edge of the creek where a new pedestrian bridge will connect the bike path along the creek with the new park above the tunnel.

In this public project, I am interested in reconsidering the border that lies between the city and the creek. Borders are areas that run along or around a space and help to define that space. Borders confine, but can also allow entrance and understanding. The edge of the creek has been severely altered by flood control management; little or no vegetation exists. The creek edge is inhospitable to wildlife and people who might otherwise utilize this barren area. My desire is to recall the original nature of the creek edge within the constraints of its urban context.

Lost Borders is the result of a collaborative process. I am the artist on a design team consisting of Mark Johnson who is an urban designer, Eric Olgeirson who is an ecologist, William Taggart who is a hydraulic engineer, and Jim Logan who is an architect. The project we have designed overlays biological, mechanical, and sculptural components to create a new system for the creek edge.

Using existing storm sewer water, as well as the fluctuation of creek water levels, to enable irrigation, we have designed a place where native plants will be reintroduced. Three terraces that respond to different seasonal water levels in the creek integrate rock, soil, and creek edge vegetation to form a cohesive biomass which is necessary during flood

Sherry Wiggins's project helps to define our need to bring the issues of reclamation to the process of designing our urban landscape.

≈

Cherry Creek
Denver, Colorado
1993

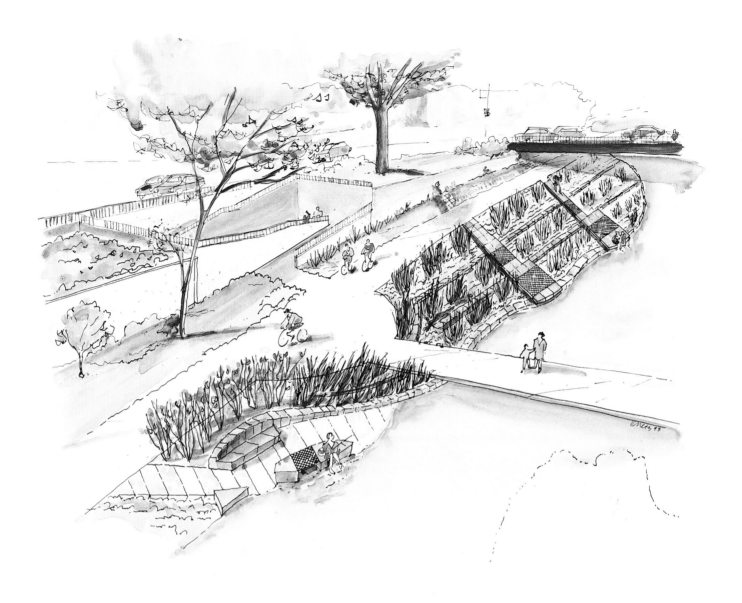

conditions. High-velocity flood waters scour the creek bed and edges several times a year. During these times the plant roots will bind the soil in pockets between the rocks to prevent scouring. The native vegetation will lay down and protect the edge of the creek. These plants include alkali bulrushes, arrowheads, arctic sedges, baltic rushes, hardstem bulrushes, hairy sedges, marsh marigolds, nebraska sedges, and sweet flag pickerel.

The terraces are reminiscent of zones where these plants would occur naturally. The plantings are not necessarily intended to reproduce Nature, but to call attention to natural phenomenon. They are arranged in decorative patterns, and as the water rises and subsides from season to season, they will eventually migrate downstream. The manipulated border will reorder itself through a natural process.

Sculptural ramps transect the terraces and offer entrance through the lush vegetation to the creek edge. These walkways have been engineered to withstand floods, and will be built from steel, large flagstones, and metal gratings. Native vegetation surrounds the bridge abutment, extending the living edge of the creek. A curved stone seating area and ramp are protected by thickets of willows which allow the area to be private.

The elements of the design represent various boundaries: zones of vegetation, water levels, urban structure, and areas of access for people. The park is a small border between the natural and built world, and it also represents boundaries between different ways of thinking. We interpreted the process of urban design as an intertwining of natural, built, and aesthetic systems. *Lost Borders* proposes a new way of using the creek, as well as a way of working with a collaborative and integrated vision.

Mel Chin

I had an exhibition at the Hirshhorn in 1989 that represented the culmination of a long period of intense and strenuous labor. I showed large-scale political pieces and a complex installation called *The Operation of the Sun Through the Cult of the Hand*. Following that show, I began to pursue a process set off by the completion of these sculptures. This process was an attempt to create situations of provocation and mutation that would challenge my personal artistic stage of development. First I asked myself what my particular passion was at the time. I realized it was a love for making things by hand, and I felt I could continue to make competent work by maintaining this direction for quite a while. After coming to this understanding, I decided to force a mutation in myself by removing the method I had come to rely on from my next work. I decided to propel an evolutionary situation—a condition of extinction and of not-knowing.

I was immersed in a period of re-education which allowed a free association/free-ranging type of research to begin. After reading an article suggesting the use of plants as remediation tools, I immediately saw the possibility for a new project. The irony was that it would require some of the most hand-intensive work I had ever done (sod busting, tilling, seeding, weeding, fence mending, ground hog chasing, and so on).

Revival Field was to be a sculpture in the most traditional sense. My primary concern was with the poetic potential of the work, besides the obvious ecological and political aspects. My desire to realize the aesthetic product of *Revival Field*—decontaminated earth—led me to a responsible search for the necessary scientific understanding and method.

I spent several months on a datura dragnet, trying to ascertain all the properties of jimson weed (*Datura stramonium*), beyond its well known psychedelic and mystical properties. I was unable to verify claims that the plant could be used to remediate soil in the way I envisioned. I continued my research in many directions until I finally found Dr. Rufus Chaney, a senior research scientist at the USDA. He specialized in soil and microbial systems, sludge composting, and the transfer of heavy metals from plants to animals to humans. Chaney's proposal in 1983 to use plants as remediation agents for polluted soil had been shelved by the conservative politics of the times. He was one of the few people in the world who had knowledge of and belief in this untested process. My desire to create a sculptural work rekindled Dr. Chaney's hope of bringing this biotechnology into fruition, and we initiated an earnest cooperation that eventually led to the first *Revival Field*.

Together we envisioned *Revival Field* as an experimental project using plants to cleanse industrial contamination from soil. These plants, which have evolved the capacity to selectively absorb and contain large amounts of metal or mineral, are called hyperaccumulators. Historically used as a method of prospecting, the plants were tested and proven to be viable toxic sponges by Dr. Chaney and Dr. R. R. Brooks. We felt that this approach to leaching heavy metals out of tainted soil by safely trapping the toxins in the vascular structure of plants and mining the ash (after proper incineration) could be not only beneficial but practical and economical as well.

We never know the true destination of each journey we begin. Revival Field *has taken Mel Chin from the artist studio and into the realm of applied scientific research and national politics. This project, begun as an art statement, has led to one possible solution for decontaminating hundreds of thousands of acres of soil.*

≈

Photo: David Schneider

**Revival Field
Pig's Eye Landfill**

Saint Paul, Minnesota
1993

Mel Chin

174 / 175

We conceived of the project as an ongoing operation until tests could verify significant improvement of a site's quality. The formal configuration of the work consists of two fenced areas—a circle within a square. The fences are standard chain links. The circular area, planted with the detoxifying weeds, serves as the test site, whereas the square, unplanted and of equal area, serves as the control. Paths that intersect in the center provide access to the site and form a crosshair target when viewed from above. In this case the plants, guided by a natural process, aim at a malignant presence in the ground.

Conceptually, the work is sculpture that involves a reduction process, a traditional method used when carving wood or stone; here, the material is unseen, and the tools consist of biochemistry and agriculture. The work, in its complete incarnation,

after the fences are removed and the toxin-laden weeds harvested, will offer minimal visual and formal effects. For a time, an intended invisible aesthetic will be measured scientifically by the quality of a revitalized earth. Eventually the aesthetic will be revealed in the return of growth to the soil.

Unfortunately, my efforts to realize the project were just beginning when controversy over funding led me into an entirely different series of negotiations. I had applied to the National Endowment for the Arts for a grant for *Revival Field* from the Inter-Arts New Forms Category. I soon learned this was the first time that a grant had been vetoed by the chairman of the NEA after being approved by both the panel and the council. I felt a responsibility to question the nature of the rejection and to expose the flaws of a system that allow autocratic control over the use of public funds. With these goals in mind, and with much support from the arts community, I arranged a formal meeting with NEA Chairman John Frohnmayer in Washington. Our constructive discussion set a precedent: an artist may now directly address an NEA chairman regarding such exercises of authority.

The meeting also resulted in reappropriating funds for the project, and I was able to begin the equally difficult and perhaps even more frustrating task of securing a site. After six months of negotiations for sites all over the country, we were finally able to began planting the first *Revival Field* in June 1991 on a portion of Pig's Eye Landfill, a state Superfund site in St. Paul, Minnesota. The area contained elevated levels of cadmium, a heavy metal that can be harmful to human health.

The Minnesota *Revival Field* was designed as a replicated field test of green remediation—the first such on-site experiment in the United States, and one of only two in the world. Three zinc and cadmium hyperaccumulators were chosen by Dr. Chaney to match the local ecotype: *Silene cucubalus*, a hybrid zea mays, and *Thlaspi caerulescens*. Merlin red fescue and romaine lettuce were also included to test for metal tolerance and food chain influence. The circular test area was divided into ninety-six separate plots to assess different soil and pH treatments as well as management techniques.

Thlaspi Caerulescens
Hyperaccumulator plant
Revival Field

Revival Field
Pig's Eye Landfill

We harvested the Pig's Eye field for the final time in October 1993, ending the first three-year test. Its formal configuration has already been erased with the removal of the fencing. *Thlaspi* samples taken from this site showed significant uptake in the leaves and stems of cadmium and zinc, verifying the potential of green remediation. A second field is already in place at a national priority Superfund site in Palmerton, Pennsylvania. We are planning an international *Revival Field* effort, sponsored by the Ministry of Culture of the Netherlands, at severely contaminated sites in that country and neighboring Belgium. These additional field tests will offer more valuable data regarding soil treatments and plant hardiness, and will extend biomarker research.

With positive results from Minnesota and additional sites secured, the *Revival Field* project is at a critical stage in its development. At this point, its focus must shift from implementing more field tests to conducting further scientific research. Thus, my most recent work on *Revival Field* has taken place in an editing studio. This indoor labor has produced a short video tape that describes the progress of *Revival Field* to date.

When I originally conceived of *Revival Field*, I was aware that it might not be fully realized in my lifetime. The project is in its infancy, and continues to progress. Whether it is viewed as an alchemic, metallurgic, social, scientific, or aesthetic experiment, its goal is to realize the full remediation of a contaminated area. The *Revival Field* project is driven by a desire to find solutions for problems, rather than express problems metaphorically. It will reach its final form, completing an evolutionary aesthetic, when the burden of heavy metal contamination is shed, when *Revival Field* is forgotten, and the mechanics of Nature can resume their course.

Photo: David Schneider

Mel Chin

Viet Ngo

My work is a fusion of engineering, architectural planning, and art. I design and build waste water treatment plants for cities and industries. Having a strong interest in horizontal architecture, I like things that stay on the ground. People have asked me if my work is public art. That is my intention, but I do not like to use these words because they segregate me from the working people. I recognized early on that to be successful in infrastructure work, one needs to be in touch with and to have the support of the general public. The work I do is utilitarian in the most basic manner—it is treating waste, and it is user-friendly and fairly simple to understand, but it is no ordinary task.

As a trained professional engineer, I sought to develop a new technology to treat waste waters using natural biological means instead of mechanical and chemical processes.

The technology that I helped develop is called the *Lemna System*. It relies to a large extent on the use of small floating aquatic plants grown in specially designed ponds to treat waste to a very fine degree. These Lemna facilities are designed as green corridors or punctuation marks in the general urban landscape. They are nice green parks in an odor free atmosphere, and sometimes they carry interesting design features to tell people about our environment, our soils, and our waters.

In general, the isolation that is associated with art concerns me since I like to be accepted by the communities I work in. In a way, one can look at a community as an organic body with many interrelated parts. These parts fulfill certain functions that can be broken down and examined from various angles. Waste water treatment is certainly a big part and a big function of any community (except in poorer countries that cannot afford treatment). Yet modern designing tends to place waste water treatment in the background and forget about it. This is evident by the odor problems common to many existing treatment facilities and the fact that international competition for treatment plant designs is rather rare.

I think it is all right to keep treatment plants in the background, but we must not forget about them. They should be designed and maintained with care, in the same manner as other parts of our infrastructure. (Incidentally, only Hollywood movie sets for Western flicks have all infrastructures in the foreground.)

Lemna Systems

In tune with the twentieth-century capitalist free market system, Lemna™ is a trademark name, and the concept is patented. Lemna plants are very small floating plants ubiquitous throughout the world. They thrive anywhere from cold climates to the tropics, even in the deserts. In Sardinia, which is rather dry and rocky, it took us less than an hour to find two beautiful species of *Lemnaceae*, the Latin name for these plants. I follow a philosophy of minimum to no interference. I serve only as a cheerleader. I take what already exists in a bioregion and encourage the plants to grow. (In contrast, only immigrants like me are supposed to emigrate to America, but no fruit and vegetables, please).

Back to the Lemna plants: they grow very fast, and will cover the surface of a pond if undisturbed by winds and waves. They act as a filter to absorb and neutralize

Viet Ngo's projects address the real issue of water cleansing and reclamation. His challenge is for his systems to work in balance with the ecosystem, surpass government regulations for clean water standards, and to create environments that are aestheticly pleasing and inviting to the general public.

≈

Lemna Plant

Approximately life size

pollutants in the water. In addition, they help stabilize the biological reactions in the pond, optimizing natural treatment processes by bacteria, micro- and macro-organisms, and by other physical processes.

Lemna plants absorb and control odors by using sulfides, methanes, and other gases as food sources; they also shield the pond to prevent odors from escaping to the air.

Lemna plants have very high protein concentrations, making them a potential alternative food source for many parts of the world. (When I started working with Lemna, I dreamt of feeding the world.)

To harvest these plants, we use mechanized pontoon boats equipped with simple hydraulic gears to manage huge quantities of biomass. The harvested plants, which represent the excess growth, are either composted to form a rich fertilizer for organic farming, or with proper testing and analyses, used as a high-protein animal feed.

The clear water produced by this process can be used for irrigation or for other beneficial purposes. In Mexico we use it at one site to irrigate city parks and golf courses. In Egypt we plan to recharge the ground water table and irrigate crops with the effluent.

The design of *Lemna Systems* is thus based on a resource recovery concept: waste water being treated in a natural way will produce clean water which can be reused for irrigation and for ground water/stream/lake recharge. At the same time, valuable biomass can be harvested for organic fertilizer or a feed source. The Sun is the main source of energy, and the Earth is reclaimed as fertile ground.

Lemna Design

To control the growth of the floating plants, a network of floating barriers that form a gridlike pattern is placed on the Lemna pond surface. These barriers can be compared to the facade of a building—they are necessary to support the system, and they carry aesthetic considerations that go beyond the practical. The ponds can also be designed into meandering channels that control the hydraulic flow of incoming water. Together they form a specific landscape that vitalizes an urban design. The facilities may occupy a vast acreage of land and yet appear unobtrusive from the ground. Only from the air can one decipher the true size and meaning of the works. The design stresses respect for Nature and natural things.

Of course, the vision incorporates a very practical side, for the treatment results must be impeccable. The facilities accomplish the routine yet awesome task of cleaning our wastes. They must be attractive for the visitors, comfortable for the workers, and satisfactory to the government regulators.

Devils Lake, North Dakota, or Snake on the Plains

The citizens of Devils Lake care deeply about their water resources. The City Elders, especially the visionary team of one commissioner and the city engineer, wanted a natural system. So, after 100 public meetings and 1001 late nights of design, we came up with a fifty-acre stylized snake that would meander across a former wetland. This Lemna facility consists of nine serpentine channels to remove the harmful phosphorus, nitrogen, and algae before releasing the treated water into one bay of Devils Lake.

Funded by the U.S. Environmental Protection Agency and the city of Devils Lake, the $5 million project was completed in 1990. The harvested biomass has been used as an organic fertilizer, and school children are frequently invited on guided tours to learn about biology, the environment, and what people can do to aid preservation.

Lemna System
Devils Lake, North Dakota
1990

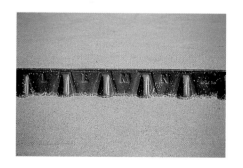

Lemna Floating Grid
Detail

From the window of an airplane, one can see the green oasis forming an intricate pattern on the Dakota prairies. It always amazes me when forms that have been prevalent throughout the ages, such as the serpent form of Devils Lake, seem to spring out of the land when they are part of a design that seeks balance with the processes of the Earth. In the case of Devils Lake, there is a little more technology involved, but the product is linked to the past.

Blue Ridge Mountain Blues Georgia

As I get further involved in my work, the undisturbed landscape interests me more and more. For this design at the foothills of the Blue Ridge Mountains, I chose a flat piece of land wedged between a trout stream and the surrounding hills. In this community, they had an old mechanical treatment plant that discharged badly treated water into the trout stream.

The Lemna facility took after the shape of the land and became a small lake blending into the contour of the hills. We created a simple visitor center above the lake, and have plans to grow a variety of native trees, wildflowers, and grasses.

It is important for me to let the land govern the design. In this case, we were digging out the bottom of the lake when we hit a large rock formation. The contractor planned to blast out the rock in order to fit our design. But as I saw it, the rock did not interfere with our design—our design interfered with the rock. I made sure that the rock stayed. The result was a much more organic meandering pattern, unlike the pure geometry of Devils Lake.

Lemna System
Blue Ridge Mountains, Georgia
1992

Viet Ngo

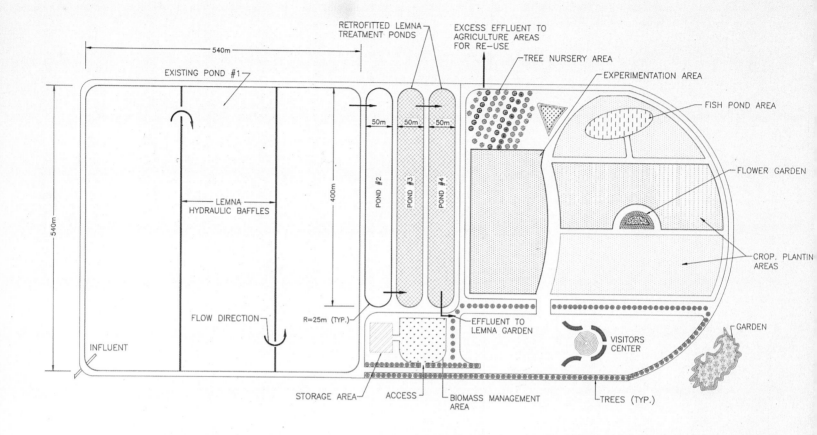

RETROFITTED LEMNA TREATMENT PONDS

EXCESS EFFLUENT TO AGRICULTURE AREAS FOR RE-USE

TREE NURSERY AREA

EXPERIMENTATION AREA

FISH POND AREA

540m

EXISTING POND #1

LEMNA HYDRAULIC BAFFLES

FLOWER GARDEN

540m

400m

50m 50m 50m

POND #2

POND #3

POND #4

CROP. PLANTIN AREAS

FLOW DIRECTION

R=25m (TYP.)

EFFLUENT TO LEMNA GARDEN

GARDEN

INFLUENT

VISITORS CENTER

STORAGE AREA

ACCESS

BIOMASS MANAGEMENT AREA

TREES (TYP.)

Egyptian Oasis

In desert countries it is especially necessary to reuse the wastewater. For Sadat City in Egypt, I have proposed a facility that will reuse every drop of treated waste water to raise fish and grow produce. We also plan to use the harvested Lemna plants to feed the fish and to fertilize the fields. The Lemna plants covering the ponds will reduce evaporation, and the Sun's energy will be exploited for growing the Lemna plants on a year-round basis. This will truly be a green oasis in the desert

People have asked me why I want to interfere with the desert. Well, this is no longer the era of Lawrence of Arabia sitting on a hot sand dune and pondering the meaning of life. There are fifty-three million Egyptians who badly need waste water treatment service. Let this green oasis be the demarcation line between urban sprawl and the pristine desert. Insidious and sometimes invisible pollution is a fact of life and must be taken care of.

**Lemna Water Park
Conceptual Design**
Plan view
Sadat City, Eygpt

Potpourri and Hors-d'oeuvres

A lady in Mississippi once complained that the city dared install a *Lemna System* waste water treatment facility next to her home. She threatened to take us all the way to the Supreme Court because of the potential odor nuisance. But the smell never came, and instead one of our staff brought her some compost for her roses. A few months later, the woman came back to thank us and asked for some more compost because her roses grew rather prettily. In a way, this was part of our odor control scheme.

An Israeli outfit contacted me and proposed an intriguing joint venture involving the sale of Lemma plants as health food. We would grow the Lemna plants under control conditions in pure water. A marketing trial has already been established in Switzerland. I liked the idea, but could not come up with an interesting design angle. It will take some time before we see Lemna cream puffs at chic parties.

Civilizations in the past have infused much spiritual thinking in their designs and their art. In my travels, I have seen many ancient sites that have given me no need to wonder how and by whom they were created. They just exist as balanced parts of the landscape, perhaps slightly frayed at the edges. The designs simply embrace you. So in the end, perhaps I am inspired to create a kind of urban ecological art with a sense of purpose and resolve.

Lemna System
Desert Installation
Boulder City, Nevada

Viet Ngo

Mierle Laderman Ukeles

For me, the possibility of locating an art-making enterprise in the midst of the most common, daily urban enterprise could be a wondrous fable, accomplished in reality.

Dazzled and frazzled by the birth of our first child, in 1969, I wrote a manifesto calling maintenance—itself—art. I posited that if, in a free culture, an artist could call anything art, then why not necessity itself, maintenance itself, the act and processes of keeping those precious things we've created precious—an individual, a life, a home, a system, a city?

Culture grows everywhere. Each of us creates culture, and every part of life is inside the cultural enterprise. Nothing is outside of it. Before our great age of common rights, culture was owned by those who had the most power. That's over. My vision since 1969, when I wrote the *Manifesto for Maintenance Art*, has been to open up the lens, to blow apart the frame. Our entire planetary home is inside, and all the practices and all the work that keep our home alive breathe culture. Formerly this "house-keeping" wasn't supposed to be talked about. It was downstairs, out-back, behind the scenes, over the edge. And so were all the people who did the keeping.

By luck, I was invited into the New York City Department of Sanitation in 1977, to consider creating art from the inside out. We—the Department and I—came up with a title for myself: unsalaried, official Artist in Residence. For me, it was proof of my vision. If art can grow out of the essence of the work of "dailiness," (i.e. keeping our common home), out of the transformation from dirty to clean, again and again, then the vision is grounded.

Since then, I have made over twenty-five large art works with the New York City Department of Sanitation. Among them was *Touch Sanitation*—the introductory work, in which I circled the city in a spiraling journey that took a year and a half. I shook hands with each of the 8,500 sanitation workers, and face to face to each one, said, "Thank you for keeping New York City alive." I also created *The Social Mirror*, a 20-cubic-yard garbage truck faced in hand-fitted tempered mirror. This project allowed citizens to see themselves linked with the handlers of their waste. The goal of these works with the department was to reveal sanitation as the beginning of culture, to erase the boundary between inside and outside.

Flow City

When the department of sanitation began redesigning the waste disposal system for the city of New York in the early '80s, they invited me to sit in on the meetings. During my *Touch Sanitation* work, I had fallen in love with one of locations they now wanted to redevelop. It was a location at the base of 59th

The work of Mierle Ukeles

delves into the very

core of any culture—

the support systems that make

all of our lives possible.

Her "maintenance art" helps

us all keep in touch with

the true bottom line.

≈

The Social Mirror
Mirror-covered garbage truck
NYC Department of Sanitation
New York, New York
1983

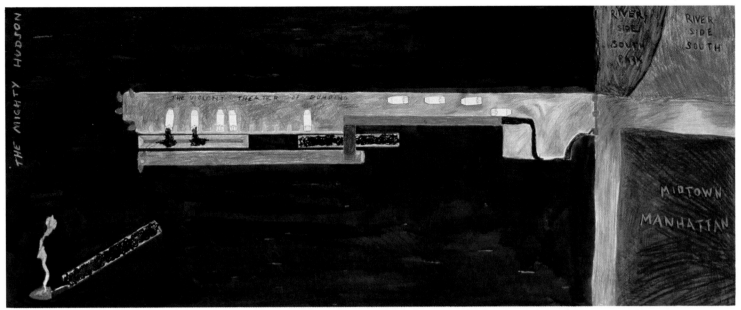

Flow City
59th Street Marine Transfer Station

Plan Drawing
NYC Department of Sanitation
New York, New York
1983–ongoing

Flow City
Passage Ramp

Elevation Drawing
NYC Department of Sanitation
New York, New York
1983–ongoing

Street, on the Hudson River. In 1983, I proposed to the department a permanent public environment that would become an organic part of an operating garbage facility. I designed *Flow City* with the design engineers from Greeley Hanson.

The site is one of the most beautiful sites on the Hudson River, midway between the George Washington Bridge and the Statue of Liberty. It is a marine transfer station that handles a waste flow equivalent to that of a city the size of San Francisco. Garbage trucks transfer their payloads into barges that wait in the finger of the Hudson River that flows through the station. The barges are then switched out in a beautiful nautical maneuver, and taken by tug to the Fresh Kills Landfill on Staten Island.

Flow City is a radical penetration of art into the workplace. The penetration begins with a *Passage Ramp* that leads to a *Glass Bridge*. From the bridge, visitors will observe the operation of the station. The end of the bridge is called *Media Flow Wall*.

It took about two years in the construction of the facility to build in public access for everybody. When we first proposed *Flow City*, the Department of Ports

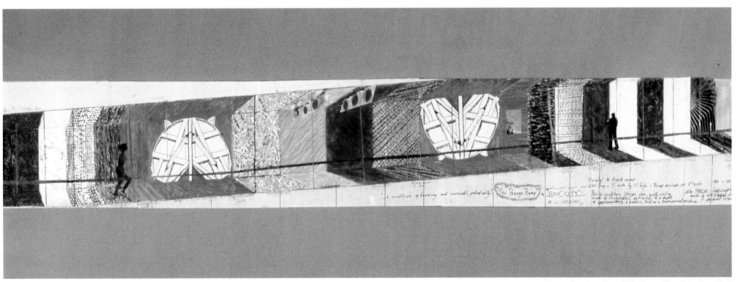

Mierle Laderman Ukeles

Flow City
The artist at the 59th Street
Marine Transfer Station
The violent theater of dumping

Photo: Daniel Dutka, Courtesy Ronald Feldman Fine Arts, New York

and Terminals said, "You can't do that because it's never been done before." The sanitation department replied, "Yes we can. It is time to lift the veil on the subject, and this is the way to do it."

Passage Ramp will be a 248-foot-long procession made of ten to twelve recyclable materials, including 20 feet of crushed glass and 20 feet of shredded rubber. I want visitors to feel the extreme diversity in different materials, because if you can appreciate this, then you can't watch them all getting dumped together in the barge without thinking, "How stupid." I want visitors to see the materials in a kind of hovering state of flux: thrown out, not yet back. I want the visitors to pass through a state of potentiality.

I have designed the recycling panels in the shape of a running spiral. A running spiral can be found in every culture, and is universally seen as a symbol of regeneration and continuity—the essence of recycling. This work is about a paradigm shift in how we relate to materials in the world. We need to grow beyond the

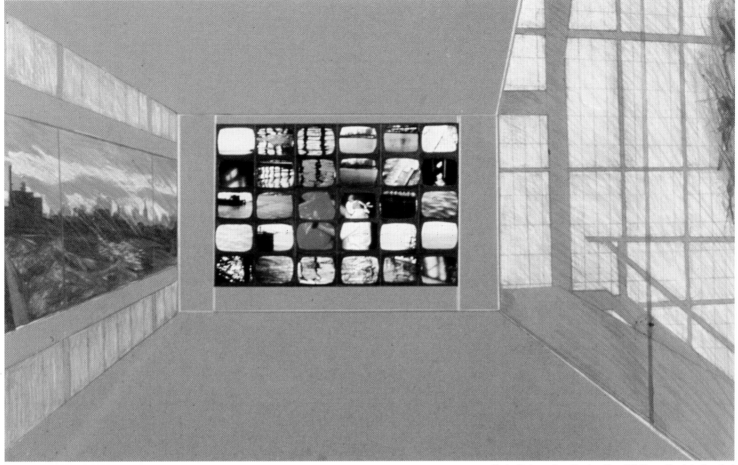

Photo: D. James Dee, Courtesy Ronald Feldman Fine Arts, New York

Flow City
Media Flow Wall

Drawing
59th Street Marine Transfer Station
NYC Department of Sanitation
New York, New York
1983–ongoing

self-destructive cycle of acquiring materials, owning them, using them, and then leaving them as if they don't exist anymore.

At the top of the ramp visitors will enter a *Glass Bridge* that is 40 feet long and 18 feet wide. On one side of the bridge is the formal city with the icons of New York: the Empire State Building and the World Trade Center. On the other side, is the city in flux. The trucks, in fourteen dumping bays, lift their hoppers, and dump their payloads into waiting barges. As the barges are loaded, the visitors will see them passing beneath their very feet, under the *Glass Bridge*. They will be able to watch all of the things they worked so hard to buy go to waste. I call it the "Violent Theater of Dumping."

At the end of the bridge is the *Media Flow Wall*, a 10 by 18 foot crushed glass wall with twenty-four monitors set into it. The video wall will be programmed with live cameras, located on and off site, and prepared disc and tape sources. It is an electronic permeable membrane that will enable visitors to pass "through" this physical point in order to get a broader understanding how this kind of place links up with the systems of the planet. The wall will transmit three kinds of flow-imagery: river, landfill, and recycling.

Six live cameras, 350 feet away from the facility, will focus continually on the mighty Hudson River. The fact that the garbage is collected and transferred in this particular place prompts a great loss, because the facility bars access to our primal source: the river. This river makes the city live. It will flow back in real time across the *Media Flow Wall*, as cameras focus downriver, upriver, midway, close-up on the face of the water, and even beneath the surface, where thirty species of fish presently live in midtown Manhattan.

The wall will also document the accumulation of our garbage at the Fresh Kills Landfill, that will eventually be the highest point on the eastern seacoast, rising almost 500 feet.

Mierle Laderman Ukeles

186 / 187

The third source of imagery is the great social revolution of our time, recycling, in which each of us becomes a sanitation worker, a participating partner in the care of the environment.

I also plan to have an intercom system set up in order to create a flow of communication between visitor and any available sanitation worker. As citizens, we consume the services of those who work in these places; we produce the product that is serviced in these places; we own these places. These are public facilities. We have every reason to be here.

There are many reasons why there are veils between ourselves and our waste. Hopefully, in a short while, we can lift these veils and see who we are, where we come from, and what we can do.

A Blizzard of Released and Agitated Materials in Flux

This permanent environmental installation was commissioned by the Research Institute for Contemporary Art and the Taejon Expo Organizing Committee for the Recycling Through Art Museum in Taejon, Korea. It celebrates the 1993 opening of the Taejon Expo, the first Universal Expo in a developing country.

I wanted to create a place to begin a new kind of journey, a place where one could pass through a blizzard of released and agitated materials in a state of flux. These surprisingly rich and abundant materials have all been thrown out. The desire that made people work to make them, and to purchase them, has passed. The materials have now been densified, and are in the first stages of reprocessing. They are not yet formed again. Visitors enter the place and see them, held for a moment in flux.

This passage, 20 feet long by 16.5 feet high by 15 feet wide, includes 14,000 hand-pulled "blobs" of extruded polystyrene, 6,000 washed and smashed steel and aluminum cans, and 1,721 bundles of spiraling metal filings—all bound onto 572 binding wires. Each of the wires is attached by a spring to the ceiling. The materials move and shimmer as visitors pass through the three-foot-wide path and cause slight shifts in the air. A 310-square-foot downpour of shattered bottle glass streams down the walls of the entire passage. This piece was created with enormous hand-labor of myself with thirty-five assistants. My intention was to show that it is our work that can connect the Above with the Below, so that both we and these materials can continue to flow. I think this work is quite at home in Korea, a place where extraordinary endurance for work is a commonly shared cultural value.

This is a place to foster a new understanding of our relationship to the material world. Each material is on a different journey from each of us. True, we can capture and shape matter, but its journey is not ours. When our journey shifts or ends, it does not mean the end of the materials we have gathered with so much possessiveness.

We need to learn to pass through materials without ruining their chances for other cycles, other journeys. We must move through them without abusing them to such a degree that their effects poison us or the Earth itself.

At the entrance to the work, there is this sign:

Dear Visitor:
As you enter this blizzard, into the land of
NO-LONGER-AND-NOT-YET,
I ask you,
"Are you passing through these revolutionary materials?
Or, are they passing through you?"
I ask us,
"Can we walk through a wall? In our mind?"

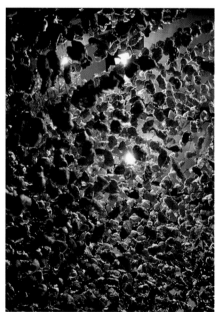

Opposite:
A Blizzard of Released and Agitated Materials in Flux
Recycling Through Art Museum
Taejon, Korea
1993

Photo: Courtesy Ronald Feldman Fine Arts, New York

A Blizzard of Released and Agitated Materials in Flux
Detail
1993

Mierle Laderman Ukeles

188 / 189

Photo: Cymie Payne, Courtesy Ronald Feldman Fine Arts, New York

Turnaround/Surround for Danehy Park

This is a work commissioned by the Cambridge Art Council's Art Insite Program for Danehy Park in Cambridge, Massachusetts. The park, designed by landscape architect John Kissida, is built atop a large, closed municipal landfill, earlier a clay pit/brickworks. Cambridge is one of the densest cities in the United States, and Danehy Park provides the community with twenty percent more open space. An integrated system of dynamic earth design, methane and erosion control, and environmental and storm water management re-established the web of life within the park. Plant, water, and animal life are returning each day. I want to add a self-consciously created symbolic place of community turnaround to the park. The effort is an experiential statement of belief in ourselves. We can see here active functioning life, for all, returning to a place of decay.

Turnaround/Surround has four parts: Access Path, Plantings, Five Circle Places, and Community Implants. I completed parts one and two by mid-1993, after intense collaboration with Pallas Lombardi, the Council's Director of Public Art and John Kissida, park designer.

**Turnaround/Surround
Danehy Park**

With the Cambridge Arts Council
Cambridge, Massachusetts
1990–ongoing

The Path

A one-half mile glassphalt path was created, fully accessible, to bring everyone to the top of the hill, the highest point in Cambridge. Any person can now climb the path (whether by foot, carriage, wheelchair, or roller blades), twirl around and around, and become king or queen of the hill.

Since glassphalt has never been used before in Cambridge, I needed to gain the confidence of the community. I conducted three large scale tests with the New York City Departments of Sanitation and Transportation, which have the longest continual track records for use of glassphalt as a safe and fully recyclable material.

The city of Cambridge dedicated one week's harvest of glass from its regular recycling program, and sorted it specifically for the project. I gave presentations and workshops to over a thousand public school students in every grade level, as well as to the neighborhood and to the art and design communities, asking all to contribute to the glass collection.

**Turnaround/Surround
Danehy Park**

Detail of glassphalt path
Cambridge, Massachusetts
1990–ongoing

After a national search, we also located ten tons of stained glass in mixed colors, donated by Spectrum Glass Company in Woodinville, Washington. The city of New York sent us crushed mirror.

Poured in June of 1993, the path is already revealing its glittering riches. The older and more worn it gets, the more beautiful it will become.

Plantings

The Plantings component was completed in June of 1993, and consists of the following.

An Allée of eighty large trees: red maple, pin oak, champagne ash, and green ash form a series of grand formal entries, as well as more grove-like spatial enclosures and framed openings all along the half-mile long path.

Smellers and Wavers on the hilltop: more than 3,000 individual plants of herbs, roses, and four varieties of naturalized grasses accentuate the wind patterns that play across the central mound. They also offer up a wonderful fragrance in a place that used to smell terrible!

Parts three and four have begun to be realized.

The Five Circle Places

Five locations have been selected at the top of the mound. Each circle place is made of a different recyclable material. It is as if these separated materials have risen up as renewed differentiated individuals from the mess of mixed wasted materials deep beneath the surface. I have designed them to be ritualistic and celebratory resting places and dance floors for the kings and queens of the hill. In this rather windy and bare location, we can face each other, and face the fact that we can create a turnaround of earlier states.

Community Implants

Here at the top of the hill, precious donated objects will be implanted to recall the special heritage of individuals selected from the fifty cultures that make up this community. This individual local richness will become part of the meaning of open common space, a place accessible to all. The precious material things will comprise a community fabric to be treasured together.

Mierle Laderman Ukeles

Fresh Kills Landfill

The mother of all landfills, Fresh Kills is the largest on the planet, occupying a site of 3,000 acres. Thirteen thousand tons of garbage are brought to it every day. When completed, it will be the largest man-made structure ever built, as well as the highest point on the eastern seacoast—a social sculpture we have all wrought in common.

This place is the live 3-D symbol of our entire culture's waste crisis.

Several recycling projects are also components of Fresh Kills. These encompass methane mining, urban composting, construction and demolition material recycling, wood-chipping, and a recycling plant that is currently being designed.

I have dreamt of transforming the site since 1977, when I received a National Endowment for the Arts planning grant. Two years ago, a jury from the New York City Department of Cultural Affairs Percent for Art Program selected me as the artist of this landfill. I will serve as a full member of the Master Plan/End-Use design, with department professionals and officials and the outside consultants. My contract says my vision, once accepted, will become part of the construction of the site. The hardest personal question? What time frame do I work within? The closure of the landfill will take ten to twenty years, at least. How many years do I work on the piece? How many years do I have?

The challenge of this site is that it consists of two kinds of spaces that are inherently in conflict. On the one hand, it's the only citywide site left to "put away" our garbage. On the other hand, this is peoples' neighborhood. It is not isolated in the desert. The largest regional shopping center is literally right across the street. One gets the image of avid consumers buying-buying-buying, consuming-consuming-consuming, and simply lobbing the undesired objects directly across the street. Not a second lost in the frenzy to waste. It's so close by that it could be funny, if it weren't so "awe-full."

My work is divided into several phases. Phase I involves research, ranging from pre-historical sacred mounds to ecological parameters of landscape restoration processes and bioengineering restoration techniques in relation to government regulations.

Concurrently, I've begun phase II, which involves rigorous experimentation with a range of recyclables. These prospective landfill construction/art materials will be used on a huge scale, in ways not yet seen. The challenge is to determine whether they are permanent, durable, and safe, and whether they make sense at this scale, artistically.

Gradually, I will increase my interaction with the more than 500 professionals, including technical and operations personnel, who work at Fresh Kills. Together with the citizens who live facing this THING, we will recreate this place.

These are the big questions:

— How transparent can we make this place, and as a result, how transparent will we become to ourselves looking at what we do to ourselves?

— How deeply and with what level of resonance can we bring the public into a penetrating interaction with the place?

— Can we literally bring the public inside without damaging the enormous tracts of wetlands being restored and the succession landscape being re-engendered here to heal this degraded landscape? How far inside?

— Can we bring them right into the daily operations area without endangering them or disrupting the work?

— Or should we bring them in via electronic highways: video-magnification lenses that plug right into the compost rows and the garbage mounds, over 400 feet below the ground, so they can watch the greatest of transformers— the microbes and the anaerobic bacteria—doing their magic?

— Can we make the place transparent as the crucible of our interaction with the material world—a free public university of ecology in real time and space?

Fresh Kills Landfill

Aerial
NYC Department of Sanitation
Staten Island, New York
1992–ongoing

Mierle Laderman Ukeles

Yes, Yes, Yes, and in this way we can transform the very notion of public culture. We will do this by centering in on the great issue of our time—how we Can change and Are changing our relation to the material world—happening before our very eyes.

The design of garbage should become the great public design of our age. I am talking about the whole picture: recycling facilities, transfer stations, trucks, landfills, receptacles, water treatment plants, and rivers. They will be giant clocks and thermometers of our age that tell the time and health of the air, the earth, and the water. They will be utterly ambitious—our public cathedrals. For if we are to survive, they will be our symbols of survival.

Dominique Mazeaud

The Great Cleansing of the Rio Grande

A garden consisting of three old linden trees planted close enough to form a dome was my grandmother's love. Water bathed my youth: be it the Atlantic of my early Brittany summers, the Mediterranean of my teenage holidays, or the river my father would require as a condition for any potential weekend house. I loved Nature—a daily walk in the woods was a family ritual during our time away from Paris.

I loved Nature, but what kind of love was it? I had inherited a tradition. How real was it? I did not know when I began *The Great Cleansing of the Rio Grande*. In September 1992 as I enter the sixth year of the project, I realize it's through "art-ing" with the river that I have reached a much deeper sense of connection toward the natural world. It's a bit of that journey I'd like to recount.

What brought me to the river? In August 1986 I drove to Taos with a friend, a traditional Navajo. Over lunch, he let out his pain about what European settlers had done to his people. What could I say in the face of his justified pain and anger? I listened with my heart, then added what I knew was true: "More and more people are waking up to what really happened, and dedicating their lives to the healing of wrong doings." After lunch we walked along the Rio Grande. Everywhere the bank was covered with trash. Disgusted, I exclaimed, "Another insult to the Earth Mother; this is too much, something must be done." At that very instant, I envisioned a work of art, *The Great Cleansing of the Rio Grande*.

Every month since September 1987, on the 17th, I do my ritual/performance. I begin in the Santa Fe River, a small tributary of the Rio Grande, making my way through the trickle, trash, disrespect, and despair, filling up uncountable garbage bags, walking toward the Great River, sending her energy, making an offering of my action. I also receive many gifts—trash turned into sculpture, encounters, lessons, and synchronicities.

The Santa Fe River is often dry because a siphoning reservoir was built to supply the growing city's water. The dying river obsessed me at the beginning. Reliving my "garbage practice" through my journal "riveries," I see how I have changed. I also see how much the river has taught me. I realize now that my attitude at the beginning was that of a well-meaning artist/activist who despaired at the river's "dammed/damned" condition. Excerpts from my journal help me remember what I learned. After encountering a homeless person under the Paseo de Peralta bridge, I have gloomy thoughts:

> *in religion, water is a sacred symbol. why have we stopped seeing all waters blessed?*
> *how long will it take to notice the trouble of our waters? how many more dead fish floating*
> *on the rhine river? how many kinds of toxic waste dumpings?*
> *how many acronyms for new illnesses?*

As I look back and study the river journal, I am surprised at what I read:

> *when are we going to turn our malady of separateness around?*

The importance of Dominique Mazeaud's work is found in the simple act of doing. It clearly demonstrates the difference an individual can make in healing the wounds of our planet.

≈

What I did not see then is that I was suffering from that malady myself. Of course, there are many, many degrees of acuteness. I had to do a lot more walking in the company of the river to experience the totality of life, to see with my own eyes that death and also life, birth, and creation are not only real and simultaneous, but also one and living inside of me.

Between my grandmother's garden and my father's waters, there were many unresolved pains that prevented me from going deeper in perceiving the world and Nature. To be able to feel a real sense of connection, one must reach a lived awareness. There are many steps to achieve this. The most important step is to discover life in its totality.

One day I skimmed the following little poem from the surface of my quieted mind. I used it in a ceremony I did when launching *The Great Cleansing of the Rio Grande*. Since then, I have come to see the performance as a contemporary ceremony.

Photo: Michel Monteaux

The Great Cleansing of the Rio Grande
Santa Fe, New Mexico
1987–ongoing

water, through you i was born
without you i could not live
i pray i remember who you are
i pray that i always respect you,
like the river of my own being...

The last words found an echo inside, and on April 8, 1988, I have a first hint:

so this is about birth, my own birth?

On May 1, I feel pain. I have to move from my beautiful little house; nobody, nothing outside seems to respond to me. I seek comfort from my friend the river:

does she feel alone, like i do today? no one
ever asked her if she wanted her blood
drained and her life weakened? do they
really ask rivers...the men who build dams?
do they realize they are setting up
death traps around the rivers' throats?

Feeling the pain of the river makes me start feeling my own pain—a new thing for the strong, "everything is fine" person I have been until then. Soon, a much bigger tornado of pain hits the shore of my being. Some old, deep family wounds reopen. The dialogue that the river had led me into—now it's been a year—intensifies.

how can we keep from avoiding sorrow? how can we use our
experience of suffering to contact and nurture our caring?

Do I find answers? I am not sure, but I keep at it. Perhaps the following quote gives me a hint that I am on the right track.

We get wise asking questions, and, and even if these are not answered we get wise, for a well-packed question carries its answer on its back as a snail carries its shell. —*The Salmon of Knowledge*, JAMES STEPHEN'S IRISH FAIRY TALES

Questions lap at my soul, river steps carve at my vision. While it's grand to have visions, the essence of a vision is as much vague as it is profound. A pilgrim knows from the depth of her or his being to go to the holy place. How to get there is the question. A pilgrimage is about trust, unfailing willingness to listen and watch for signs, to retrace some steps, unload a heavy, useless bundle. For twenty-two years, my life has been woven of art—first, working with established artists and then guiding younger ones—I am now directed to join the ranks myself and do "heart work." I tread on unknown territory. I answer, "heart is my medium," when asked what I do. I listen for clues on my path of "heartist." I can't help but notice that heart, as a word and an idea, holds ear and earth!

Artists are catalysts. At the beginning, I don't miss a chance to plant a seed. Religiously, I send releases to the local press and write labels for the bags. At first I dispose of the trash myself with the help of a friend and his pickup truck. Then one day I see the city sanitation come by while I am in the river—the labels must have worked. I keep my attention on doing. I feel so responsible I talk of "putting in my day." Little by little, however, I relax my activist mentality, pay attention to the whole of me. I stop counting the bags. At one point, I even stop being interested in the river's gifts.

> *today i feel it was buying into the present system of art that's so much object oriented.*
> *is it because i am doing art i need to produce something?*

In August I write a poem titled *moment*. In the acronymically inclined river tongue, *moment* stands for "making out my existence now truthfully." This increasing attention to moment helps me remember my intention.

> *what i do in the river is a ritual. it is important that i prepare and reiterate one more time*
> *to myself (or, to be more precise, to the higher part of myself) what it is i am really doing here.*

I reflect. I relax. Yet, I see how I give myself a hard time if I relax too much. The river—even though she has no water per se—is always present. On the first anniversary, I happen to be traveling between two destinations. An inner battle is raging. I hear a voice say:

> *don't be so hard on yourself. it's about flow, remember... there are certain dates that stand like*
> *boulders in the middle of your river...the only thing you can do is to flow around them...*

Helped by the philosopher Gaston Bachelard who wrote the seminal book, *Water and Dreams: An Essay on The Imagination of Matter*, I want to discover the "matter of my river." Again the despair,

> *my matter is non-matter. my matter is a trickle, trash, disrespect, and despair.*

Though the waters are gone, life is there in myriads of forms. A certain light-heartedness replaces my one-way obsession with the beginning litany, trickle, trash, disrespect, and despair...

> *another bag full. i throw it over the supporting stone wall first, and follow it by climbing...*
> *i never played in rivers or climbed walls when i was a child...i am the child...truly, listen*
> *friends...come and see for yourselves...i got it... this is the born again children movement!*

On December 26, 1988 I decide to do a ritual of thanks to my river. I go all the way up to where she is a little singing stream, in a rocky enclave that I always saw as a place for ceremony. I notice how I have to struggle not to use the bags that I took as a matter of habit. I see how mechanistic one becomes, even with good intentions. Finally, a voice, speaking through the water, or is it inside of me, says:

Photo: Dwayne Rourl

The Great Cleansing of the Rio Grande
Santa Fe, New Mexico
1986–ongoing

i pray…actually, i try to just be…listening, i image the water pouring down
its magical substance through my body…letting myself be purified..
letting her open to the gates of the "river of my life" wider and wider…

In February 1989 a year and a half into the project, I review my journal. The language of my earlier entries hinting that perhaps my action would have some influence, horrified me. This had not been conscious, yet "showing them" is the last thing I want my art to be about. At the time, I realize now, I was confusing missionary and visionary.

as i pick up a can, and then another…what matters more and more is the depth of my relation-
ship with the river, my awe at the miracle of her beingness. what matters…the matter—my matter
—is the truth behind my action, her presence, my love, our oneness, our moment…drop by drop,
it seems, from the silence we share, a new way, a new understanding—our healing—is flowing.

In April 1989 I was asked to speak at the Elmwood Institute's yearly conference. (Founded by nuclear physicist Fritjof Capra, the institute refers to itself as a think-do-tank). The assigned topic was *Heroism in Dangerous Times*. Together with my teammate, the poet and educator Anne Valley-Fox, I had come to a nice, thorough script à la Joseph Campbell. Two nights before the conference, however, a nightmare sounded the alarm bell. I chucked the script thinking, this is who I was yesterday, but no longer today… and began afresh. Asking the river for help, something entirely different came. I was scared to deliver it—remember, I was among people who prided themselves in being think-do-tankers:

talking about doing, that's less and less what matters…simply, i am…in the truest and deepest
sense of the word, just as you, my river, you are…i am a being, not a doing…

It was then I finally understood a native quote, a favorite of mine: "to know, to believe, to be." For a long time, I did not know whether I had heard the quote correctly, so would always say "to know, to believe, to do or to be." I was understanding that the doing flowed out of the being, but certainly was not doing for the sake of doing. Because I was experiencing it, I could joyfully and knowingly talk not only of the "child-born-again movement," but also of being a mother, a mother of the Earth. It was no longer a pure intellectual impulse or even a moral obligation:

two years later i don't talk much of prayer anymore; i bow. yes, my pickup gesture is simply
bowing…in the acronymic river tongue, to bow is to be one with. and as i said to be is to do…

By Thanksgiving 1990 the consciousness of a gesture faded altogether:

an apron of joy festooning my heart, this day dedicated to thanksgiving, i really want to be
here, to be fully me, partaking of the river's feast: hop on a stone here, move the body,
a near dash, a little splash…some "unriverly" material calls me to take a sweeping
plunge…who said i was doing anything? i am simply dancing the song of my heart.

When I am in the river, I feel on top of the world. Yes, it's easy, take a breath with me, close your eyes and imagine:

visualize the Earth—you know the image well, you can practically put Her in your lap
with your mind's eye…imagine a river, the rio grande—our holy river. next, you see
the whole american network of rivers. soon, it's a diamond web stretching over the Earth—
her blood stream—her life. and you, i, stand and walk in one of these streams,
we become one with the life of the Earth…what a privilege…

…these riveries make me explore territories that are foreign and dark; the non-matter of my river, makes me explore different matters within myself…

to heal heals,   the question i keep asking myself, when is one ready for that? it sounds so simple…
it should be…
do people realize the miracle of our river, of all rivers…
that their life is being taken away.
healing with ablution is a thing of the past…
we have switched to a new era…
the era when things have dried up… our work, our reveries, and our healing, is to bring the waters back.
today there is no need of a priest for exorcism…we can do our own as we are doing our little bit on the Earth …actually, since each one of us is a miniature Earth (yes, we are made of the same chemical elements and our water proportion is very similar!), whatever healing we do will benefit the "other" Earth.

Newton Harrison
Helen Mayer Harrison

The Serpentine Lattice

We come to a place only by invitation and only when somebody agrees to network us into the conversation of place. As a consequence, we speak with many people, questioning and engaging in the dialogue of place before anything will happen at all. Thus, we never have the control that an artist in a studio has because "chance is always operating." Who we will meet? Who will raise what issue? Who we will not meet? Who has invited us and why? How much money and other resources will be available? Above all, what will emerge as central to our perception of the well-being of this place?

A good example of this is a man named Istok Geister, a principal ornithologist in Slovenia, who came into our life while we were working with the European Heritage Fund on the *Sava River Project*. We asked him, "Aren't you afraid that the life of the river is at risk from human desires that are encroaching upon it?" and he said that he was an animist and that "Nature exists in secret places and invisible spaces and will find ways to co-exist." We used this belief as one guide for our design of the Sava as a whole, paying careful attention to the secret places (We have always focused on invisible spaces.)

Few of our ideas develop independent of outside influences. Our ideas are in constant interaction, growing and changing with the accrual of each new information bit, until, like a stew, the disparate contents gradually develop a taste of their own. In fact, we hold that the Universe, as a whole, is a conversation in which we all necessarily participate, though we may choose where to focus our attention or how to respond.

When Susan Fillin-Yeh asked us to Reed College to see if we wished to consider the area for a new project, the first thing she did was to have people take us to various areas of old growth in the vicinity of the college and various areas that had been clear cut. After that, we were taken up in an airplane to look from above. We began to ask three very fundamental questions. The first was, "Can it be that people have permitted the cutting of 95% of these great conifers in an accelerating rate up to the present?" And the answer was "Yes." The second question was, "What are all the ecologists and other informed people doing?" And the answer was, "fighting to save the 5% of old growth." The third question was, "Who is looking after the other 95%?" Since the answer was no one in particular, we decided that we would think about how to plan for that 95%, if we could, in a work. And that is when *The Serpentine Lattice* [1] started to take shape.

We decided to take the perspective of the coast range, from San Francisco Bay to Vancouver Island, as a start—an area about 2,000 miles long and 20–30 miles deep. Including islands it is about 54,000 square miles. We decided that saving the old growth, while vitally important, would not save the forest. The only thing that would save the forest was actually reconstructing it in all of its biodiversity. We came to understand that land undergoing healthy succession will become the most valuable land, because if it is held in trust now, it will be the basis for old growth 200 or 300 years from now. We decided to put a concept in place that would offer an alternative to cutting the new growth every 30 to 60 years.

Helen and Newton Harrison

are a husband and wife team

who pursue the art of conversation,

primarily addressing the issue

\of global survival.

Their conversations often generate

new metaphors which in turn

provide starting points for proposals

and projects. The following text

comes directly from transcripts of

conversations I had with Helen and

Newton about their project,

The Serpentine Lattice.

I have distilled the Harrisons'

answers to a series of questions.

The Harrisons would hope that the

readers can intuit the questions

from the answers.

≈

Right:
Serpentine Lattice
Map based upon a
map originally produced by Eco-Trust

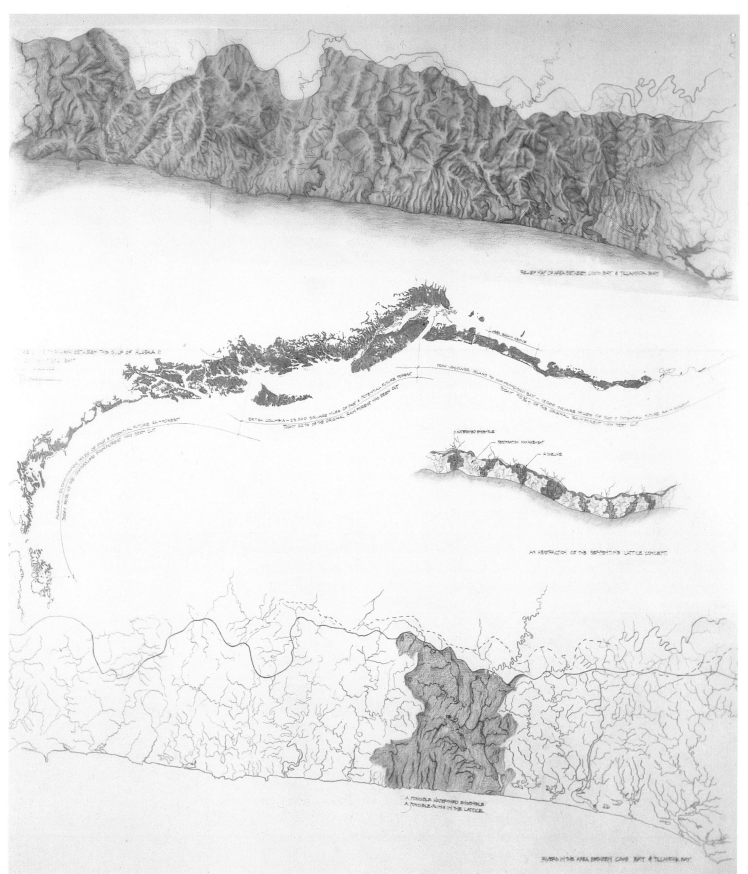

RELIEF MAP OF AREA BETWEEN COOS BAY & TILLAMOOK BAY

AN ABSTRACTION OF THE SERPENTINE LATTICE CONCEPT

A POSSIBLE WATERSHED ENSEMBLE
A POSSIBLE RUNG IN THE LATTICE

RIVERS IN THE AREA BETWEEN COOS BAY & TILLAMOOK BAY

Newton Harrison and Helen Mayer Harrison

The map that we drew for this project is a reproduction, elaboration, and clarification of a map done by Eco-Trust. It looked like a strange map, for it implied that everything was green from northern California to southern Alaska. However, we realized that the green area represented the former extent of the Coastal Rain Forest, and in our minds, we took the canopy off, and noticed rivers and tiny little water sheds running from the ridge line to the sea in very complicated and interesting patterns. When we drew a line around a watershed along the high ground, it looked almost like a leaf. Patterns began to emerge.

Look at the lower ridge line of the forest from San Francisco Bay to Yakutak Bay. It is a winding serpentine. Look at the shoreline, a second winding serpentine that runs somewhat parallel. Thus, two sides of a lattice are formed. From the ridge line, looking for cross pieces, there are the leaf-like watersheds making an intricate lattice form. It became immediately clear that we would want to network the watersheds. The question then was, "How?"

Now by networking, we mean finding the connections, the corridors, that link the watersheds, one to the other. One of us said, "Network the watersheds," and the other said "A game of Go." The game of Go is really about forces joining and forces broken apart, disassociated. It is an ancient Chinese game that appears simple but that in reality is formidably complex—a guiding metaphor for *The Serpentine Lattice*.

Why choose watersheds? For the last twenty years, we have been interested in watersheds. A watershed is a discreet bioregion with many subregions: estuaries and wetlands, perhaps meadows and forests, and other diverse terrain. As you move uphill, there is a complex and changing biota. As topographical entities, watersheds offer the greatest opportunity for biodiversity.

Paying careful attention, you can see that the north/south ridge line actually exists. Were you to imagine buying the private lands and attaching them to the public lands, a mile wide path along the ridge line for thousands of miles could be made. Calculate the cost. There are 640 acres to a square mile. Multiply it by two thousand miles and then multiply again by two hundred to a thousand dollars per ruined acre; more for tree farmed privately held acres. Imagine subtracting for the state parks and public lands and you come up with a figure that is not so far from three billion dollars. That is not a lot of money. If issues of private property arise, remember that there are ways in the public domain to condemn lands to make a freeway or a railroad. Why not to save terrain? We believe that in due course there will be ways to condemn lands for Earth regenerative corridors coupled with the grouping and clustering of critical habitat. In fact, an eco-security system needs to come into being, perhaps parrallel to the social security system.

At one point in time, human activity existed only in isolated areas within a matrix of pristine habitat. At present, there is practically no place on the globe that is not affected in some way by human activity, if only from airborne or waterborne pollution. There are relatively pristine areas here or there operating in a matrix that is, in the main, altered by human activity. *The Serpentine Lattice* proposes the reverse, so that areas moving toward the pristine reconnect to form a matrix, and human activity finds itself imbedded within this matrix: a reversal of ground. Think about the figure-field relationships every artist used to study.

On the map, the green spots are proposed watersheds moving toward the pristine and the white areas are human activity: tree farming, mixed use forestry, farming, human settlement, fish farming and industrial production.

The ground can be reversed, but an image of sufficient power needs to be produced to accrue belief to it. We work with the image of the disappearing forest. The forest is disappearing, first in one place, then another, all the way up the coastline from northern California to southern Alaska. Imagine the images on the following pages as part of a ten-minute slide presentation of this disappearing forest. Imagine the collective image to be eight feet tall and thirty-six feet wide. Imagine the image six feet off the ground on a wall, so it can be walked around and looked it. The sense of loss and disappearance becomes palpable. Belief accrues that the other 95% best be looked at and quickly.

We hope that the best of our work is self-evident. When something seems so sensible to you that you integrate it into your thoughts, so that often you simply don't remember where you first heard it, it seems that you always thought it and were only missing a small piece. Sometimes our image supplies that small missing piece that lets the gestalt form. Reversing the ground is such a piece.

We work with a concept that we call conversational drift. Conversational drift implies that conversations have a way of drifting, like clouds. Thus, often times, they drift away from you and you can find yourself left out of the very conversation that you began. The conversation has drifted off in another direction, and nobody may even remember you. Perhaps it will drift back again, and all of a sudden there you are, as if you had always been there. Such events happen to us frequently.

Because of this, the larger the work, the more anonymous we become. It's not that we set out to become anonymous. It's simply that our participation may become less vital over time, since the larger the scale of a work, the more critical the issue, the more imperative the outcome, the more necessary the participation of many, the less important how it began.

We have also proposed works that unfold according to forest time and geologic time; sometimes even urban time.

To the degree that we are successful, many of our works will reach maturity long after we are gone.

We are often asked how we can stay engaged in a project such as *The Serpentine Lattice*. We consider that question a very serious and tough one. For instance, we have been invited by the University of Oregon to work with a group in the watershed areas of Deadwood City. This will be the first site of the first rung in the lattice. The Deadwood people literally would not even talk to us unless we were willing to commit ten years. The answer is that we will commit ten years or more, but we can only stay deeply engaged by request. Essentially, we can be available because we don't have to be continuously with a project. It can operate in Nature time and have quiet periods. Thus, when we take up a project of significance, we can continue to be available for the rest of our lives.

In Oregon, in the Deadwood watershed and in collaboration with the University of Oregon in Eugene, we have begun to work with a proposal of assisted migration which will help species move back into the destroyed areas. A forester named Dave Perry provided us with some additional ideas for it. He is working with a 40–70-year-old monoculture, trying to bring about a return to biodiversity. We have some other ideas involving the inoculation of dead soil with healthy soil.

However grand, most so-called ecological problem solving consists of spot solutions. No one is looking at the whole figure-ground relationship of our culture, to the habitat that it has emerged from. There is a bit and piece mentality that comes out of entrepreneurial modernism and has affected all problem solving. The practice of isolating information bits from their contexts in the laboratory, in politics, and the marketplace does not work well at eco-scale. Remember "the flavor of the soup." Notions about human as well as animal and plant behavior must undergo some type of phase shift. This, of course, is the relevancy of the game of Go. But, there are many, many ways in which to go.

---

1. *The Serpentine Lattice* is an installation composed of an 8' x 36' slowly shifting slide mural with three slides to an image, diverse texts, drawings, photography, and a 38' x 8' drawn map of the Pacific Northwest Coastal Rainforest. Commissioned by The Douglas F. Cooley Gallery at Reed College. Director, Susan Fillin-Yeh. Photography from the archives of Trygve Steen whose work enabled the mural. Ecological and Mapping Research, Heather Diefendurfer.

THE SERPENTINE LATTICE

A multimedia installation proposing a new history for the
North American Pacific Coast temperate rainforest.

FROM SOUTHERN ALASKA
TO NORTHERN CALIFORNIA
NORTH AMERICA'S
LAST GREAT TEMPERATE RAIN FOREST IS DYING
EVERYBODY KNOWS THERE'S LESS THAN 10%
OF THE OLD GROWTH LEFT
BETWEEN SAN FRANCISCO
AND VANCOUVER ISLAND
PERHAPS 40% IN BRITISH COLUMBIA
AND NOBODY CAN AGREE ABOUT ALASKA

BY NOW
EVERYBODY KNOWS
THAT A TREE FARM IS NOT A FOREST
THAT IS
EVERYBODY KNOWS
WHO THINKS ABOUT SUCH THINGS

AND EVERYBODY KNOWS
THAT THE DOUGLAS FIR
CANNOT GROW IN ITS OWN SHADE
ALTHOUGH IT MAY LIVE A THOUSAND YEARS
AND EXIST THREE TO FOUR HUNDRED MORE
AS A SNAG OR A NURSE LOG
AND EVERYBODY KNOWS THAT
THE WESTERN RED CEDAR IS AS STOUT
THOUGH NOT AS TALL
RESISTING DECAY
SOME SPECIMENS
LIVING MORE THAN TWELVE HUNDRED YEARS

AND THE WESTERN HEMLOCK
AS UNDERSTORY
COMPLETES ONE OF THE ARBOREAL TRIADS
FROM WHICH
THROUGH WHICH
IN AND ABOUT WHICH
UNDER WHICH
A WHOLE ECO-SYSTEM RESIDES
AND ONCE FLOURISHED

NOW
THERE IS ENOUGH NEW INFORMATION ABOUT
AND ENOUGH OLD WISDOM AROUND
FOR ANYBODY
WHO THINKS ABOUT THESE THINGS
TO KNOW THAT THE DEATH OF A GREAT FOREST
IS A GLOBAL TRAGEDY

THINKING ABOUT THIS FOREST
STRETCHING ALONG THE COAST
FROM THE WESTERN HEMLOCK
OF SOUTHERN ALASKA
DOWNWARD THROUGH SITKA SPRUCE
WESTERN RED CEDAR
AND DOUGLAS FIR
TO NORTHERN CALIFORNIA

WHERE THE COAST REDWOODS CARRY ON

KNOWING THAT EMBEDDED
IN THIS TERRAIN
THIS ONCE GREAT
PACIFIC COASTAL FOG FOREST
IS THE WHOLE NORTH AMERICAN
RAIN FOREST
THEN
WHO CAN SERIOUSLY VALUE
ITS TOTAL DESTRUCTION

WE
BEING GRATEFUL
FOR THE OPPORTUNITY
TO JOIN THIS PERILOUS CONVERSATION
WHERE SOMEBODY SAID
HOW WILL YOU CROSS STATE BORDERS
WHEN THE LAWS ARE DIFFERENT
AND NATIONAL BORDERS
WHERE THEY ARE EVEN MORE DIVERSE

AND SOMEBODY SAID
IN PARTS OF CANADA
THE CLEAR CUTTING IS FAR WORSE
AND SOMEBODY SAID
IT'S TOO LATE ANYWAY
THERE'S NOT ENOUGH LEFT
AND SOMEBODY SAID
WHAT WILL YOU DO
ABOUT THE LUMBER INTERESTS
AND WHAT WILL YOU DO
ABOUT THE CASH FLOW FROM JAPAN
AND WHAT WILL YOU DO ABOUT JOBS

AND SOMEBODY SAID
SURELY YOU WILL CONSIDER ALL POINTS OF
VIEW
AND SOMEBODY SAID
IN ONE WAY OR ANOTHER
YOU CAN'T DO THIS BECAUSE OF THAT
OR THAT BECAUSE OF THIS

WE
BEING GRATEFUL
FOR THE INVITATION TO JOIN
THIS PERILOUS CONVERSATION
BEGAN TO IMAGINE AN ACT OF RESTITUTION
YOU SEEING A SERPENTINE
I SEEING A LATTICE
WE BEGINNING TO IMAGE
NORTH/SOUTH CONTINUITIES
FROM YAKUTAT BAY
TO SAN FRANCISCO
CONTINUITIES THAT WOULD BESPEAK
THE ECO-POETICS OF THE WHOLE

ONCE INTERRUPTIONS IN THE FOREST CANOPY
WERE ANOMALIES
NOW SUCH INTERRUPTIONS
AS CLEAR CUTS

Newton Harrison and Helen Mayer Harrison

AND TREE FARMS
AND ROADS
AND OTHER ARTIFACTS OF CIVILIZATION
HAVE BECOME A NEW NORM
AND
THE RARE INTACT CANOPIES OF OLD GROWTH
HAVE BECOME THE ANOMALIES
WITHIN THE MANAGED FOREST
AN UNFORTUNATE REVERSAL OF GROUND

NOW LOOKING AT HEALTHY SUCCESSION
LOOKING AT OLD GROWTH REMAINING
WONDERING ABOUT A MATRIX
IN WHICH TO INSERT A NEW VISION SUDDENLY
YOU SAID A LATTICE
AND I SAID A SERPENTINE
AND YOU SAID NETWORK THE WATERSHEDS
AND I SAID A GAME OF GO

IMAGINE THE SERPENTINE FORM
OF THE CREST OF THE COASTAL MOUNTAINS
IMAGINE THE SERPENTINE FORM
OF THE PACIFIC COAST
IMAGINE SOME OF THE RIVERS
REALLY WATERSHED ENSEMBLES
EXTENDING FROM CREST TO COAST
CONNECTING THE SERPENTINES
AS NEARLY LEAF SHAPED RUNGS
OR CROSS MEMBERS OF THE LATTICE

THEN
WITHIN THIS LATTICE COULD BEGIN
THE RESTORATION
OF THE MORE PRISTINE ENVIRONMENTS
BY LEAVING THEM ALONE
BY ENGAGING IN MORE ACTIVE RESTORATION
ONLY
WHERE CLEAR CUTTING HAD BEEN MOST
SEVERE
BY CLOSING OFF ENTRY ROADS
WHEN FINISHED

A WILLFUL GETTING OUT OF THE WAY
A FELICITOUS WITHDRAWAL

THEN
WITHIN THIS LATTICE
THE OPENING UP OF DENSE MONOCULTURE
COULD BEGIN
BY ASSISTING THE MIGRATION
OF SPECIES THAT ONCE FLOURISHED
AND REINTRODUCING SPECIES
THAT ARE NO LONGER PRESENT

THEN
WITHIN THIS LATTICE
SILVICULTURE
AS WELL AS CITIES
AND FARMS
AND ROADS
AND OTHER AMENITIES

COULD EXIST
IN THE AREAS BETWEEN
THE RESTORED CROSS MEMBERS

THEN
WITHIN THESE CROSS MEMBERS
A MINIMALLY MITIGATED ENVIRONMENT
MOVING TOWARDS THE PRISTINE
WOULD EXIST AND COULD FLOURISH
AND EXPAND

THEN
A NEW REVERSAL OF GROUND
COMES INTO BEING
WHERE HUMAN ACTIVITY BECOMES A FIGURE
WITHIN AN ECOLOGICAL FIELD
AS SIMULTANEOUSLY
THE ECOLOGY CEASES BEING
AN EVER-SHRINKING FIGURE
WITHIN THE FIELD OF HUMAN ACTIVITY

WE
BEING GRATEFUL
FOR THE INVITATION TO JOIN
THIS PERILOUS CONVERSATION
CONTINUE
THINKING ABOUT A NEW HISTORY
FOR THIS ONCE CONTINUOUS
ALTHOUGH CHANGING
REMAINDER
OF THE
NORTH AMERICAN
COASTAL TEMPERATE RAIN FOREST

FOR INSTANCE
IF
ACCORDING TO THE LAWS
OF THE CONSERVATION OF ENERGY
THE TRANSFER OF ENERGY
FROM ONE FORM TO ANOTHER
GENERATES A NET LOSS
THEN
THE CLEAR CUTTING OF OLD GROWTH FOREST
MUST INVOLVE A NET LOSS EQUAL TO MORE
THAN THE ENERGY GAINED
FROM TRANSFORMING IT INTO PROFIT

FOR INSTANCE
WHO WILL PAY THE LONG TERM COSTS
OF CHANGING WEATHER PATTERNS
AS THE MOISTURE RETAINING PROPERTIES
OF THE LARGER TREES
DISAPPEAR
AND THE CARBON SEQUESTERED BY THE GIANTS
IS RELEASED INTO THE ATMOSPHERE
AND THE OXYGEN REPLENISHING PROPERTIES
OF THE QUADRILLIONS OF LIVING NEEDLES
ARE SUBTRACTED
AND THE GRANDEUR
OF THE ANCIENT
FOREST SYSTEM OF THE GIANTS

Newton Harrison and Helen Mayer Harrison

DISAPPEARS

WHO WILL PAY THE COSTS
OF THE LOSS OF PLANTS AND HERBS
WHOSE MEDICINAL VALUES
ARE AS YET UNKNOWN
AND THE PRICE
WHEN THE SEQUESTERING OF CARBON
BY
SUCCESSION ECOLOGIES
DIMINISHES
AND WHO WILL PAY THE COSTS
OF APPARENTLY UNSUPERVISED
AGGRESSIVE CLEAR CUTTING ON PRIVATE LANDS

AFTER ALL
THIS LONG TERM ENERGY DEBT
COMES DUE
IN THE NEXT GENERATION
WITH THE TURNING
OF TENS OF THOUSANDS OF SQUARE MILES
OF BIOLOGICALLY PRODUCTIVE LANDS
INTO FUNCTIONAL DESERTS
AND THE ELIMINATION
OF PRODUCTIVE ECOSYSTEMS
FROM OVER ONE-HUNDRED-THOUSAND MILES
OF RIVER-STREAM HABITAT
AND THE WATER PURIFYING PROPERTIES
OF THE WETLANDS
DISAPPEAR

WHO WILL PAY THIS ECO-DEBT
AND WHERE WILL WE FIND ECO-CREDITS
TO PUT AGAINST IT
AS ECOSYSTEMS SIMPLIFY
AND BECOME MINIMALLY PRODUCTIVE
AND THEREFORE
MINIMALLY SUPPORTIVE OF HUMAN
EXISTENCE

FOR INSTANCE
IF THE GROSS NATIONAL PRODUCT
IS 5.7 TRILLION DOLLARS
AND
PRODUCING THE GROSS NATIONAL PRODUCT
IS THE OUTCOME OF EXPLOITING
THE GROSS NATIONAL ECOSYSTEM
AND
THE GROSS NATIONAL ECOSYSTEM
IS NOT INFINITELY RENEWABLE
THEN
IT IS NOT DIFFICULT
TO IMAGINE THE GROSS NATIONAL PRODUCT
SHRINKING
IN CONCERT WITH AN OVEREXPLOITED
LESS PRODUCTIVE
GROSS NATIONAL ECOSYSTEM

HOWEVER
IF
AS A FORM OF RECYCLING

WE TAKE 1%
OF OUR GROSS NATIONAL PRODUCT
AND ESTABLISH
AN ECO-SECURITY SYSTEM
NOT UNLIKE
OUR SOCIAL SECURITY SYSTEM
THEN
ROUGHLY 57 BILLION DOLLARS
BECOME AVAILABLE YEARLY
FOR RESTORATION/RECLAMATION

NOW
IF
10% OF THE PROPOSED
ECO-SECURITY SYSTEM FUNDING
OR 5.7 BILLION DOLLARS YEARLY
COULD BE PUT AT THE DISPOSAL OF
THE RAIN FOREST OF THE PACIFIC NORTHWEST
FOR A 25-YEAR PERIOD
THEN
PERHAPS 140 BILLION DOLLARS
COULD
BE MADE AVAILABLE
FOR THE REGENERATION OF
THESE FORESTS
RIVERS
WETLANDS
CREATING JOB OPPORTUNITIES
FAR IN EXCESS
OF THOSE THAT WOULD BE LOST
BY LIMITING LUMBERING

THEN
THE RIDGE LINES
NOT NOW IN THE PUBLIC DOMAIN
COULD BE PURCHASED
RIVERS AND WATERSHED ENSEMBLES
BROUGHT TO MORE PRISTINE CONDITION
MONOCULTURES COMPLICATED
AND OLD GROWTH EXPANDED

FINALLY
GROUND WOULD BE REVERSED
SO THAT
THE ECOSYSTEM
BECOMES THE FIELD
AND HUMAN USE
THE FIGURE WITHIN IT

THEN
THE GROSS NATIONAL ECOSYSTEM
WOULD TAKE ITS PLACE
PRIVILEGED
APPROPRIATELY
AS THE FIELD WITHIN WHICH
THE POLITICAL SYSTEMS
SOCIAL SYSTEMS
AND
BUSINESS SYSTEMS
THAT COMPRISE
OUR ECO-CULTURAL ENTITY
CAN EXIST

Newton Harrison and Helen Mayer Harrison

Andy Lipkis

I've always had trouble with the question "What do you do?" which really means "Who are you?" I have difficulty choosing a bailiwick because I truly believe my work is healing the planet. A longer list of my occupations would include citizen forester, urban forester, communicator, educator, inspirer, executive, tree planter, community organizer, student, teacher, fund-raiser, author, video producer, event coordinator, policy analyst, commentator, activist, bridge-builder, radical, practical dreamer, and magician. Perhaps only the titles artist and healer integrate all others.

How could a forestry professional possibly be called an artist? I take a piece of the world everyone recognizes, and put a frame around it in a way that encourages the public to connect with it emotionally, intellectually, or spiritually. This heart connection crosses cultural, political, economic, age, and racial boundaries.

My first work of art was fairly simple. I was a fifteen-year-old kid in smoggy Los Angeles. I'd escape the oppression at summer camp in the forested mountains one hundred miles east of town. I thrived in the fresh air and supportive community atmosphere. One summer, the U.S. Forest Service announced that smog from L.A. was reaching the forest. I learned that trees are air filters, taking in pollutants and producing fresh oxygen. And I learned that these trees I knew and loved—and potentially all the trees in the forest—were dying from the smog.

My fellow summer campers and I wanted to save the trees. We planted smog-tolerant trees and a meadow in a piece of "dead" forest that had been used as a camp parking lot and baseball field. In three weeks, we dug through tar, moved rocks, hauled cow manure, laid pipe, and planted. Twenty-four young men and women brought back life to that piece of Earth. New grass popped up, and squirrels and birds were immediately attracted back to the site. I was stunned that we could do something so profound with our hands. I'd grown up in a culture where every institution, including school and the media, seemed to be telling me that I didn't count, that I couldn't do anything to change anything. Yet this work, which most would compare to prison labor, was challenging, stimulating, and fun. I gained a vision of what needed to be done to heal the environment, and to heal society.

That summer ended, but I went on for three years trying and mostly failing to find ways to share the work with others. Ultimately, I rescued 8,000 seedlings from being destroyed, and prepared to give them to other summer campers so they could repeat my experience.

The *Los Angeles Times* ran an article that told my story. It presented the frame I'd put around the issue. Thousands responded, and in a matter of weeks, my Johnny Appleseed tale had garnered $10,000 in contributions that averaged $2 each, and offers of help from corporations and government agencies. The incident turned out to be the birth of an organization. To handle the money and legal matters, I formed a nonprofit corporation and named it the California Conservation Project. I then hired four buddies, and we spent the summer planting with thousands of kids who consistently reported that the experience connected them to a new part of themselves and their environment. Although we had the formal name, everyone we worked with called us "the tree people." Ultimately I renamed the organization TreePeople, dropping the formality and combining the two words into one.

Andy Lipkis' art is that

of inspiration and empowerment.

It lies in his ability to

understand what actions need

to be taken to help heal our planet

and then facilitating events that help

individuals to not only understand

the problems but be presented the

opportunity to be part of the solution.

His work with TreePeople

has brought together hundreds of

thousands of people by creating the

Citizen Forestry movement.

The results of this work has

literally moved to action

individuals, corporations,

and government agencies

world-wide.

≈

TreePeople
Martin Luther King, Jr. Blvd.
Tree Planting

Citizen forestry in action
Los Angeles, California
1990

TreePeople stresses the critical and inseparable need to have both people and trees working together to heal the environment.

Supportive letters flooded the mailbox. Believers of every religion, as well as people from the far right and the radical left expressed some certainty that I was one of their own. Everybody was responding to the integrity and simplicity of my story. I had discovered the artist in me.

The First Urban Forest Run

Through my work I saw everybody believed that nothing could be done to improve L.A.'s air quality. Linked to "You can't fight city hall" was an almost religious conviction about the power of the automobile. We build monuments and places of worship for cars even more powerful than the objects of desire themselves; we call them freeways. Built by human hands, their qualities of function, mass, form, material, and mortal power unite nevertheless to form a powerful monument to human powerlessness.

About eighty percent of L.A.'s air pollution is attributable to automobiles. Cleaning the air means messing with our relationship to cars—a taboo subject in the late '70s.

Though TreePeople had been around a few years, the concept of the urban forest was still unknown, and I felt that media involvement could make the term part of the public conversation. The urban forest was my way of defining and helping people see that the city was actually a living ecosystem. Urban forestry was a means for having the city population understand a bit about their ecosystem and participate in its management and improvement. But to get things started, it was important for people to start hearing the term.

I designed a ten kilometer run on a freeway. It provided a popular, healthy mass medium with a unique venue that would attract a big crowd and give me the "frame" needed for my message. If we can crack the invulnerable monument to the automobile, then we can break down other barriers to environmental solutions.

The First Urban Forest Tree Run
A ten kilometer run and tree planting
Los Angeles, California
1979

The Marina Freeway was five kilometers long, with a 5,000 car parking lot at a shopping mall on one end. A ramp led from the parking lot right onto one end of the freeway. It was built for the run! With the date set, I sought permission to close the freeway.

Caltrans officials had a melt-down. When I reminded them of precedents, they reminded me of the rules—that a project must demonstrate significant local interest and commitment, and that it must meet the following requirements: legislative resolutions from the California State Assembly and Senate, the L.A. County Supervisors, and the city councils of L.A. and Culver City; a $10 million liability insurance policy; and a $5,000 performance bond to guarantee we'd cover their costs.

The First Urban Forest Tree Run
California Assemblywoman Gwen Moore
planting aleppo pine
alongside Marina Freeway
Los Angeles, California
1979

I had six weeks to find a funding sponsor, recruit and train volunteers, and recruit runners, as well as write, introduce, and pass legislation through five lawmaking bodies and find someone to sell us a small insurance policy.

There was nothing I could do but do it.

We found friendly legislators who agreed to introduce and carry the legislation on a fast track. I recruited a local radio station to help with publicity and a lumber company to buy the T-shirts. I worked up a logistics plan and turned it over to a team of specialized volunteers—ham radio operators and off-road vehicle club members—while I appeared before the assembly Transportation Committee in Sacramento. I needed to testify on the purpose of the run before they would approve the bill and send it to two other committees, the full assembly

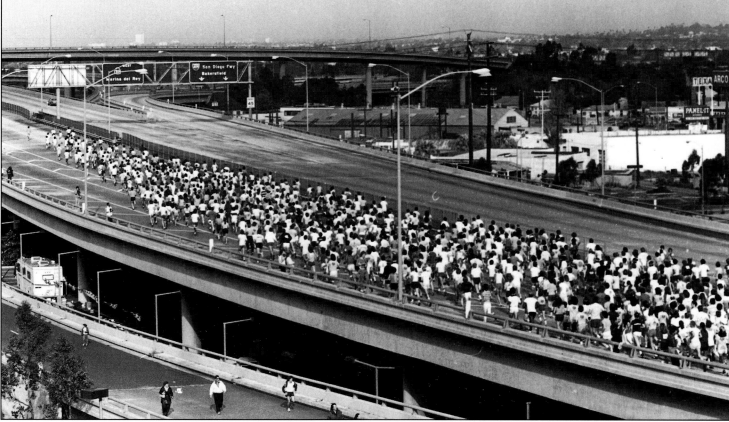

TRAFFIC JAM — Traffic moves at a trot on the Marina Freeway during 10-kilometer Urban Forest Run. Freeway was closed to autos for the occaision — a California first. Jeff Clark was first man across finish line, and women's winner was Andrea Hardy.

Photo: Art Rogers, Courtesy of the *Los Angeles Times*

The First Urban Forest Tree Run

A ten kilometer run and tree planting
Los Angeles, California
1979

and the senate. With three days to go, the resolution was approved by the senate and faxed to Caltrans. Officials were so stunned they pulled out all the stops to help with final details.

Meanwhile, I'd discovered that only Lloyds of London would sell us the insurance—and at a cost greater than the projected run proceeds. Happily, our radio sponsor was a subsidiary of ABC, which ultimately covered us under its insurance umbrella at no cost.

Nearly 10,000 people showed, and 5,000 ran. Everyone took home seedlings, and some even stopped to landscape the freeway! The event received heavy media attention, including front page cover photos in the local dailies, both of which used the term "urban forest" in a headline for the first time.

I organized three more runs in succeeding years. Perhaps we put a crack in the freeway belief system. Who knows? At any rate, a lush grove of trees now shades the Marina Freeway.

Martin Luther King Jr. Boulevard

As I expanded my understanding of the human role in ecosystems, I translated my knowledge into projects that invited people not only to participate but to commu-

Andy Lipkis

nicate the message. Hence the notion of "citizen forestry." I coined the term to give credence to our super-volunteers. People had begun to respond to what was happening in their neighborhoods, and I wanted to nurture the power they possessed to reshape their communities.

Citizen Foresters were being trained and supported by TreePeople. Yet despite the impact on their neighborhoods, they didn't seem to be valued for the incredible work they were doing. To everyone, neighborhood-scale revitalization appeared insignificant next to L.A.'s overwhelming scale and its mounting problems.

Citizen Forestry needed a media frame so that practitioners could be recognized and regular citizens could begin to participate at the neighborhood level, block-by-block, across the entire city.

The perfect opportunity, as usual, presented itself.

Martin Luther King Jr. Boulevard is a seven mile long street running through south central Los Angeles. As has happened in many U.S. cities, this street was renamed as a monument to Dr. King. As is also frequently the case, L.A.'s King Boulevard runs through many economically depressed neighborhoods, and is not very pretty. Eudora Russell, a Citizen Forester, shared with me her feeling that the street should be a beautiful symbol of hope and strength instead of another ugly boulevard.

Eudora had written the mayor, but to no avail. She asked me how to get the city to act. Aware of its escalating budget crisis, I knew the city wasn't likely to commit several million dollars anytime soon. I suggested we challenge the entire community to do the job itself, and added that it would be especially potent if we could plant trees the entire length of the street in one day—on Dr. King's birthday. Eudora loved the idea. We wanted to see who else might go for it.

We called a meeting, inviting another Citizen Forester, Fred Anderson, and representatives of the three city council offices whose districts were involved. The group was noncommittal. Fred was so excited, he left his job to coordinate the entire project.

Martin Luther King, Jr. Blvd.
Tree Planting

A 7 mile long tree planting of 400 trees
by 3,000 people
Los Angeles, California
1990

**Martin Luther King, Jr. Blvd.
Tree Planting**

Los Angeles, California
1990

The story of the project is documented in TreePeople's manual, *The Simple Act of Planting a Tree*. The following is a summary.

The King Boulevard Memorial Committee was formed with four months to pull the project together. The work included planning, fundraising, and outreach to local schools, community groups, and churches. Volunteers canvassed the street, inviting the participation of residents and shopkeepers. We negotiated with police and city agencies for required permits. Volunteer management included recruitment, training, assignment, and rehearsals for more than 1,000 people. Many agencies, groups, and corporations joined in, including the Gas Company and the Chevy-Geo Environmental Program.

The committee organized a poster and writing contest for students to further deepen the educational and involvement aspects of the project.

A day before the planting, we realized the contractors who were cutting planting holes in the concrete sidewalks were way behind schedule. We called the Gas Company, which recruited employees as volunteers. Emergency jackhammer crews broke concrete into the night.

The big day arrived—it was raining! Nevertheless, 3,000 people appeared and took up positions on both sides of the seven mile long boulevard. To make it more manageable and intimate, we divided the street into twenty-five two-block-long units. Each unit had a host, a greeter, a planting teacher, a portable toilet, tools, supplies, water, a birthday cake, and a two-way radio.

People came from all over southern California—as individuals, as families, as employee teams. Dr. King's message has touched a great diversity of people, and

Andy Lipkis

the planters reflected that diversity in a youngster-to-old-timer mix of African, Asian, Hispanic, and European Americans. Strangers dug, sweated, and laughed together. Most worked in teams of four to six.

Mayor Tom Bradley planted a ceremonial tree, and was moved to tears by the sight of miles upon miles of his citizens lining the street, helping to heal their city.

Three hours later, 400 trees were in the ground and watered. Planting teams recruited a resident or shopkeeper to adopt each tree and commit to its watering, care, and protection. Together, team members named and dedicated their trees and signed their own names to vinyl stickers affixed to the support stakes. The trees were only six feet tall, but still they transformed the street. As cleanup was completed, a rainbow graced the eastern sky, bringing a final blessing to a miraculous day.

Participation went beyond the 3,000 people who picked up shovels. Those who watched—on the street or on television—shared the accomplishment. Political leaders saw, perhaps for the first time, the real power and potential of coordinated grass-roots community involvement. Those who participated understood that they could personally make a visible difference.

That was four years ago. Every month since, TreePeople and the King Boulevard Committee have organized events for watering, weeding, and feeding the trees. All are thriving and many are over fifteen feet tall. Numerous community groups in the area have since organized their own planting projects.

The Next Frontier!

Given the urgency of the global environmental crisis, it is critical that we quickly find a way to galvanize human ingenuity and energy, and harness it to yield long-term sustainability.

Imagine every human being on Earth educated, technically equipped, motivated, and charged with the responsibility to manage the environment where they live, work, and play. Imagine this simply being a part of each of our daily lives. The information, resources, and technology exist, but none in a widely-accessible form.

Even given access, most people need role models to help convert them from house-potato to healer. Along with role models and technology, we usually also need to observe the success at the end of that different pathway before we'll risk eschewing old familiar ways.

This, therefore, is my next challenge: to heal the environment by combining hard science and technology with entertainment and environmental management.

I'm currently developing a simulated model for an entire operating ecosystem, using computers to condense space, time, and supposedly unconnected pieces of reality. It will enable people to quickly see the long term results of their actions. The goal is to demonstrate that:
   — many disparate elements are closely linked,
   — the world can and should be viewed from a global,
   whole systems perspective,
   — every daily human habit has either a positive or negative
   impact on the environment.

My goal is to see this used as a planning tool for individuals, corporate leaders, and elected officials, to help them gauge the local, regional, and global impacts of their decisions and actions.

I believe another needed element is a high-visibility TV drama series that makes heroes out of everyday people committed to environmental healing. The storyline would reveal all the challenges (bureaucratic red tape, physical, emotional, and psychological roadblocks, and seemingly hopeless situations) and all the pathways to success, including the "win-win" problem-solving style.

Finally, it's critical to include a demonstration of integrated urban ecosystem management.

It is my hope that this project will change not only the way people relate to their environment, but the way urban infrastructures are managed. It's the culmination of my 25-year vision to reconnect people with their vital role in Nature. It would enable us all to realize, on a practical level, that our thoughts, our energy, our emotions—even our technologies—are part of Nature. Our personal health, happiness, and success are linked to the role each of us needs to play in the repair and operation of the ecosystem.

To realize this project, I am developing a number of models that demonstrate the basic cycles and mechanisms of an ecosystem. I am using the simplicity of a forest ecosystem as my visual metaphor. The forest model is easily overlaid on a city model to demonstrate where Nature's cycles have been broken and where positive human intervention can assist Nature in repairing itself.

The models will range from living demonstrations to posters and public service announcements to interactive multimedia presentations. Some will be designed to generate cost/benefit analyses, and to demonstrate the difference in the two paths we face, calculating the resources used or conserved by a certain action, the pollution generated or dissipated, the economic opportunities developed, etc.

The first model is for the thousands of students and families who visit TreePeople's headquarters annually. They will be invited to be part of a mini watershed, and to play with it as it works. Visitors will be issued umbrellas as they walk into a simulated urban rainstorm and watch stormwater rush across asphalt and pavement, carrying with it spilled oil, beer cans, and other litter. They will observe an identical site retrofitted with a forest—trees surrounded by mulch—and cisterns. They'll note how rainfall is absorbed and pollutants either stay put, or in the case of some toxins, are treated by soil micro-organisms. They'll return to the urban scene to follow the polluted run-off into the storm drains. Sliding down a slide through a huge drainpipe, they'll follow the path of the water to a beach where the runoff and pollutants are dumped. Viewing the results of rainwater on two city settings, they'll see the opportunities accessible to them to make an improvement.

The project doesn't stop with presentations; it creates opportunities for people to participate as environmental managers of their homes, neighborhoods, and places of work. The first demonstration will involve residents managing the land around their homes as a watershed. They'll plant trees to shade and cool their homes, make mulch and compost of the "green waste" from their trees and gardens, and install cisterns to capture the rainwater for landscape irrigation.

For individuals, this will:
— reduce the energy needed for air conditioning,
— potentially cut in half their consumption of city-supplied water,
— cut by one-third the waste they send to the landfill,
— sharply reduce the amount of potentially polluted stormwater
that leaves their property, thereby lowering the amount of toxics
flowing into rivers and bays downstream.

When applied to an entire city, these individual actions yield a powerful economic tool that can lead not only to the creation of sustainable jobs, but to substantial environmental healing. These are current examples of the path of expression I feel driven to take to help steer us away from the brink.

Human beings are viewed as the most destructive force on the planet. My personal mission is to effect a perceptual shift in the population that will enable people to use their energies—creative, spiritual, intuitive, and physical—to become the most efficient and effective healing force available. Given the right communication tools, this shift can happen practically overnight, and it can yield an environmental force bigger than anything that can ever be created by government action.

Betsy Damon

No doubt the first success occurred in water—the biological equivalent of the big bang of the cosmophysicists, very likely a singular phenomenon.
— LEWIS THOMAS, *The Fragile Species*, SPECULATING ON THE ORIGINS OF DNA

I believe that a group of committed people can address any challenge concerning water, or any other issue, and solve the difficulties in ways that respect the dynamic Universe and every individual. The key to our success is relationships!

My art rises from an awareness that all things are interconnected. But it is not a conceptual dialogue about connections. My work is action—action that motivates, connects, and possibly at times, changes lives, which I hope invites or offers the possibility of connections.

Becoming aware that relationships are the core of all activities was an evolutionary process for me. It began in 1972 when I founded the Feminist Art Studio at Cornell University. It developed further through my workshops on power and creativity with women in the '70s. Looking back, it is clear to me that my life, and in particular my art, has been about stretching for aliveness, and essential to this process is being in community and building relationships.

Water is Life.
— AN AFRICAN PROVERB

A Memory of Clean Water

Water forms and informs every movement and detail of our world including the shape and motion of our hearts. Human beings and water are in every way absolutely interdependent, yet most people know very little about water. Turn on the tap and there it is. If it is polluted, buy bottled water or a purifier. With modern technology, our understanding of water has become extremely specific and yet considerably foreign. It is difficult to conceptualize the fact that 83,000 possible contaminants exist in our water. Testing, monitoring, and understanding the actual impact of these chemicals is virtually impossible. Bottled water and purifiers are certainly not true solutions. (The Environmental Protection Agency recently set standards for only 83 of the contaminants.)

My interest in water issues was first triggered in 1984 during a seven week camping trip with my two teenagers in the Southwest. En route to a Native American Sun Dance, I encountered dry

Water is the most abundant element on the planet's surface as well as in the composition of our bodies. No wonder we take it for granted. We have been asleep as clean, living water has become a memory. Betsy Damon has dedicated her art to awakening our memory.

≈

In Memory of Clean Water
Paper casting of dry river bed
Castle Valley, Utah
1985

Your Body Is Water
River Delta and Human Artery System
1993

In Memory of Clean Water

Lifting off of paper cast
Castle Valley, Utah
1985

river beds everywhere. I learned these bared "bones" of the Earth were caused by damming and excessive use of water. Later in the year I started No Limits for Women Artists, a support network that had nothing to do with water issues, but prompted me to explore my passions. One day I asked two friends a "no limits" question—"If you could do anything, what would you do?"—and they in turn posed the question to me. I then verbalized my fantasy of casting one of the dry river beds.

By October 1985 I found myself in Castle Valley, Utah, casting 200 feet of dry river bed in hand-made paper. This large scale undertaking was funded by a grant from the Massachusetts Council on the Arts through the Danforth Museum. The installation eventually traveled to many museums and was included in numerous exhibitions during a seven year period.

A crew of ten remarkable people worked with me for three weeks. We named the piece *A Memory of Clean Water* after I heard that uranium tailings, fertilizers, and other toxic wastes had destroyed the water quality in the region. I thought to myself, "If the water here is undrinkable, then this must be true all over the place."

It was this work that inspired me to commit myself as an artist to clean, living water. I deliberately made water central to my life, both as an issue and as a metaphor. In doing this I soon learned that I had chosen the ultimate teacher. I realized that keeping the ecosystem alive and myself alive were one and the same activity. The project set me on a road that insisted I learn about myself.

Everything flows; nothing remains
one cannot step into the same river twice.
—HERAKLEITOS, *translated by Guy Davenport*

Keepers of the Waters: Citizens Rights and Responsibilities

Subsequent to *A Memory of Clean Water*, I spent several years researching water issues and creating a series of water-related artworks. My reading led me to consider the physics, spirituality, and history of water, as well as the relationship between disease and water. Daily life in our society hardly lends access to such knowledge. The tremendous damage caused by the floods of the summer of 1993 is testimony to the fact that respect for the dynamics of rivers and modern hydraulic engineering have not been one and the same. From straightening rivers to building on flood

Betsy Damon

plains to dumping toxic waste near water sources, it is evident that many people are unaware of, or disregard, basic laws of the water cycle.

By 1989 I had conceptualized a community outreach effort called *Keepers of the Waters: Citizens Rights and Responsibilities*. I moved from New York to Minnesota because Minnesota contains the head waters of the Mississippi and is the home to more water than any other state. *Keepers of the Waters* might be viewed as a metaphor for water in that it is inclusive, flexible to any

In Memory of Clean Water
Danforth Museum
Farmingham, Massachusetts
1986

situation, and able to nurture and sustain a community. The project builds relationships among artists, scientists, and community members by focusing on solutions to water issues through art and education. It seeks to do the following: connect people, inspire initiative and hope, educate the community about water, point people in the direction of caring, create a new imagery and language about water, and facilitate change in the treatment of water.

The project was difficult to fund because it was difficult to categorize: was it art, science, environmental education, or (?). I eventually developed *Keepers of the Waters* with the Humphrey Institute of Public Affairs. They supplied a full time administrator, and the Jerome Foundation provided a grant for workshops that brought artists and scientists together, and assisted artistic involvement throughout communities.

Keepers of the Waters inspired many divergent groups to work together on water issues. All of the 4H groups in the state devoted a year to water; the Minneapolis Institute of Art developed a docent led program using works in their collections that related to water; and churches and garden clubs organized activities around water.

With funding from 3M, I did a pilot program in Anoka, a small community near the Twin Cities. An unprecedented number of people came to the project's open meetings. Citizens passionately wanted to do something to preserve their water, but many were not even aware that it came from a fragile 12,000-year-old aquifer threatened by development. With support from the mayor's office, the high school initiated an excellent water program, and the community created murals, plays, and poetry and organized a festival around water quality issues. The city made plans to create a park that would include water education.

I received funding to do *Out of Site; Out of Mind*, an event that involved the capping of a well. Between 10,000 and 30,000 wells in this country are left uncapped and often abandoned. They can be thought of as direct openings into the Earth's body, open arteries into which anything can be and is dumped. If a person owns land with a well on it, then that well is theirs to tend to or mistreat. The law protects the property owner, regardless of what effect their dumping has on the underlying aquifer.

As word of this project got around, I was asked by Jill Jacoby of the Pollution Control Agency in Duluth to do a *Keepers of the Waters* project for the St. Louis River. In April of 1993 the St. Louis River Watch, a program administered by the Pollution Control Agency, began collaborating with local artists, Citizen Advisory Committee members, teachers, activists, and scientists in the Duluth area to pilot the program.

The primary goals were to preserve and improve the water quality of the St. Louis River and Lake Superior; to provide education and outreach using art as a medium for communication; to provide information to citizens so that they could participate in collective decision making; and to create an opportunity for artists

Your Body Is Water
Apex of the Heart
1993

and scientists to work together in devising practical ways to disseminate technical information.

We have organized artist/scientist teams who work with people of all ages in the schools, the Art Institute, and the Lake Superior Center. Some of the projects include an invitational art exhibit and Earth Day Gallery Hop for Earth Day 1994 with a theme on water quality concerns; a recipe book, *Slug Bread and Beheaded Thistles, Non Toxic Methods of Pest and Grunge Control*, and satirical theater presentations from Colder by the Lake focusing on fish consumption advisories, fish deformities, and the newest fashion statement—the litmus bathing suit. Radio and television spots appear frequently.

These projects will culminate in a multimedia estuary park on the grounds outside the Lake Superior Center. The environmental walk will integrate sound and visuals created by many segments of the community to illuminate the thousands of life forms that thrive in the estuary and to identify the sources of the toxins that threaten them with extinction. Young people, seniors, and many other sections of the community will work with an artist to contribute visuals that will be organized to emulate the ebb and flow of the estuary. Finally, we will have a human board game showing the environmental consequences that human actions have on water quality and a book documenting all the events of the *Keepers of the Waters* program in the St. Louis River Watershed.

Keepers of the Waters is being adopted by numerous communities who want to use the model or adapt it to their needs. Each community has different issues, challenges, and resources, and this model builds on the initiative, enthusiasm, and resources that various organizations and individuals contribute to the project and their community.

One of the foundations of my work is the belief that water quality means more than processed, chlorinated, or filtered water; it means water that creates and sustains life. In pursuit of this truth, I went to Chengdu, China to study a sacred water site and learn about the role of water in traditional Chinese medicine. Through talking about my art in China, I got artists and others thinking about contemporary water issues as related to art. Water became the theme of the first Ecology and Traditional Chinese Medicine Conference in Chengdu. At the conference, I talked about water, health, science, and art. Their relationships were readily understood, since they have been fundamental in Chinese medicine and society for thousands of years. The notion that art can empower, inform, and incite discourse about living water, as well as inspire actions that insist on change, was immediately comprehended. It was only a small step to conceptualize programs that begin to address the large environmental issues facing China today, where rivers are sewers for everything from factories to fields.

I was able to return with renewed determination to persist in models that invite collaborations. I had new ideas for approaching the Mississippi, with its cancer corridor, and addressing the separation not only between information and activities but the deeper separation between people and the source of their water and the reality that water is the source of everything.

Betsy Damon

Vijali

The seeds of ritual, earth art, and world family were embedded in my early childhood. My mother and father divorced when I was two years old and I was placed in child care homes. Eventually I lived with my grandmother and enrolled in a private girls' school. At fourteen, I made the decision to enter the Vedanta Convent, where I stayed for ten years. I feel very thankful for my early beginnings. Because of my childhood, I have always had need of family, but since I didn't experience a conventional upbringing, my idea of family grew to become a world family.

At the age of six I remember going behind my grandmother's house to a place where I could hide behind tall weeds. I would sit for hours in a circle of stones that I had thoughtfully gathered, and arrange the dandelions I had picked from the front lawn. This space was so special. I never revealed it to anyone, not even my closest playmates. How comforting to be there as I mourned the death of a girlfriend or wept for my mother and father.

The objects of ritual are always at hand. Stones are altars. Sunlight shining through leaves is stained glass. Trees are pillars holding up the vaulted sky. Rivers are baptismal waters. Flowers are incense of the Earth.

As an Earth artist, the processes of carving, painting, and performance are themselves rituals. When I became frustrated with the commercialism of the art scene in 1975, I closed my studio and started creating art and eventually community through a process of ritual.

I kept expanding the borders of my sculpture and art, so that my art became life itself. The media was not only the stone, but the people around me—their problems, their hopes and dreams for the future. For many years I traveled in various countries, and at the completion of each stone sculpture, created rituals as a voice of the community. These creative expressions evolved into the concept of the *Theater of the Earth*, embracing the whole of life.

World Wheel: Theater of the Earth

The form of the *World Wheel* emerged from dreams and meditations over a period of many years. In 1986, I started on a journey around the globe, creating stone earth sculptures and ritual performances in twelve nations. These works create a physical circle around the world close to the 40th parallel: Malibu, in the Los Angeles area; the Seneca Reservation in the state of New York; the Alicante area by the Mediterranean Sea in Spain; the Umbrian Forest outside Gubio, Italy; the island of Tinos in Greece; the desert of Egypt; the banks of the Dead Sea in Israel/Palestine; a village in West Bengal, India; a cave in Shoto Terdrom, Tibet; Xishan Forest Park in Kunming, China; Lake Baikal in Siberia; and the completion of this *World Wheel* in Japan. My intention was to work within a community in each of these areas of the world. I planned to ask three questions:

— Where has our spirit come from?
— What is our imbalance, our sickness?
— What can heal us, what can bring us back to harmony?

I would base my performances and sculptures upon the responses to these questions.

Vijali's World Wheel *project has taken her to twelve sites along the 40th parallel. She has reached into the communicative power of the visual and performing arts to carry the message around the world that we are ultimately one people from one common origin— the Earth*

≈

**World Wheel
Western Gateway**

Site 1, Earth Wheel
Malibu, California
1987

Western Gateway

Performance by Georgianne Cowan
Representing our origins

Malibu

Before I had the right to involve other communities, I felt I needed to begin this work within the community of my place of birth, Los Angeles. A few of us from the community would go to the ocean and gather colored stones, then bring them to the site in the Santa Monica Mountains, overlooking the Pacific Ocean. We used the stones to develop a large earth wheel. This work was performed as a ritual in the silence of meditation.

The first question: Where has our spirit come from? was interpreted as a meditation by Georgianne Cowen, a visual and performing artist. She created a performance piece representing our origins, emerging out of the water of a lake at the site. She had a membrane skin suit made for herself and another performer. The performance began as the two emerged out of the water onto the sandy shoal as androgynous beings. As they peeled out of their skins, they were revealed as man and woman, black and white. People with animal masks were standing on the stone outcropping of the surrounding

Vijali

hills, silhouetted against the sky. Their sounds punctuated the silence.

Since I always like to dissolve the barriers between the audience and the performance, we all moved together from the lake to the slope of the hills where the earth sculpture lay. Here, Anne Mavor developed a piece around the second question: What is our imbalance, our sickness? On the slope our problems were depicted as the arrogance found in the United States, our thinking that we know what is right for other people, other countries. This arrogance has only brought on the death of people, the death of other cultures.

As Anne's performance ended, I emerged above the Earth Wheel with my response to the third question: What can heal us, what can bring us back to harmony? Silhouetted against the sky with my hair woven in a tumbleweed, my body and clothes stained with mud, as Gaia, I beckoned people to come up the hill, to come back to the understanding that we are Earth, that we are not separate beings but one community, one Earth Family.

The healing of the audience/participants took place as they responded personally to the three questions. In this last segment the people came into the circle, into the ritual of pouring water over the stone, allowing the heat of the fire, stone, water, and air to become one in the rising steam. All joined in, following the performers as they danced into the evening in celebration of the unity of animals, plants, stones, people, and all life as one world family.

**World Wheel
Western Gateway**

Vijali performing as Gaia, beckoning the participants to come back to the understanding that we are Earth

Western Gateway

Vijali as Gaia performing Purfication Water Ceremony with Dan Kwong

Bengal, India

While in India, the seventh site of the *World Wheel*, I was traveling on a train when I heard lively music down the corridor. The musicians came to my compartment; they looked so fascinating in their ocher clothes, beads, and long hair wound on top of their heads. Their music was so vital that I kept giving them coins so they would stay. I found out that they were Bauls, folk musicians from West Bengal. Before they left my compartment, they invited me to their village.

Their village is very poor. The wife of one of the Bauls brought out a straw mat for me and laid it under a tree by their hut. When I peeked in their house, it had a dirt floor, three pots hung on the wall, and a wooden board with a cloth on it for their bed. The wife brought me delicious spiced tea. The children of the village put garlands of jasmine around my neck and danced and sang for me. Bauls from another village were passing through and joined in the singing. The stars and Moon appeared. This community gave me the most hospitable and beautiful evening of my life.

They found a hut for me, and I moved into the village. As I stayed with them, I became aware of their poverty and felt that a sculpture would be totally inappropriate. I kept imagining them all sitting down in one circle. Finally I realized what was needed: a communal house—a commons—a lodge where they could come together, for many of the Bauls were wanderers with no home. Here they could practice and perform their music, have their own pujas (ceremonies). The house could also serve as a schoolroom for their children.

Western Gateway
Closing Celebration of our One Earth Family
of animals, plants, and stones

Photo: Eric Lawton

Vijali

World Wheel
Baul Kutir
(Heart of the Bauls)
Site 8,
Start of construction of the community house
Shyambati, Subhas Pally,
Santiniketan, District Birbhum,
West Bengal, India
1991

I decided to build a round house with one door and eleven windows, representing the unity of life of the *World Wheel*. With a string tied to a stick in the center, I made a circle on the ground. The children came and sat in this circle, knowing it was their place. The house that became known as Baul Kutir, the Baul Heart, was built out of the same materials as the homes: mud, bamboo, and rice grass for the thatched roof. I hired and worked alongside an outcast who badly needed the work and who had experience in building huts. The Bauls only sing—they don't do any physical work. At first they just watched me, their honored guest, hanging out with the low castes in the mud. One Baul started to help, then his brother came, then the father, and soon someone else in the village would stop and say, "Oh, my goodness, you don't do it that way, here, let me show you." That's how it happened.

We had a ceremony at the completion of the house that was attended by everyone. The Bauls sat all together in a circle, in spite of the very strict caste rules of the village. They sang the responses to the three question.

Baul Kutir

Above:
Starting the roof

Left:
Building the Dhuni, the sacred fire pit

World Wheel
Baul Kutir

Ritual burying of the earth from
the other World Wheel sites.

Baul Kutir

Baul musician, Basuev Das Baul, playing
during the opening ceremony of the house

Baul Kutir

Finished community house

« WHERE DO WE COME FROM?
We come from the womb of our mother, from the mother who is the Earth.
We are part of the great cosmic goddess, Kali.
WHAT IS YOUR IMBALANCE?
We are exhausted and under strain all the time.
We have to leave our homes to wander and sing so we can earn money.
When we return home, we often don't even have enough for food.
WHAT COULD HEAL YOUR PROBLEM?
To really love our singing and not worry about the future. Just to keep
on doing what we are doing, but give up the anxiety and be present
with every moment of our day. »

I returned in May 1992 for the first annual celebration of the house's completion,
attended by 450 people from all over West Bengal. I was very happy to see that
everyone was using the house. The children were using it as their school, which the
Bauls were teaching five days a week. It had also become a gathering place for the
village festivals and pujas.

Vijali

World Wheel
Tenkawa Ancient Shinto Site
Site 12,
Priest, Mikinosuke Kakisaka,
during World Wheel ceremony
Nara Prafecture, Japan
1993

Japan

Japan was very different for me. I collaborated with Japanese artists and with Dominique Mazeaud, an artist and curator from Santa Fe, New Mexico. Her contribution was the weaving of a web of connection between ourselves and the places and people of Japan.

Three events took place at three separate sites in Japan. The first was a ritual performance in the center of Ichi Ikeda's Breathing Water Circle and Action. The next event was at the performance artist Rui Sekido's family property in Yuguchizawa, where he holds a yearly festival for performance art. The climactic third event was at Tenkawa, an ancient Shinto site, in the mountains of Nara Prefecture, that honors Benzaiten, the goddess of arts, wisdom, and water. It was a full harvest Moon on October 30, 1993, the moment of completion for the seven year pilgrimage of the *World Wheel*.

It rained heavily on this day, jeopardizing our planned outdoor activity with Ichi Ikeda. Two hours before we were scheduled to begin the ceremony/performance, the head Shinto priest, Mikinosuke Kakisaka, talked with us and asked me about the content of the ceremony. I told him, "The ceremony is a prayer for the realization of our true nature without boundaries, that will lead us to world peace." He said, "Benzaiten has brought this rain. God's grace has brought us together in this way because she wants you to join us inside her shrine."

In my first days at Tenkawa, I carved twelve stones with patterns found in Nature that represented the twelve countries of the *World Wheel*. These carvings were moved to the center of the shrine and placed in a large circle with sacred cedar branches and candles. The priest encompassed my offering within another circle of cedar branches.

As he walked in at the beginning of the ceremony, I thought, "This is what I was trying to have happen. But the Universe created it in its own way; the rain brought a strong male energy into this circle, bringing a balance of the yin and yang, a pattern of completion and harmony of the *World Wheel*."

The ceremony began with the priest drumming on the giant Shinto drum and chanting. I stood in the dark at the center of the circle, all in black with my face painted as emptiness—an open blue sky. One half hour passed. I slipped into the stillness and borderlessness of my own essence. When the drumming came to an end, we both walked to the altar and gave offerings and prayer. When I returned to the center, an assistant priest lit the twelve candles in the stone circle, and I began to slowly move to the south with the sound of a digeridu. When I stopped, the digeridu stopped, and the tones and wail of Earth's sadness and the sorrow of her children poured from my belly. Then slowly I returned to the center, sensing the loss of my individual identity and an opening up to our shared universal energy. I stood at the center until the music drew me to the other cardinal directions of the circle. I stopped in the east and stood, as Emptiness, at the point of new beginnings, the rise of a new Sun. An ancient Sanskrit hymn to the Divine Mother of the Universe leapt from my mouth. Without planning, my movements and voice embodied the answers to my three questions.

The priest then came to the circle and sat in the south to perform a Shinto fire ceremony. He asked Dominique and me to sit in the west and east with the goddess Benzaiten to the north. We held the energy of the four directions as the fire burned in the center.

At the completion of the ceremony, the priest took the stone that the Dalai Lama had blessed and the earth from all twelve nations of the World Wheel and led me to a rectangular piece of earth honored by a braided rope with white ties. He said, "This is the most sacred spot of Earth. Not even the priests are allowed to enter." He asked me to reach into this holy ground and bury the stone and earth. He turned to me and said, "The Earth and Cosmos have heard your sincere prayer dance, and it will be answered." His words aren't necessarily the truth, but I felt they came from the energy of the evening, from a larger part of the Universe than his personality.

The next day the stone carvings were placed around the crystal shrine as a permanent installation. Our closest new friends and family came together in a final ceremony. To my amazement, there were twelve people, six men and six women. This symbolized for me the balance that I had hoped for, a pattern of harmony and peace, set in motion, that can infiltrate the world.

The closing twenty-four hours of the *World Wheel* came about without any conscious plan on my part. Its completion was truly honored by the support and participation of the priest and by his desire to have earth from the other countries mix with the shrine's sacred ground. It was an acknowledgment of the essence of the *World Wheel* pilgrimage: of the unity of the world family, of all people, animals, plants, and stones coming into the wheel as one mind, one body, and one heart.

**World Wheel
Concentric Circles;
With One Heart, One Mind**

One of a series of carved stones
that were left at the shrine
Nara Prefecture, Japan
1993

Vijali

226 / 227

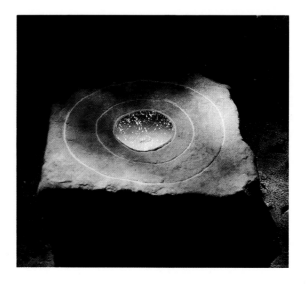

Tom Van Sant

The GeoSphere Project

In the 1960s, Buckminister Fuller advanced the idea that we are all travelers on the spaceship Earth. His analogy helped us begin to realize that we share the same habitat and live in a closed system. The Gaia hypothesis, which was set forth by Dr. James Lovelock, represents the next level of understanding. Named after the Greek goddess, the Gaia hypothesis interprets the Earth as organism-like because of the interdependent and self-regulating aspects of its systems. The Earth is not a spaceship; it is a planet of which we are a part, from which we emerged, so to speak. The elements that make up our planet are debris from the explosion of stars. We are surely children of the Universe, and our life is a product of this great system.

I believe that Earth resource management will be the primary issue of the coming decade and century. *The GeoSphere Project* ™ intends to make the complex issue more easily understood by providing a giant reality model of the Earth. Growing up, I spent a lot of time in the forests, on the desert, and in the mountains where Nature prevailed. I am also very sensitive to all the various species of the world. We are not the only occupants of the planet, and have traditionally dealt with other species with less respect than I wish we did. I think one of the ways human beings will start treating each other with more respect is by treating other species and ecosystems with respect as well.

The deterioration of Earth's resources—tropical forests, the ecosystem of the ocean, ozone depletion, loss of species habitat, and consequently loss of species— concerns me greatly. There are no shortcuts for turning around man's attitude toward Nature. It doesn't help to lobby decision-makers unless you can inform their constituents. My vision of the *GeoSphere Project* emerged as I began to see no other alternative but the education of everyone.

The global issues of deforestation, desertification, global warming, acid rain, and toxic waste disposal are so complex and involve so many factors that the only way I believe we can understand them is through visualization. It is fine to look at globes that show all the political boundaries, but I think it is also time to start seeing the reality of the Earth.

Responsible Earth resource management must be humankind's highest priority. Presently, all countries and institutions report their gross national products without taking into account any of the nonrenewable resources utilized in the production of these GNPs. There is nothing more fundamentally flawed than this accounting, as it is not an accurate indicator for any future projection. Good management is the ability to project the consequences of resource allotment, and this is what we must do with regard to the Earth's resources. It is as though we were running a company in which we eat away at our principle and pretend that it is profit. Is there any better formula for failure through bad management? The *Geosphere* visualization system will provide for understanding these kinds of relationships as never before.

Should the World Bank contemplate giving support to a developement project in the Amazon, it could not now see through the *GeoSphere* all the ramifications of that decision. Policy-makers should be allowed to see what the Amazon basin looked like in the past, what it is today, and what it will be in the future with present

Tom Van Sant's work with

The GeoSphere Project is providing

a valuable resource that helps us to

visualize the impact that

we are having on the planet.

His GeoSphere is the

first visually accurate image of the

entire surface of the planet.

With his Global Visual Library,

he has begun the process

of setting up a

worldwide computer network

that provides images which help us

to see and understand the

complex global relationships

that are affecting

all of our lives.

≈

Above and Right:
**Reflections from Earth
Shadow Mountain Eye**

Mirrors creating an image for
a *Landsat* satellite. Image can be seen in
upper right corner of larger view at right.

**Reflections From Earth
Shadow Mountain Eye**

Placing mirrors
Mojave Desert, California
1980

Ryan's Eye

Man-made image of submicron scale

Tom Van Sant

policies in place. We can visually show them what the rain forests will look like in 2010 if the same rate of deforestation persists. Earth resource studies are essential ingredients to the formation of public policy. It makes perfect sense for an artist to head a scientific project with this goal. The world of technology needs the service of artists to take on these issues and communicate them in visual terms.

Artists throughout history have worked with the tools of their time. I love everything that has to do with the sky, and I love looking at the Earth from above. I became fascinated with remote sensing from satellites. In 1980, I placed sunlight-reflecting mirrors in the Mojave Desert to overexpose the sensors of the *Landsat* satellite passing overhead. The mirrors were set out in the shape of a giant eye when viewed from 500 miles above the Earth. The overexposure created a drawing of a giant eye, about 2.5 kilometers across, or 100,000 times the size of a human eye. This mirror reflection project with the *Landsat* satellite was an effort to come to terms with the issue of scale—our human scale versus planetary scale. Two years later, I created a tiny eye, 100,000 times smaller than the human eye, at the National Research and Resource Facilty for Sub-micron Structures at Cornell University. In working with these technologies, I came to understand how multi-specture scanners and electron microscopes work. Also through my work with geographic information systems, I learned about the geographic organization of materials. As an artist, former city planner and architect, I understand the organization of information as seen from inside and from above. *The GeoSphere Project* draws upon all the different dimensions of my professional career, providing me with a great sense of purpose and sastisfaction.

Before committing to the *GeoSphere Project*, I had a very personal experience that was related to my eyesight. An infection developed after I received a cornea transplant, and nearly claimed my vision. Treatment called for the administration of five different antibiotics in my eyes every half-hour, twenty-four hours a day, for ten days. I was never able to go to sleep. So instead of fighting it and trying to sleep, I pursued meditation for ten days. Meditation has been a part of my life always, but never for such an extended time. My bed remained in an upright position, and I continued to meditate ceaselessly. By the second day, I no longer experienced any effort in dismissing the movie that plays in our heads—the movie about the past or the future. There weren't even any thoughts left to dismiss. I had this extraordinary experience of being truly in neutral gear. When the period ended, I was quite content to stay where I was. I felt no urge to re-involve myself with the world. When I did, I discovered something very surprising—an inability to pay much attention to anything but the *GeoSphere Project*. The experience committed me to the project without allowing me to spend time doing anything else.

It was in the hospital that I began to visualize the *GeoSphere* system: a whole new level of scientific visualization—not a level of greater complexity, but of greater simplicity. The key was in removing secondary symbolism, removing color-coding, removing the levels of language one is forced to learn to understand the issues. Now, the issues become straightforward.

In June of 1989, I began developing the *GeoSphere* image, the first satellite composite view of Earth. I worked with Lloyd Van Warren, James Knighton and Leo Blume, scientists from the Jet Propulsion Laboratory (J.P.L.). NASA agreed to release Warren for six months to work with me. I sold the lot on which I had been planning to build my dream house, and bought a $200,000 Stardent GS 1000 Graphics Supercomputer. My son Ryan and I moved into a Santa Monica garage apartment, and I went to work on *GeoSphere*. The satellites that collect the data we needed follow a polar route—north to south—and after enough orbits they blanketed the globe to transmit pictures in digital form. I hunted through thousands of photo negatives at a government library before buying about $10,000 worth of satellite computer tapes. The tapes held seven days of photos taken over two years on days when the cloud cover was thin. The goal was to find at least one cloud-free satellite picture of every area of the planet. From these we could use Van Warren's computer program to assemble a single mosaic-style tile picture of Earth.

GeoSphere
The artist working on first prototype
1990

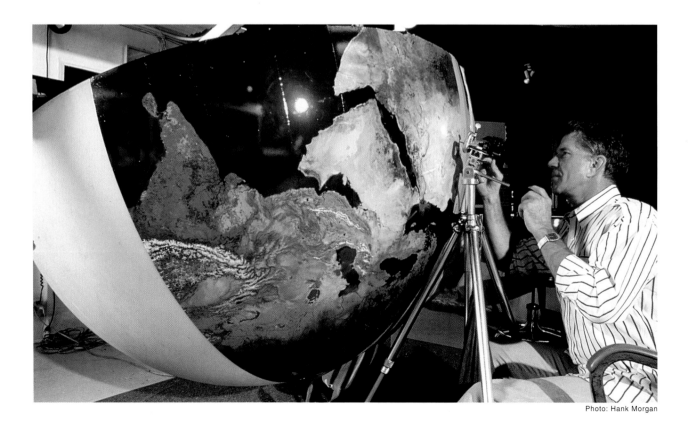

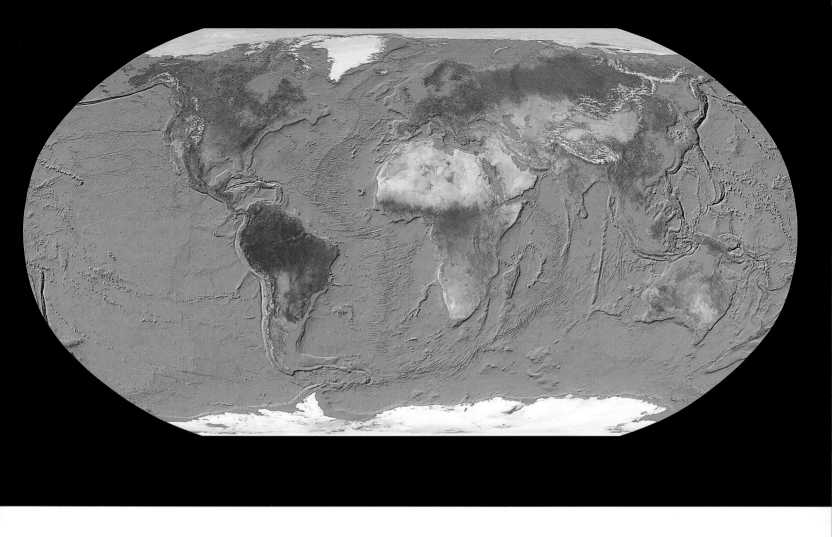

Robinson Projection with Bathymetry
1992

Some areas, such as parts of the Amazon, the Congo, and southern New Zealand, were always covered with clouds. We needed help from Jim Knighton, who had purchased charts and tables, originally compiled by the CIA, describing various rivers and coastlines. Even before we met, Knighton had been using computer graphics to convert these data into picture form. The image of the Earth remained seriously flawed, however, because the colors, coded by scientists concerned with such topics as surface temperature and infrared radiation, were wrong. Heavily forested areas, for example, typically came out red instead of green. Leo Blume, another computer graphics consultant who then worked for J.P.L., designed a program to correct the colors. At every turn, we could move forward with the mosaic only after a technical team created a workable computer medium.

The image that emerged is not quite a photo, though it looks like one. Surface features in perpetually cloud covered areas were traced in through computer graphics and colored as they would appear. Green areas were made a little greener to compensate for natural factors that convert green to a dull brown when viewed from space. Other surface features, such as rivers, were enhanced to make them more visible. The resolution enables us to show any object on the surface that is four kilometers or larger, although a person might need a powerful magnifying glass to see it. The image was printed on a photographic stock that allowed the emulsion to be peeled from the paper. The resulting transparency was then applied with adhesive to the surface of a translucent globe.

Our *GeoSphere*, completed in November of 1990, is the first visually accurate, three-dimensional model of Earth. The globe uses advanced computer technology to control rotation, lighting, audio, projection, and informational programming. We constructed the sphere from translucent fiberglass to allow the surface to be illuminated from within.

Tom Van Sant

The Earth Situation Room Network is a major goal of the *GeoSphere Project*. The room constitutes a clearing house, research center, and software and hardware interface for worldwide research on global change and Earth resource management. It also provides a center for tracking and visualizing topical news events of global concern. The Earth Situation Room will be a combination global file research center, public venue, television studio for producing global change programs for international distribution, and global graphics production station for publishing and computer software industries.

The function of the *GeoSphere* is to provide a three-dimensional icon/screen. A series of projection systems, including video, laser, and 35mm, are used to produce a wide variety of programs. Special interior lighting allows city lights to be viewed on the night side of the planet. The live weather from the GOES or TIROS weather satellites can be projected or applied to the inner or outer surfaces of the clear atmosphere. Time lapse sequences will be used to show global change. These will be projected onto continental overlays acting as area selective screens.

Eventually, the *GeoSphere* will enable us to zoom from a whole-Earth context to a regional high resolution display. By connecting such a zoom to high and low altitude aerial photography, it is possible to perform a complete zoom from the whole Earth to an individual standing on its surface.

We have developed a "Living Earth" visualization featuring the migration of the vegetation band and the seasonal migration of ice down into the oceans and back to the poles. If we project six or eight of these systems onto the *GeoSphere*, overlaying one on top of the other and compressing an entire season's visualization down to twelve seconds per cycle (twelve seconds representing twelve months),

The GeoSphere
Himiji Gas Energy Hall
Osaka Gas
Osaka, Japan

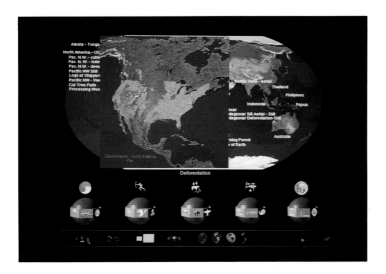

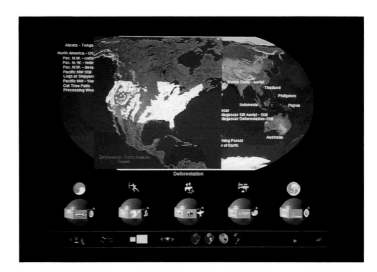

The GeoSphere Project
Global Visual Library

Depicting deforestation pattern
in North America
Image on the left shows the historic forest
and the image on the right shows
the extent of the predicted forest cover

we'll be able to see Earth as a living and breathing entity, as opposed to the rather mechanical model we were brought up with in school. For the first time, we will be able to visualize and understand the wholistic aspects of Earth systems.

The foundation of the visualizations will be vested in the *GeoSphere Project Global Visual Library* ™. This library will consist of global, regional, and site specific databases, coregistered and recolored to the one kilometer resolution *GeoSphere* whole-Earth image. An array of monitors will allow viewers to closely inspect active work stations, monitor individual Earth resource issues, and participate interactively in the management and overlay of the full range of global change issues. The basic Earth Situation Room contains a two meter *GeoSphere*, a set of three monitors, and Macintosh computers running the *Global Visual Library*. We are currently putting together live input portions of live weather, seismic activity, population clocks, shuttle flights, and communications from other expeditions.

The Earth Situation Room is a vehicle and outlet for many types of educational programs. Our images are shown on Whittle Communications Channel One, which now broadcasts into most middle and high schools, reaching half of all the teenagers in America. The same visualizations that we're making for education serve purposes of further research. We're just making them very beautiful and very intuitive, and for the first time we're providing interactive management of the data base. We're writing software that enables users to create their own videos by running multiple overlays—a personal document of inquiry.

The GeoSphere Project
Global Visual Library

Depicting deforestation pattern in South
America. Left image is the historic rainforest
and the image on the right shows
the extent of the rainforest in 1985.

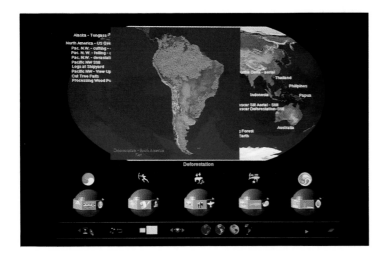

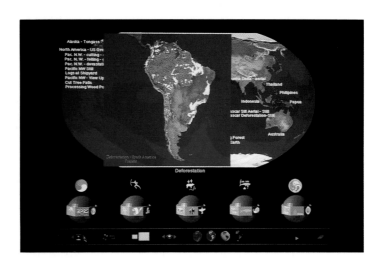

Tm Van Sant

We're making Earth Situation Rooms for locations all over the world now. The electronics and the globe and the live input are all the same, but because each institution has its own character, the results are always unique. Recently, we formed a group technology consortium with other software and hardware developers for our whole management system and the *Global Visual Library*.

The first Earth Situation Room was demonstrated in 1992 at the Earth Summit in Rio Di Janeiro. Delegates viewed the visualizations from the center of the Global Forum. However, the first true Earth Situation Room with the monitors and the *Global Visual Library* was established at the Brazilian National Center for Space Research in 1993.

Future visualizations will come from the Earth Situation Room network system itself in one of two ways. The first is through our technologies exchange agreement, whereby visualizations will be produced from the raw data generated by institution members of the *GeoSphere Project*. The visualizations will then be coregistered with all the other global databases in the world. The second and ultimately most effective way the visualizations will be produced is through an agreement with the individual venues of the Earth Situation Room network. As the network expands, each venue will be given the opportunity to produce one visualization per year in exchange for a break in their licensing fee. These visualizations will be made accessible to all other Earth Situation Rooms, so that when, let's say, there are 40 locations, each location will receive 39 other visualizations per year for their *Global Visual Library*.

We are creating a visually orientated electronic library for the 21st century. Libraries today are based on a linear form of access, such as alphabets or numerical systems. Under the current system, you can't have a universal library because there are many alphabets. We are following an alternate path of holistic and spatial organization. We're using the Earth itself as the reference for the library and using icons for selection instead of words. Geography and pictures are the languages upon which everyone can agree. Organizing the library spatially was not just an alternative—it was the only alternative we could find. This knowledge obligated us to design a program for everyone, a program that will grow creatively and rapidly without controls.

It is wonderful to speculate on the social and cultural consequences of the project, which may perturb some people. The implications are obvious, for power is held by those who control information. Our project will change everything by giving this control over to people of all ages. When a child has equal access to pertinent worldwide information, and you change the way information is delivered, the whole concept of education changes. Teachers will grow more into the role of facilitators of learning. Instead of spanning kindergarten through 12th grade, education will span zero through whatever, with equal access for everyone all the time. Within a dozen years, we will access this information through interactive computers in schools and offices, and interactive television at home.

I presume the rest of my life will probably be spent attending to the *GeoSphere Project*. We have just begun the adventure into visualization of Earth systems. We are visual beings. Who better to help us become aware of the reality of Earth than a visual artist.

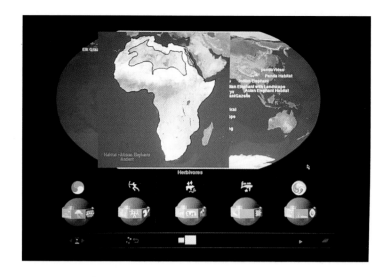

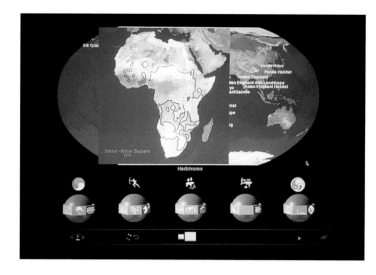

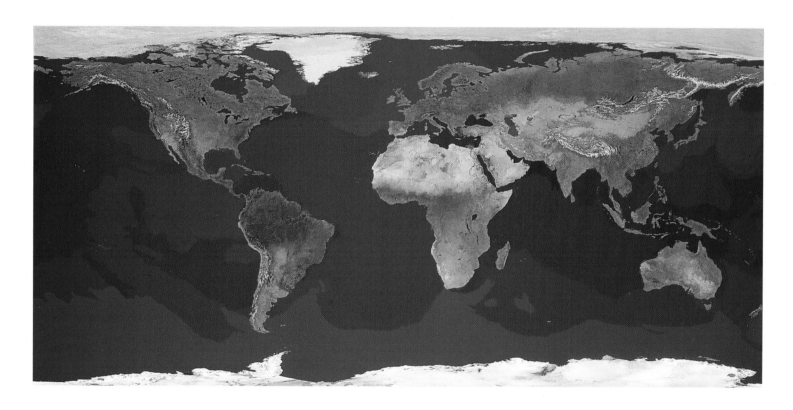

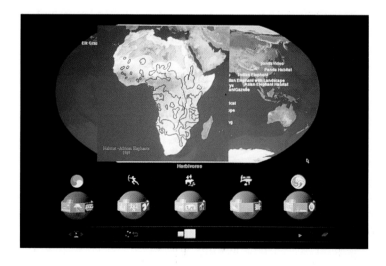

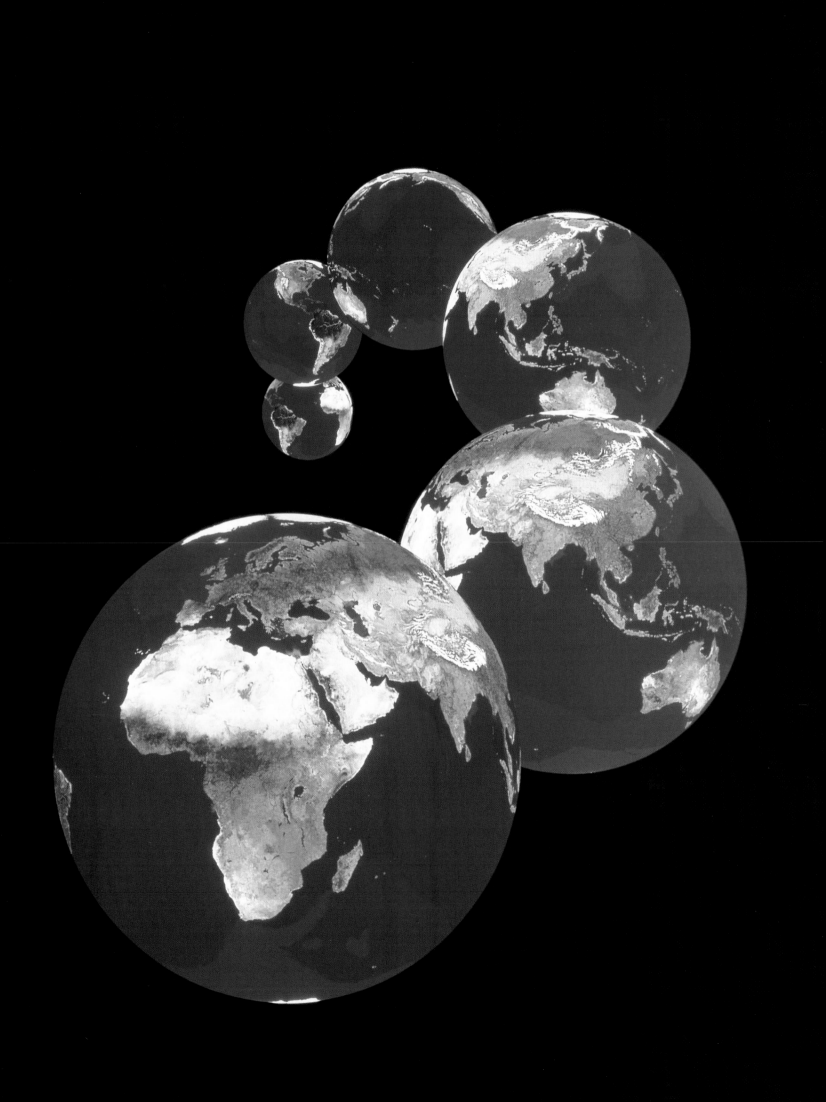

Afterword

And so in our time now, as the works and words of these thirty-five artists attest, we learn again to see. We begin to see and relate to our planet home in new ways. Adapting the words of Saint Paul, we could say, "Once we saw in a mirror darkly, but now face to face." Once we saw the world as separate from us, but now we sense it as our own body. Once we viewed Earth as a mass of resources to exploit, but now we turn to behold its true face—which is our own.

The significance of the artwork pictured and described in these pages lies not in their individual or arresting or original qualities, so much as in the spirit that pervades them. This spirit breaks out of the tired and tiring dichotomies that have separated us from the living Earth, trapped us in prison cells of our own making. It reveals a shift in perspective that is imperative for the survival of our planet as a home for conscious life. And this shift, praise be, is not limited to the artists presented in this volume. I see it today in countless places and walks of life—an awkward, beautiful, and sometimes painful awakening to our mutual belonging in the living body of Earth.

George Spencer Brown, the British engineer who developed an algebra to express the nonlinear relationships of living systems, said, in effect, I can only conclude that the Universe is so constructed as to be able to know itself. This is what we behold in these artists' work—Earth recognizing itself. And this is what each of us can practice every day; discovering and unleashing Earth's creativity, through our own eyes and hands and hearts.

Joanna Macy

JOANNA MACY

Acknowledgments

My deepest appreciation goes first to my family. Their endless patience, willing support, and understanding enabled me to dedicate myself entirely to the realization of this book. My wife Kathleen was there in numerous ways to shoulder many daily responsibilities alone. Our children Galen, 8, Taryn, 4, and baby Conor made honorable attempts to understand how this project could, so often, be worthy of cutting into our family time together. My father, Robert Bannon, was also there, with encouragement, support, and belief in this project.

I am honored by and thankful for the involvement—time, imagery, and friendship—each artist and contributor brought to the project. I applaud their vision, committed to furthering an awareness of our environment—Nature, Earth, and Universe. I also enjoyed the intimate one-on-one process of collaboration with each one, as we worked to develop a dialogue that would reveal the artist's unique thought process and creative intent to the reader. I am also grateful for the generous support and good faith of the photographers, who elevated the quality of this presentation beyond our budgetary means.

Many thanks to Wendy Lochner, executive editor at Van Nostrand Reinhold, for recognizing the value of publishing this work—exposing to city planners, landscape architects, and many others how art and design can help to foster ecological awareness and understanding. Her continued support during every working stage has been invaluable. My editor, Jane Degenhardt, deserves special praise for her dedication and extra hours spent attending to endless details.

My compliments go to all the VNR staff on this project, for their professionalism and guidance. Of special note are Leeann Graham, Anthony Calcara, Veronica Welsh, Mike Suh, Margaret Harrison, Henry Flesh, Renee Guilmette, Jackie Martin, and Val Zaborski.

Of special value here is the research assistance given to me for the section on Ancient and Contemporary Art. In this endeavor I commend John Carlson, director of the Center for Archaeoastronomy; Janet Saad-Cooke; Virendra Sharma; Dave Dearborn; and Ed Krupp, Director of the Griffith Observatory, for their involvement and interest.

Many appreciations go to the Graham Foundation, and the encouragement of its director, Carter Manney, for their generous financial contribution. Their grant enabled me to commit myself to the book full-time, thus accelerating the entire process of the work.

During the 1992 International Sculpture Center (ISC) conference, I was fueled by the zealous efforts of Nora Clow. Her support was essential to the mounting of the exhibition, *Artists Who Interpret the Earth and Its Systems*, that I curated for the conference which included works by several of the artists discussed in this book. These works triggered strong interest by the ISC to present a new touring exhibition to highlight the public sculpture presented in this book. I credit all involved at the '92 exhibition, especially Marsha Moss, Barry Parker, and Leah Douglas. The ISC, together with the aid of the District of Columbia Commission on the Arts and Humanities, and Ms. Clow's ongoing support, has made the *Sculpting with the Environment, A Natural Dialogue* exhibition possible. The ISC's efforts of outstanding note are Carla Hanzal's motivation and knowledge in coordinating the exhibition, Cecilia Miesner's help in raising the essential funds, and Tom Yarker's production of the exhibition panels and management of its tour logistics.

Throughout this project I found myself in need of guidance. I am appreciative of all the friends and acquaintances who lent helping hands along the way.

Special thanks go to Dorine Real and Lee Tepper for making their computer equipment available to me whenever the need arose, especially Lee's loan of his equipment during the design phase of the *A Natural Dialogue* exhibition and Mac wizard Justin O'Connor for his technical support guiding me through the vast world of computers and endless perils of the megabyte forest.

I am very grateful to designer Mark McGowan, for sharing his expertise and keeping flexible during the initial creation of design grids and style. And to designer Sharon Jacobs for her keen eye and assiduous assistance, providing me with an objective critique, and intelligent solutions for numerous design and technical issues.

Thankful recognition is credited to Peter Beren for his consultation, legal advice, and facilitating my negotiations with the publisher.

In one way or another, our lives are all shaped daily by interactions with the people we meet. Too numerous to name, I credit many with anonymous support.

Over the years, I continue to savor a goodness in my life; that of being encircled by many strong relationships, generous friends and family—who inspire, challenge, and renew my growth.

The kindness and support of one such friend, Bill Alexander, has made a special difference in my life. My dreams have often sprouted wings, thanks to his understanding, appreciation, and support of my artistic endeavors.

In closing, listen. The voice of the future speaks loud and clear in each passing moment through mountains, skies, rainforests, oceans, cities... The healing of Earth does lay within reach. Look within. Solutions are plentiful and ripe, resting in our field of vision, eternally nourished by the inherent powers of all LIFE and the miracles of all CREATION.

CARPE DIEM!

BAILE OAKES.

Artists' Acknowledgments and Resumes

The following section does not

follow any set format

for I wanted to respect the

needs of each individual artist.

This section allows each artist

to recognize the others

who have contributed to the

development of their work or

to supply the reader with

additional information concerning

their respective careers.

∞

Robert Lee Adzema

The artist is well known for his Sundial Sculptures. His work uses sunlight and shadow in unique and often surprising ways so that we experience light as a tangible form and "time and place" as inseparable. He has an intense love of architecture and is committed to integrating sculpture with buildings and landscapes. Mr. Adzema, a native New Yorker, was born in Staten Island in 1944. He chose to study industrial design at Pratt Institute and went on to receive a Masters of Fine Arts in figurative sculpture from Indiana University in 1968. Since then, his work has been commissioned for private and public sites throughout the U.S.A and in Europe and is in the permanent collections of the city of New York, The New York City Board of Education, The New York and New Jersey Port Authority and the Museum of Fine Arts of Indiana University.

Mr. Adzema has been honored as an Artist in Residence at the McDonnell Colony in New Hampshire, the museum of Holography in N.Y.C. and in Lemberk at the International Sculpture Symposium, Jablonne v Podjestedi, Czechoslovakia, 1990. He is also co-author of *The Great Sundial Cutout Book* which has been published in the United States and currently in a German edition.

Robert Adzema is also a professional landscape watercolor painter. He is resident of Palisades, NY and also maintains a studio in New York City.

Commissions (Selected)

Central Connecticut State University, New Britain, CT
The City of Maribor, Slovenia
The George and Annette Murphy Center. New York, NY
The T.W.U. Park, Carona, Queens, NY
P.S. 12, Woodside, Queens, NY
Thorpe Village, Sparkill, NY
Lemberk 1990, Jablonne v Podjestedi, Czechoslovakia.
Sundial sculpture for Port Richmond High School in Staten Island, NY
Sundial for the Robert Yeager Health Complex in Pamona, NY

Adzema Studio
Box 67A Ludlow Lane
Palisades, NY   10964

533 Greenwich Street
New York, NY   10013

Othello Anderson

Education

1987–88, School of the Art Institute of Chicago: Post-graduate study in 20th Century Art Theory and Criticism
1973–77, MFA, School of the Art Institute of Chicago
1970–73, University of Chicago
1969–73, BFA, School of the Art Institute of Chicago

Solo Exhibitions (Selected)

1991, Artemisia Gallery, Chicago, IL
1985, Morton College, Cicero, IL
1981, N.A.M.E.Gallery, Chicago, IL
1978, N.A.M.E. Gallery, Chicago, IL

Group Exhibitions (Selected)

1994, Studio Museum in Harlem, NY
1994, Spertus Museum, Chicago, IL
1994, Betty Rymer Gallery, Art Institute of Chicago
1992, Betty Rymer Gallery A.I. Chicago
1991, Struve Gallery, Chicago, IL
1990, Chas. Wustum Museum, Racine, WI
1989, Sundered Ground, NY
1986, Brunner Museum, Ames, IA
1984, Museum of Cont. Art, Chicago, IL

Public Collections

Harold Washington Library Center Art Institute of Chicago
Museum of Contemporary Art, Chicago, IL

Publications

Suzi Gablik, *Michigan Quarterly Review*, Sp. 1993 Vol. XXXII, no. 2, p. 231
From America's Studio, Catalog, Art Institute of Chicago, 1992
Garrett Holg, ART NEWS, Jan. 1992, Vol. 91, no. 1, p. 135
Suzi Gablik, *Art in the Ecology*, RESURGENCE, July/Aug. '91 Is. 147, p. 42
Visions, School of the Art Institute of Chicago, Spring/Summer 1991, p. 12
Timoth Porges, Review, CONTEMPORANEA, Jan '91, no. 24, p. 24
Suzi Gablik, *The Re-enchantment of Art* Thames & Hudson, 1991
Suzi Gablik, *Towards an Ecological Self*, NEW ART EXAMINER Jan, '91, Vol 18
Jeff Abeil, Review, NEW ART EXAMINER, Dec. 1990, Vol. l8, No. 4, pp. 41–42
Joyce Hanson, *Can Art Save The World?* , NEW CITY, Sept. 13, 1990, Vol. 5, No. l19
Gloria Orenstein, *The Reflowering of the Goddess*, Pergamon Press, Athena Series

Anderson Studio
400 N. Racine
Chicago, IL   60622

Thomas Berry

Thomas Berry is a historian of cultures and a writer with special concern for the foundation of cultures in their relations with the natural world. He comes from the hill country of North Carolina and was born in 1914. He began his life in a monastery in 1935. His doctoral degree in history is from the Catholic University of America. He studied Chinese language and culture in China in 1948, then continued his study at Seton Hall in the United States. Later he studied Sanskrit at Columbia University.

He taught the cultural history of India and China at Seton Hall University in New Jersey and at Saint John's University in New York. He was director of the graduate program in the History of Religions at Fordham University from 1966 until 1979. Founder of the Riverdale Center of Religions Research in Riverdale NY, he has been its director since its beginning in 1970. He was president of the American Teilhard Association from 1975 until 1987.

Besides a book on *The Historical Theory of Giambattista Vico*, a book on Buddhism, and one on *Religions of India: Hinduism, Yoga, and Buddhism*, he has also published a number of papers on the more significant human issues of the present. For the past fifteen years his writings mainly have been concerned with the industrial devastation of the Earth and the need to recognize our human responsibility for the fate of the Earth.

His book entitled *The Dream of the Earth* was published in October, 1988, by Sierra Club Books. Among the essays contained in this book are: *The Ecological Age; The Cosmology of Peace; Technology and the Healing of the Earth;* and *Bioregions: The Context for Reinhabiting the Earth*.

A book written with the cosmologist Brian Swimme entitled *The Universe Story: From the Primordial Flaring Forth to the Ecozoic Era, A Celebration of the Unfolding of the Cosmos*, was published by Harper San Francisco in the Fall of 1992. The story of the Universe presented there is proposed as the context for an educational program from the earliest years through university and professional training, an education suited to the needs of the emerging twenty-first century.

In recent years he has lectured extensively on the theme that the human community and the natural world will go into the future as a single integral community or both will experience disaster on the way.

Fritjof Capra, Ph.D.

Fritjof Capra, physicist and systems theorist, is the founder and president of the Elmwood Institute, an educational institution dedicated to fostering ecological literacy. Dr. Capra is the author of three international bestsellers, *The Tao of Physics; The Turning Point* and *Uncommon Wisdom*. He coauthored *Green Politics* with Charlene Spretnak, *Belonging to the Universe* with David Steindl-Rast, and *EcoManagment* with Ernest Calenbach et al. He also co-wrote the screenplay for *Mindwalk* the feature film based on Capra's books, starring Liv Ullmann, Sam Waterston, and John Heard, created and directed by Bernt Capra.

After receiving his Ph.D. in theoretical physics from the University of Vienna in 1966, Capra did research in particle physics at the University of Paris (1966–68), the University of California at Santa Cruz (1968–70), the Stanford Linear Accelerator Center (1970), at Imperial College, University of London (1971–74), and the Lawrence Berkeley Laboratory at the University. of California (1975–88). He also taught at U.C. Santa Cruz, U.C. Berkeley, and San Francisco State University. Today, Capra is engaged in research in systems theory and its applications at the Elmwood Institute and is on the faculty of Schumacher College in England.

In addition to his research in physics and systems theory, Capra has been engaged in a systematic examination of the philosophical and social implication of contemporary science for the past twenty years. His books on this subject have been acclaimed internationally, and he has lectured widely to lay and professional audiences in Europe, Asia, and, North and South America.

Capra has been the focus of over fifty television interviews, documentaries, and talk shows in Europe, the United States, and Japan; and has been featured in major European, American, and Asian newspapers and magazines.

Fritjof Capra lives in Berkeley, California, with his wife and daughter.

The Elmwood Institute
P.O. Box 5805
Berkeley, CA 94705

Mel Chin

Born in Houston, TX, 1951
Lives and works in New York City

Awards/Grants

1988 NEA Fellowship
1989 Pollock Krasner Fellowship
1989 Louis Comfort Tiffany
  Foundation Grant (Catalogue)
1990–91 NEA: Artist's Proj./New Forms
1991 Englehard Award
1991 Penny McCall Foundation Award

One Person Exhibitions

1987 *The Operation of the Sun Through the Cult of the Hand*, Loughelton Gallery, NYC, (Catalogue)
1989 *Directions: Mel Chin*, Hirshhorn Museum and Sculpture Garden, Washington, D.C. (Catalogue)
1990 *Viewpoints: Mel Chin*, Walker Art Center, Minneapolis, MN, (Catalogue)
1991 *Mel Chin*, Menil Coll., Houston
1991 *Degrees of Paradise*, Storefront for Art and Architecture, NYC
1992 *Soil and Sky*, The Fabric Workshop & Swarthmore College, PA (Catalogue)

Projects and Installations

1989 *Conditions for Memory*, installation: Central Park, NYC
1990 *Ghost*, site specific installation: Real Art Ways, Hartford, CT (Catalogue)
1991 *Support: Installation and Response to June 10, 1991*, Simon Watson, NYC
1992 *Gallery*, simultaneous installation: Capp St. Project, San Francisco/Three Rivers Arts Festival, Pittsburgh, PA

Group Exhibitions

1992 *Allocations: Art for a Natural and Artificial Environment*, Floriadepark, Zoetermeer, the Netherlands
1992 *Fragile Ecologies*, traveling exhib., Queens Museum of Art, (Catalogue)
1993 *Exposition Differentes Natures*, traveling exhibition, La Defense, Paris
1994 *Landscape As Metaphor*, Denver Art Museum, CO, traveling exhibition
1994 *Equal Rights and Justice: Thirty Years and Counting*, High Musuem, Atlanta
1994 *Fifth Biennial of Havana*, National Museum of Fine Arts, Centro Witredo Lam, Cuba

Ongoing Projects

Echo, Headlands Center for the Arts, Marin County, CA
Heartfelt, Eco Tec International, Corsica, France
Rage/Rap, Public Service Announcements, BRAT, NYC
State of Heaven, collaborative international project, U.S., Canada, Turkey

Betsy Damon

Baile, first I want to thank you for the spirit in your work and life. The word that comes to mind is the quality of your caring.

Requests like Baile's invite me to look backwards and forwards. Behind me are the folks who have supported me and been with me, the friends from school, the women and men who in the past twenty-five years have been a net of support and in particular the women in "No Limits for Women Artists." Around me are all of you who are working passionately for things to be right. I want to mention, Robyn Stein and the crew of *A Memory of Clean Water*, along with all of you who have supported my recent work in Minnesota as I struggle to implement new ideas. I particularly want to thank Carole Fisher, Yvonne Cheek, and Cynthia Gehrig of the Jerome Foundation. I am also grateful for the enduring support of Audrey Cenedalla, Jane Loechler, Mary Linn Hughs, Stephen Schaffer, Clarissa Sligh, Gail Tremblay, my dad, Hunt Damon, and my beloved children Tamara Damon and Jon Otto.

A special thank you to Theodor Schwenk, whose books *Sensitive Chaos* and *Water* have been a great inspiration.

Even as I write dreams are coming true. Last week the artists in Duluth have begun to initiate larger and larger projects in Duluth around the issue of clean water. As we realize the implication of such a bold move, ripples of excitement pass through all those present. Nearby communities are hooking on to the Duluth project with their own water/art projects. We are planning to begin "keepers" projects at remedial action sites on the Great Lakes. My drawings of sacred water sites are getting done. Designs and projects that have long been on the back burner are moving on to the front burner. And best of all, the necessity and possibility of artists assuming central places in their communities is becoming a closer reality. What I love about this work is that my ideals, aesthetics, and relationships are converging as one voice. The water brings us together. We are remembering together and we will flourish together.

Agnes Denes

The artist combines art with science, mathematics, languages, and philosophy. Her work deals with environmental, cultural, and social issues that address the challenges of global survival, and are often monumental in scale. She is a pioneer of the ecological/environmental art movement. She has had over 250 solo and group exhibitions on four continents since 1965. She has participated in such major international exhibitions as Project '74, Cologne; the 1976 Biennale of Sydney, Australia; Documenta 6 in Kassel, Germany; and the Venice Biennales of 1978 and 1980. In 1992 the Herbert F. Johnson Museum at Cornell University organized a major retrospective of her work, accompanied by a fully illustrated monograph. The show will travel in the U.S. and other continents.

Among her numerous awards are the prestigious Eugene McDermott Achievement Award from M.I.T. (1990), and an honorary Ph.D. from Ripon College, Wisconsin for her "Environmental Responsibility" (1994). Agnes Denes has received four National Endowment Fellowships, she is a Fellow at M.I.T., Carnegie Mellon University, and DAAD in Berlin. She has published four books, including the *Book of Dust— The Beginning and the End of Time and Thereafter* (1989). She lectures extensively at universities in the U.S. and abroad and participates in global conferences.

One of her best known environmental works is *Wheatfield—A Confrontation*, a two acre wheatfield she planted and harvested in downtown Manhattan in 1982.

Another project, *Tree Mountain*, commissioned by the government of Finland and sponsored by the Ministry of Environment and the United Nations Environmental Program is Finland's contribution to help alleviate the world's ecological stress. A spiraling forest of ten thousand trees planted by ten thousand people from around the world, *Tree Mountain* will remain undisturbed for four hundred years to serve as example of successful teamwork, land reclamation and the fostering of wildlife. The project was announced on Earth Environment Day, June 4, 1992 at the Earth Summit in Rio de Jainero. It is planned to be completed in 1994.

Michele Oka Doner

Works in Public Places

1996 *Lexicon Justice*, Criminal Justice Center, Philadelphia, PA
Ceremonial Entrance, Central Library, Florida International University, University Park, FL
1994 *A Walk on the Beach*, Concourse A, Miami International Airport
1992 *Two Obelisks*, Accreted Coral and Steel, City of Santa Monica, CA
Cellular, University of Connecticut Public Safety Complex, Storrs, CT
Winged Figure, Distance Markers for Bayshore Blvd., Tampa, FL
1989–91 *Venice Accretion Project*, Italy
1991 *Codex Sacramento*, Sacramento Central Library, Sacramento, CA
Radiant Site, Herald Square Subway Complex, New York, NY
Radiant Circles, Ingalls Mall, University of Michigan, Ann Arbor, MI
1989 *Radiant Sidewalk*, Children's Museum of Manhattan, New York, NY
1988 *Bronze Memorial*, Woodstock Artist's Cemetery, Woodstock, NY
1987 *Celestial Plaza*, American Museum of Natural History, Hayden Planetarium, Bronze and Concrete, NYC
1986 *Two Garden Seats*, Bronze, Bouverie Audubon Preserve, Glen Ellen, CA
1980 *Fallen Leaf*, Franklin Historic Cemetery, Franklin, MI

One Person Exhibitions

1991 Feigenson/Preston Gallery, Detroit, MI
Gloria Luria Gallery, Miami, FL
1990 Art et Industrie, New York, NY
The Pewabic Society, Detroit, MI
Alice Simsar Gallery, Ann Arbor, MI
Meadow Brook Art Gallery, Oakland University, Rochester, MI
1989 Art et Industrie, NY, NY
Furniture of the Twentieth Century
1988 Gloria Luria Gallery, Miami, FL
1987 Diane Brown Gallery, NY, NY
Forecast Gallery, Peekskill, NY
1986 Studio E Architettura, Rome, Italy
1984 Germans Van Eck Gallery, NY
1978 Detroit Institute of Art, Detroit, MI Works in Progress: Michele Doner
1975 Gallery Seven, Detroit, MI
1971 Gertrude Kasle Gallery, Detroit, MI
1968 Forsythe Gallery, Ann Arbor, MI

Doner Studio
94 Mercer Street
New York, NY 10012

Peter Erskine

Born: June 17, 1941, New Haven, CT
1963 B.A., Political Science, Yale
  University;
1967 M.F.A Sculpture, University of
  Pennsylvania

Erskine has participated in numerous
exhibitions throughout the United States
including two Whitney Annuals. He is
represented in national and international
collections including several site specific
installations.

An hour documentary on the *S.O.S.*
Rome exhibition is being prepared for
television broadcast in 1995. Erskine has
received numerous awards and grants
beginning with a 1963–64 Fulbright
Grant to India.

Documentation on *S.O.S.* installations is available from the artist including
full color catalogs of *S.O.S.* Rome and
Berlin; the Rome documentary; a nine
minute video of *S.O.S.* Berlin and a world
wide bibliography of articles, books and
broadcasts.

S.O.S. Los Angeles is planned to
open in March 1995 at Union Station.
The *S.O.S.* installation will travel to
Washington, D.C. and tour the United
States. An Australia/Asia tour is in the
planning stages. Erskine hopes that these
tours will lead to permanent site specific
installations for *S.O.S.*

Stonehenge 2000 is a global component
of *Secrets of the Sun: Millennial Meditations.*
It is a solar eclipse of all satellite TV
transmission. *Stonehenge* is scheduled for
broadcast to seven continents every
Spring and Fall Equinox through the
year 2000. In this ritual performance
piece millions of viewers receive a direct
TV transmission, not from the Earth, but
from the Sun itself.

S.O.S. solar spectrum art has been
created for large public sites and small
residential spaces. Some of these use
high technology heliostats and computers, others use only the rotation of the
Earth to produce their changing rainbow
displays.

Erskine Studio
1100 Palms Blvd.
Venice, CA 90291

Suzi Gablik

Suzi Gablik lectures widely and writes in
the areas of cultural philosophy and criticism. Her books include *Has Modernism
Failed?*, *The Reenchantment of Art*, and the
forthcoming *Conversations Before the End
of Time* (1995). She has taught at the
University of the South in Sewanee, TN,
the University of California at Santa
Barbara, Virginia Commonwealth
University in Richmond, and was C.C.
Garvin Endowed Professor at the College
of Arts and Sciences at Virginia Tech during 1989–90.

The Re-enchantment of Art
Although art criticism sometimes
speaks to a rarefied, highly specialized
audience, Suzi Gablik's last book, *Has
Modernism Failed?*, won an astonishing
number of readers with its passionate yet
scathing description of an enervated contemporary art scene. Her portrait of the
post-modernist art world, in which the
revolutionary sources of modern art had
devolved to a market-driven form of par-
ody and calculated indifference, left readers wondering what hope Gablik held out
for the future of art.

Now, in *The Re-enchantment of Art*,
Gablik describes how her hope for that
future is dependent on her hope for our
culture's spiritual and ethical renewal. As
she puts it: "the psychic and social structures in which we live have become too
profoundly anti-ecological, unhealthy and
destructive" to indulge the modernist
sense of alienation and social antipathy.
In the course of her redefinition of art
and culture, she introduces a number of
exciting new artists seeking a fresh
approach to making "meaningful" art,
among them Rachel Dutton, a sculptor
whose atavistic subjects are made of hay
and mud; and the visionary landscape
painter Gilah Yelin Hirsch. The impera-
tives of the new cultural paradigm she
suggests include a revitalized sense of
community, an enlarged ecological perspective, and greater access to mythic
and archetypal sources of spiritual life—
a "re-enchantment" to challenge and
to inspire.

Reiko Goto

1955 Born in Tokyo, Japan

Education

1987 San Francisco Art Institute; MFA
1976 Women's College of Fine Arts;
  Tokyo, Japan, Bachelor of Fine Arts

Awards

1993 An Isadora Duncan award for out
  standing achievement in visual design
  for the dance performance *Cho-Mu*
1993 Capp St. Artist in Residence
1990 Calif. Arts Coun. Artists Fellowship
1989 Artist in Residence at the
  Headlands Center for the Arts

Civic Art and Planning Projects

1993 San Francisco Redevelopment
  Agency, An artwork for the Yerba
  Buena Garden in San Francisco
1994 City of Oakland CA; public art
  program. An artwork for the China
  town branch public library
1993 San Francisco Arts Commission,
  Art in Public Places. Artwork for San
  Andreas Water Treatment Facility
  Collaborative project with Tim Collins
1991 Washington Art Commission, Art
  in Public Places. Artwork for the
  Edmonds Community College
1990 Athenian School, Danville CA.
  Collaborative design with Tim Collins
  and teachers and students of the school
  We were asked to design an artistic
  response to the school future sale of
  1/2 it's property to developers. The
  project was constructed in a single day
  with all the students constructing the
  work in a barn raising style.

Selected Exhibitions

1993, *Cho-Mu (Butterfly Dream)*
  An installation/performance by Reiko
  Goto and Joanna Haigood. Music com
  posed by Lauren Weinger, performed
  by Zac-Cho Dance Theater. *Cho-Mu*
  was commissioned by Capp Street
  Project in San Francisco, Dancing in
  the Streets in New York, Walker Arts
  Center in Minneapolis, and Jacob's
  Pillow in Massachusetts The project
  was shown at each place.
1993 *If I were a Pigeon* An installation for
  the Intersection Gallery, San Francisco
1989 *Nezumi*, Installation presented for
  San Francisco Art Inst. Annual Exhib.
1988 *1000 Wingless Cranes*, An installa
  tion presented for Artist on the rock.
  Alcatraz Island, CA
1988 *Emergence*, A collaborative tempo
  rary public work presented at the
  Marin Civic Center. The project was
  developed with Jeff Brown. Marin, CA

Juan Geuer

The Truth Seeker Company

It is certainly important that the world becomes aware of the anxiety and the concern that exists among so many artists about the livable future of our wonderful planet. It is also important that we, with younger and upcoming artists, are willing to struggle and to sacrifice for a profound paradigm change in our basic value systems and our attitudes.

With all who believe to be partners of the same all embracing "Truth Seeker Company" I love to share insights gained and discoveries made. Please ask for information by writing to my address below.

There are catalogues of my work available and I have given lectures and workshops among others at the Tech University in Delft, Holland (in Dutch); at the Hocheschule ruer Medienkunst in Colgne, Germany (in German); and at MIT, Cambridge, Mass. Topics relate to my life experiences: Global, Social, and Ecological issues; Geophysics; Perception and the choices we have as artists in our Post-modern society.

And for one thing it would be interesting to show my *People Participating Seismometer!*

Juan Geuer
P.O. Box 1210
Almonte
Ontario, K0A 1A0
Canada

Helen Mayer Harrison and Newton Harrison

Single Exhibitions (selected)

We have been collaborating since 1971 and have been with the Ronald Feldman Gallery in New York City since 1974 with exhibitions in 1974,'75,'78,'80 (uptown as well as downtown),'82,'85,'91 and '93.
Los Angeles County Museum of Art
The Chicago Museum of Contemporary Art
The Johnson Museum at Cornell Univ.
San Francisco Museum of Modern Art
The San Francisco Art Institute
The Museum of Modern Art, Ljubljana, Slovenia
Neuer Berliner Kunstverein, Berlin

Group exhibitions (selected)

1971, *Art and Technology*, Los Angeles County Museum of Art
1974, *Projekt '74*, Koln
1987 *Documenta 8*
1976 & 1980, Venice Bienale
Collaboration in the 20th Century, The Hirshhorn Museum, Washington, DC.
1985, *The Sao Paulo Bienale*
Artec '91, the Second International Bienale in Nagoya, Japan
1992, *Fragile Ecologies*, traveling exhibition initiated by the Queens Museum

Projects Completed or Under Way

1977–78, Art Park, Meadow Reclamation *Baltimore Promenade*, Conceptual design which is partially built
1987, Conceptual design for the reclamation of Devil's Gate Debris Basin, Pasadena, California, (in process)
1992, Conceptual design for the master plan for the San Diego Landfill (with Martinez, Cutri and McArdle)
A Wetland Walk for Boulder Creek ,design for the tertiary treatment for the sewage outfall in Boulder, Colorado
1993, California Wash at Pico-Seagate in Santa Monica, California
Disappearing Path, Newport, California

Also in process are invited proposals for the reclamation of a 50 square kilometer strip mine in Bitterfeld, Germany with the Bauhaus at Dessau, including a separate proposal for the Muldeaue; the strip mines of Northern Bohemia in Czechoslovakia
A Forest Promenade for Cergy Pontoise in France
Design for the Yarkon River in Israel
Designs for *A Serpentine-Lattice for the Pacific Northwest Temperate Coastal Rain Forest*
Design for resiting the city of Terre Haute back into its original ecology

Collections

The Los Angeles County Museum of Art
Powers Collection in Australia
The La Jolla Museum of Contemporary Art
The Brooklyn Museum of Art
The Museums of Modern Art in New York and Chicago
Tel Aviv Museum, Israel
Metromedia
The Chase Manhattan Bank
The First National Bank of Chicago
ARCO, Inc., Dallas, Texas
The Art Gallery of Washington University in St. Louis
Chicago Office of the American Medical Association.
Also listed in Who's Who in American Art and Contemporary Artists.

Professors:
University of California, San Diego
Department of Visual Arts 0327
La Jolla, CA 92093

Donna Henes

Chant For Peace There's a Chance for Peace for Peace on Earth for Peace of Mind There's a Chance for Peace There's a Chance for Earth for Peace on Earth for Peace of Mind for Peace for a Chance For a Change for Peace for Earth for Peace for Earth for Us There's a Chance Still a Chance Still a Very Good Chance for Peace for a Change for a Chance for a Change Chant for Change for Peace for Earth for Peace on Earth for a Change for a Chance for a Peace of Mind a Peace on Earth a Chance for Earth Chant For Peace There's a Chance for Peace for Peace on Earth for Peace of Mind There's a Chance for Peace There's a Chance for Earth for Peace on Earth for Peace of Mind for Peace for a Chance For a Change for Peace for Earth for Peace for Earth for Us There's a Chance Still a Chance Still a Very Good Chance for Peace for a Change for a Chance for a Change Chant for Change for Peace for Earth for Peace on Earth for a Change for a Chance for a Peace of Mind a Peace on Earth a Chance for Earth Chant For Peace There's a Chance for Peace for Peace on Earth for Peace of Mind There's a Chance for Peace There's a Chance for Earth for Peace on Earth for Peace of Mind for Peace for a Chance For a Change for Peace for Earth for Peace for Earth for Us There's a Good Chance for Peace for a Change for a Chance for a Change Chant for Change for Peace for Earth for Peace on Earth for a Change for a Chance for a Peace of Mind a Peace on Earth a Chance for Earth Chant For Peace There's a Chance for Peace for Peace on Earth for Peace of Mind There's a Chance for Peace There's a Chance for Earth for Peace on Earth for Peace of Mind for Peace for a Chance For a Change for Peace for Earth for Peace for Earth for Us There's a Chance Still a Chance Still a Very Good Chance for Peace for a Change for a Chance for a Change Chant for Change for Peace for Earth for Peace on Earth for a Change for a Chance for a Peace of Mind a Peace on Earth a Chance for Earth Chant For Peace There's a Chance for Peace for Peace on Earth for Peace of Mind There's a Chance for Peace There's a Chance for Earth for Peace on Earth for Peace of Mind for Peace for a Chance For a Change for Peace for Earth for Peace for Earth for Us There's a Chance Still a Chance Still a Very Good Chance for Peace for a Change for a Chance for Earth

Douglas Hollis

I would like to acknowledge and thank the following organizations for their sponsorship of the projects discussed in this essay.

Field of Vision, sponsored by the National Fine Arts Committee for 1980 Winter Olympics with additional funding by the National Endowment for the Arts. Several other works of environmental art were located in and around Lake Placid including projects by Siah Armajani, Richard Fleischner, Lloyd Hamrol, Nancy Holt, Robert Irwin, Mary Miss, George Trakas, and Ellen Zimmerman. There was also a video work by Skip Blumberg entitled *Earle Murphy's Winter Olympics* which features *Field of Vision*'s sport supportive aspects.

A Sound Garden, commissioned by the National Oceanic and Atmospheric Administration. Project shepherds: Jim Watkins, NOAA Project Manager, and Richard Andrews, then coordinator of the Seattle Arts Commission's Public Art Program. A book on the project *Five Artists at NOAA; A Casebook on Art in Public Places* by Patricia Fuller, was published in 1985 by Real Comet Press, Seattle, with funding from the National Endowment for the Arts.

Listening Vessels, commissioned for the UC Berkeley's University Art Museum's "Matrix" experimental exhibitions series, curated by Constance Lewallen. After this exhibition I gave this work to the San Francisco Exploratorium where it resides in good company with other exhibits on sound perception. It has been shown at the Kennedy Center in Washington, D.C., and the World Financial Center in New York City as part of *Art from the Exploratorium*.

Carnegie/Armory Park Design Project, Sponsored by the Tucson/Pima Arts Council, Dian Magie, Director. The project was funded in part by a grant from the National Endowment for the Arts Visual Arts/Design Arts Program. The design was well received by the community, and funds are being sought to realize the project.

There are many other projects which could not be discussed in the essay that the reader might encounter in their travels. Some of these are:
Wind Organ, Lawrence Hall of Science, Berkeley, CA
Tidal Park, (done in collaboration with artist, Charles Fahlen), Port Townsend, Washington
Singing Beachairs, Natural Elements Sculpture Park, Santa Monica, CA
Rain Column, Rincon Center, S.F, CA

Nancy Holt

While constructing *Sun Tunnels*, I was simultaneously filming and recording the process in order to make a 26 minute, 16 mm, color film, *Sun Tunnels* (now also a videotape). Using time lapse photography, the shifting patterns of sunlight on a summer day and the rising and setting of the sun through the tunnels can be seen in a few minutes of cinematic time.

With assistance from Julia Keydel and others, I made a 33 minute, color videotape, *Art in the Public Eye: The Making of Dark Star Park*. This videotape and *Sun Tunnels* is available for rent or sale at the Film library, Museum of Modern Art, New York.

Dark Star Park, mentioned in the introduction, came into being as a result of the cooperation and support. of Arlington County employees: Thomas Parker, Economic Development Chief; Gary Kirkbride, Planning Section Supervisor; and David Pierce, Parks Department Landscape Architect, as well as, J.W. Kaempfer, Jr., private developer, Mark Wilkenson, contractor, and the engineers at Urban Engineering, among others.

Many people contributed to the realization of *Sun Tunnels*. Essential to the project were Leslie Fishbone, astrophysicist and Harold Stiles, surveyor, along with 2 engineers, 1 astronomer, 1 surveyor's assistant, 1 road grader, 2 dump truck operators, 1 carpenter, 3 ditch diggers, 1 concrete mixing truck operator, l concrete foreman, 10 concrete pipe company workers, 2 core-drillers, 4 truck drivers, 1 crane operator, and l rigger.

The late Donald Thalacker, Director of the Art in Architecture Program at the General Services Administration in Washington, DC administrated the *Annual Ring* project with intelligence and sensitivity. Robert Struthers, Director of the Saginaw Art Museum organized the exhibition that introduced my art to the community. Kim Koehler efficiently oversaw the fabrication and installation of the sculpture.

The *Sky Mound* project is also the result of teamwork. Contributors at HMDC include Anne Galli, Director of Environmental Operations; Thomas Marturano, Director of Solid Waste, and Katherine Weidel, Landscape Architect. Outside collaborators include Cassandra Wilday, landscape architect; James Mavor, archeoastronomer; and the engineers at G.S.F. Energy.

Lynne Hull

With gratitude for the generosity of friends, human and other, who have helped along the way.

In search of a new compact between the species who share the planet. In search of a life with reduced impact on the other species who so enrich our time on this planet. We used to call it Mother Earth. Perhaps now we need to think of her as Grandmother Earth—a bit frail, seriously depleted, and in need of reduced demands and some return nurturing.

Environmental Site Works:

1994, *Tree of Life*, nature trail enhancement, A.F.E.W. Giraffe Center, Nairobi, Kenya

1993, *Salmon Stones*, Colin Glen Forest Trust, Belfast, Northern Ireland

Predator's Gate, Connemara, Dallas, TX

Missoula Beaver Trade, Missoula, Mont.

The Uglies' Lovely, Art Awareness, Lexington, NY

1992, *Riverworks I*, Williamstown, MA

Scotts Bottom Nature Trail, Green River, WY

Flowing Water Moon, hydroglyph, Canyonlands, Utah

Predator Acceptance Gesture Series, temporary locations

1991, *For the Birds (and Bats)*, Grizedale Tarn Project, Grizedale Forest Sculpture Park, Curebrig, England

Pine Bluffs Project, Pine Bluffs, WY

The Bird Garden at Navaho Mountain, UT

Marten Havens, Sierra Madre Mountains, WY

1990, *Lightning Raptor Roosts*, Interstate 80, WY

Wind Raptor Roost, Shirley Basin, WY

Badger Basin Raptor Roosts, Cody, WY

1989, *Marten Havens*, Medicine Bow National Forest, Wyoming

Island for Waterfowl, temporary installation

1985–1988: *Raptor Roosts and Hydroglyphs*, Wyoming and Utah

Patricia Johanson

Bibliography and Resume

A Conversation with Patricia Johanson, Heritage Cablevision, 1985, video tape,(Dallas Public Library Media Collection)

Patricia Johanson's Environments, Balken, Debra, ART NEW ENGLAND, Feb. 1988

Patricia Johanson at Usdan Gallery, Balken, ART IN AMERICA, Jan., 1992

Patricia Johanson: Drawings & Models for Environmental Projects, 1969–1986, Berkshire Museum, Pittsfield, MA, '87

Art for Earth's Sake, Couture, Andrea, THE AMICUS JOURNAL, Summer 1993

Patricia Johanson: Leonhardt Lagoon, Duwadi, Jyoti, , 1992, videotape,avail able from Smithsonian Instit. Traveling Exhib. Program, Washington, D.C.

Patricia Johanson, Foster, Hal, ARTFORUM, May 1981

The Changing Landscape, Garris, Laurie, ARTS & ARCHITECTURE, vol. 3, no. 4, '85

Patricia Johanson at Twining, Henry, Gerrit, ART IN AMERICA, February 1988

The Transparent Thread: Asian Philosophy in Recent American Art, Hofstra University Museum, Hempstead, NY

Art and Survival: Creative Solutions to Environmental Problems, Johanson, Patricia, 1992 (Gallerie Publications, 2901 Panorama Dr., North Vancouver, B.C. Canada, V7G 2A4)

From the Other Side, Johanson, Patricia ART JOURNAL, Winter, 1989

Patricia Johanson, GALLERIE, Vancouver, B.C., 1989 Annual

Differentes Natures, La Defense Art Galleries, Paris, France, 1993

Overlay: Contemporary Art & the Art of Prehistory, Lippard, Lucy, Pantheon, '82

Sculpture for Public Spaces, Marisa del Re Gallery, New York, 1986

Fragile Ecologies, Matilsky, Barbara, Rizzoli, New York, 1992

Art & Ecology, Matilsky, Barbara, MUSEUM NEWS, March-April, 1992

Patricia Johanson: Some Approaches to Landscape, Architecture, & the City, Montclair State College, N J, 1974

Originals: American Women Artists, Munro, Eleanor, Simon & Shuster, '79

Johanson, Munro, Eleanor, ARTS, Feb. '81

Patricia Johanson, Nadelman, Cynthia, ART NEWS, June 1981

Tres Cantos da Terra, National Museum of Fine Arts, Rio de Janeiro,Brazil, 1993

Patricia Johanson: Public Landscapes, 1991, Painted Bride Art Center, Philadelphia

People Are Talking About…Patricia Johanson, VOGUE, February 1, 1969

Patricia Johanson, Perrone Jeff, ARTFORUM, Summer 1978

Andy Lipkis

Andy Lipkis is the founding president of TreePeople, a nonprofit organization based in Los Angeles.

TreePeople is a guiding light for the rapidly growing Citizen Forestry movement in this country. Andy's creative programs include airlifting bare root fruit trees to Africa, inspiring the planting of one million trees in L.A. before the 1984 Summer Olympics, numerous disaster relief efforts during flood and fire, and many versions of training designed to increase the number of citizens involved in urban tree planting and care. He is currently designing, with the L.A. Dept. of Water & Power, the largest utility tree program in the country to increase energy efficiency and reduce output of CO_2.

Along with running the organization, Andy has used his skills in many other capacities.

He served on the Earthquake Preparedness Task Force for the state of California and consulted in the de-sign and development of L.A. City's Disaster Volunteer Coordination Program.

He was on the team that designed L.A.'s curbside recycling program.

He coined the term "citizen forester" to refer to the hundreds of people TreePeople trains to plant and maintain trees on urban streets.

With his wife and colleague, Katie, he wrote *The Simple Act of Planting a Tree—A Citizen Forester's Guide to Healing Your Neighborhood, Your City and Your World*. It serves as a cookbook for organizing tree planting programs and is in use by thousands of community groups and government agencies throughout the U.S.

In 1991, with KCBS staff, he co-produced the Emmy award-winning news series *How Does Your Garden Grow?* He also produced a series of videos designed to help urban forestry professionals and citizen tree groups market their cause to local government.

After L.A.'s 1992 civil unrest, Andy co-created the Urban Greening Initiative of the USDA Forest Service, which brought L.A. $2.5 million in jobs programs and urban forestry and gardening projects.

Andy and Katie were named to the UN Environment Programme's Global 500 Roll of Honour. They hold American Forests' Lifetime Achievement Award.

TreePeople
12601 Mulholland Drive
Beverly Hills, CA   90210

Joanna Macy

Eco-philosopher Joanna Macy, Ph.D., is a scholar of Buddhist philosophy, general systems theory, and deep ecology. Weaving these threads together, she has created both a groundbreaking theoretical framework for a new paradigm of personal and social healing and responsibility, and an accessible, effective workshop methodology for its application. Her wide-ranging work includes working with psychological and social issues in the nuclear age; the role of religion and ethics in Sri Lankan economic and social development; developing and maintaining ecological awareness; and discovering the resonance between Buddhist thought and modern scientific theory which offers new approaches to personal and global change. These and other studies are explored in her books *Despair and Empowerment in the Nuclear Age*, New Society Publishers, 1983; *Dharma and Development*, Kumarian Press, 1985; *Thinking Like a Mountain*, (co-edited with John Seed, Pat Fleming, and Arne Naess; New Society Publishers, 1988; *Mutual Causality in Buddhism and General Systems Theory*, SUNY Press, 1991; and *World as Lover, World as Self*, Parallax Press, 1991.

Macy's important work over the last decade has focused on developing and implementing a workshop model for acknowledging the numbing despair in the face of the overwhelming social, political, and ecological crises of our times, and working through it to a sense of empowerment which generates positive, creative action. In these healing environments, Macy presents a new way of seeing the world as an extension of ourselves—an integrated and eloquent blueprint for reversing the destructive attitudes that have led us to the brink of planetary extinction. In 1989, the Center for Psychological Studies in the Nuclear Age, affiliated with Harvard Medical School, honored Joanna Macy for her groundbreaking work.

Joanna Macy travels widely, attending conferences, lecturing, and offering workshops in Europe, Asia, and the United States. As founder of the Nuclear Guardianship Forum, she is involved with efforts to find workable solutions to the worldwide radioactive waste problem. She teaches at the California Institute of Integral Studies, and the Starr King School for the Ministry.

P.O. Box 7355, Berkeley, CA 94707

William Jackson Maxwell

Education

1975, M.F.A.. Claremont, Claremont, Ca

1973, B.A., California State University, Sacramento, CA
Scholastic Award
1973–74, Claremont Graduate School Fellowship, Claremont, CA

Commissions

1993, University of Washington, Pullman, The Friendship Mall, Washington States Arts Commission

1993, *China Skies*, Tulsa Park & Recreation Department, City of Tulsa Zoo, Ethel Crate Fountain, Tulsa, OK

1990–93, *Tunnel Vision*, New Denver Airport, Denver, CO

1990–93, Dallas Convention Center Expansion/Vertiport Proj. Dallas, TX

1990–93, University of West Florida, Center for the Fine and Performing Arts, Pensacola, FL

1990–93, International Center for the Preservation of Wild Animals, Inc., Biopark, Zanesville, OH

1990, New Denver Airport Design Team

1989, Nevada State Supreme Court Building Project, Nevada State Council on the Arts, Art in the Public Places Program, Carson City, NV

1989, City Hall Project, City of Las Vegas Department of Park & Leisure Activities, Las Vegas, NV

1988, Aspen Art Museum, Aspen, CO

1986, Metro Dade Art in Public Places Prog., (Miami Site), Key Biscayne. FL

1986, Connemara Conservancy, Dallas

1986, Site-Specific Adobe, NCECA, University of Texas at San Antonio

1983, Winning Sculpture Design for

1984, Louisiana World Exposition, New Orleans, LA

1981, Commission, Permanent Collection, Crocker Art Museum, Sacramento, CA

1976, Restoration of Seal Pond, Scripps College, Claremont, CA

Grants and Fellowships

1992, Nevada State Council on the Arts, Carson City, NV

1990, National Endowment for the Arts, Art in Public Places Grant, University of West Florida, Pensacola, FL

1990, National Endowment for the Arts, Art in Public Places Grant, City Hall Project, Las Vegas, NV

1989, National Endowment for the Arts, Artist Fellowship in New Genres

Maxwell Studio
3340 Broadway
Boulder, CO 80304

Dominique Mazeaud

Fifteen years ago Dominique Mazeaud began to search for "the spiritual in art in our time." This exploration led her to doing art for the Earth where "heart is the form." She considers her performance and community work new expressions of ritual and pilgrimage, and relates it to the tradition of sacred art.

For her, all work of life, art-curating, writing, lecturing, teaching, collaborating are informed by the same impulse— doing art for the Earth.

For six years she has been involved in a monthly ritual/ performance, *The Great Cleansing of The Rio Grande*. In 1993 she launched *The Road of Meeting*, a pilgrimage empowering and connecting environmentalists throughout the state of North Carolina and resulting in a multimedia installation at SECCA, Winston Salem. She plans to make it a national project (one state per region) over the next four years.

Collaborating

Keeping the whole in view as more than the sum of its parts, collaboration or co-creation is central to her way of working. Her interests in global consciousness have led her to work with Ichi Ikeda of Japan (*Water Wheels*) and Zdzislaw Gniadek of Poland (*The Erotic Picture of the World*).

Writing

A book, *riveries*, inspired by her experiences in the Rio Grande, is in progress. With New York artist Donna Henes, she has been writing *Peace: Piece by Piece*. A book of inspiration, it draws on stories of innovative international peace and environmental projects and the "ordinary" heroes who created them.

Lecturing, Teaching, Curating

She expresses her support of other artists by lecturing on Doing Art for the Earth, (formerly called Transformative Art: The Artist as Healer and Peacemaker) and curating, *Revered Earth* traveled through museums in the U.S. and *The Meeting of the Black Madonnas* to the Ethnographic Museum in Warsaw in 1991 and 1992. In university residencies and workshops, she weaves the various threads that spun from her quest and explores the depth concepts of "life/art" and "The Heartist"

Viet Ngo

The work invested in any Lemna project has been enormous. It cannot be done by any single person. I am indebted to my staff at Lemna Corporation in St-Paul, Minnesota and in other parts of the U.S.A. who have been diligently working on these proj-ects to serve the public and to protect the environment. The encour-agement, support, and partnership with numerous city officials, design engineers, universities, and state and federal govern-mental agencies across the U.S.A. and around the world have also been instru-mental in making Lemna facilities func-tional, useful, and hopefully a long-last-ing public infrastructure.

I am also greatly indebted to Ms. Poldi Gerard-Ngo.

Baile Oakes

I once heard that one will find happiness in life once one has found a way to serve another. I must have been responsible for much happiness for I have been served well by many who have crossed my path.

I am thankful to all who made *Gestation* possible through their generous support: Nora Clow, Peter Norton and the Norton Family Foundation, The Santa Monica Arts Foundation, Mark and Sharon Bloome and the Heart of America Foundation, and the city of Santa Monica, CA. To everyone in the Santa Monica Arts Commission and the city of Santa Monica who helped to bring *Gestation* to Palisades Park, especially Lindsey Shields, Henry Korn, Bruria Finkel, and Barbara Moran.

To all those who helped during con-struction, especially Martha Willard who brought an exceptional skill and dedica-tion to her work and the late Ken Bisbing who brought a joy to all the work we did to align and install the sculpture to the Winter Solstice sunset.

Gaia was made possible through the support of the Santa Barbara County Arts Commission and the Santa Barbara County Parks Department. I am grateful to Maria de Herrera of the arts commis-sion for her encouragement and support and Mike Pahos of the parks department who made sure that everything that was needed for the success of the project was made available to me.

Once more Martha Willard proved to be an invaluable help as my assistant, as well as Gerardo Reyes who helped us with all of the on-site work of this proj-ect. I am also grateful to Mike Crookston of Pyramid Tile and Marble for his help with the granite slide.

Silver Sands Park was supported by the city of Palm Desert and the Public Arts Advisory Panel. My thanks go to Catherine Sass for all her support. I am greatly indepted to Bryan Spangle of the Hudson Pacific Alliance, his wife Katie, and his partner Steve Yarabek for their help throughout the project.

I am forever thankful to the late Charles Macintosh who engineered all the projects presented in this book and who always reminded me to have fun.

Other Public Works (selected)

Legacy, Grape Day Park, Escondido, CA
Spiral of Life, Civic Center,
   Beverly Hills, CA
Gestation, Roma Street Forum,
   Brisbane, Australia

Oakes Studio
Box 203, Westport, CA   95488

Jody Pinto

Papago Park/City Boundary Project was initiated in 1990 by the Phoenix Art Commission and the Scottsdale Cultural Council. It was completed in April, 1992. Funding was provided by the City of Phoenix Parks Department and Street Transportation Department Percent for Art funds and by Artscape (The Public Art Program for the City of Scottsdale). The project was administered by the Phoenix Arts Commission, a division of the Phoenix Parks, Recreation and Library Department.

Bibliography (selected)

The Once and Future Park, editors, Krasov/Waryan, essay, Patricia Phillips, Princeton Arch. Press, 1993
1992 ASIA Awards, LANDSCAPE ARCHI TECTURE, November, 1992
Public Art in Philadelphia, PA, Penny Balkin Bach, Temple Univ. Press, 1992
Breaking Ground: Art in the Environment, SCULPTURE, J. Schwendenwien, Sept. 1991
Art for the Public: New Collaborations, ed. by P. Houk, essay, Penny Balkin Bach, Dayton Art Institute, Ohio, 1988

Public Works (selected)

1993, *Remembrance Park*, Collaboration with M. Paul Friedberg, Syracuse, NY
1988–93, *Southern Avenue Streetscape and Patrick Park Plaza*, Phoenix, AZ.
1990–92, *Grand Center Master Plan Extension*, St. Louis, MO
1990–92, *Papago Park/City Boundary*, in Collaboration with Steve Martino, landscape architect, Phoenix, AZ
1988–92, *Metro-Link*, Collaboration artist-team, architect, engineer, land scape architect, St. Louis, MO
1989–91, *East/West Arbor and Gift Gardens*, International Agriculture-Trade Center, Spokane, WA
1981–87, *Fingerspan Bridge*, Fairmount Park, Philadelphia, PA

Works in Progress

1993–, *Mill Brae Water Facility*, San Francisco, CA
1993–, *Park One Park*, Miami International Airport, Miami, FL
1993–, *Sea Wall*, Roosevelt Island, NY Collaboration Weintraub & diDomenico, landscape architects
1994–, *Public Art Fund Project*, NYC

Born NYC / Lives and works NYC

Peter Richards

Peter Richards was born in Pagosa Springs, Colorado in 1944 and attended Colorado College where he received a B.A. in sculpture in 1967. He earned a M.F.A degree from the Rinehart School of Sculpture in Baltimore in 1969. His work has been exhibited in a number of group and one-artist shows, including *New Music America '81, Creative Times* and the Nassau County Museum in New York, New Langton Arts in San Francisco, and venues in Australia and India. He has lectured at the Center for Experimental and Interdisciplinary Arts at San Francisco State University, and has organized seminars and workshops on the inter-relatedness of art and science. In 1986, with George Gonzales, he installed *Wave Organ*, a permanent wave-activated sound garden in the Marina Small Boat Harbor in San Francisco.

He completed a permanent installation at Artpark in Lewiston, New York in 1989 and in collaboration with Michael Oppenheimer and George Hargreaves Associates, developed a master plan for 145 acre Byxbee landfill Park in Palo Alto. The first 45 acre portion was completed in 1991 and was honored by the American Landscape Society through its 1993 Annual Awards.

He is Director of Arts Programs at The Exploratorium, a museum of science, art and human perception located in San Francisco and is responsible for commissioning artists to create works that are related thematically with the content of the museum. He joined the museum staff in 1971.

Charles Ross

Commissions (Selected)

1993, *Year of Solar Burns*, Chateau d'Oiron, Oiron, France commissioned by the French Ministry of Culture

1992, *Spectrum Hours*, Harvard Business School Chapel, Cambridge, MA

1990, *Latitude 41°*, Central NaugaLuck Higher Education Center, Waterbury, CN. Connecticut Arts Commission

1987, *Tumbling 12*, Alaska International Airport, Anchorage, AK. Commissioned by the Alaska Percent for Art Program.

1987, *Light Lines*, San Francisco Int'l. Airport, San Francisco. CA

1986, *Light, Rock and Water*, Wells Fargo Plaza, San Diego, CA

1985, *Light Gates*, Linclay Corporation, Kansas City, MO

1985, *Lines oF Light, Rays of Color*, Plaza of the Americas, Dallas, TX

1983, *West Light*, Towson State University, Towson, MD, Commissioned by the Maryland State Arts Council with N.E.A. support.

1983, *Rock Bow, Cumberland Station*, O'Hare Rapids, MI

1982, *Toward Seven*, Grand Rapids Art Museum, Grand Rapids, MI

1980, *Spectrum Building*, Denver, CO

1979, *Prism Sky Ball*, Dietrich Foundation, Philadelphia, PA

1976, *Prism and Spectrum Installation*, GSA Art and Architecture Program, Federal Courthouse, Lincoln

Collections (Selected)

Whitney Museum of American Art
Los Angeles County Museum of Art
Walker Art Center
Nelson Atkins Museum
Indianapolis Museum of Art
San Diego Museum of Contemp. Art
Berkeley Art Museum
Herbert F. Johnson Museum of Art, Cornell University
University of Pennsylvania
Des Moines Art Center
Albuquerque Museum
Foundation Center, New York City
Arizona Salt River Project
Butler Institute of American Art
General Electric Corporation
Becton Dickinson Corporation
Security Pacific Bank
Witco Chemical Corporation
Koll Company
Champion International Corporation
Harvard Business School
French Ministry of Culture

Ross Studio
383 West Broadway
New York, NY   10012

Fern Shaffer

Education

1991, M.A. Interdisciplinary Arts, Columbia College, Chicago, IL
1983–89, Grad. Study, U of IL School of the Arts Institute
1981, B.F.A., U of IL., Chicago, IL

Solo Exhibitions (Selected)

1991, Artemisia Gallery, Chicago, IL
1989, Common Boundary, Wash, D.C.
1988, Artemisia Gallery, Chicago, IL
1986, Artemisia Gallery, Chicago, IL
1985, Artemisia Gallery, Chicago, IL

Group Exhibitions (Selected)

1993, Bucamanga, Columbia
1993, Cali, Columbia
1992, State of IL Art Gallery
1992, Bogota, Columbia
1992, Ceres Gallery, New York City
1990, Blackfish Gallery, Portland, OR
1990, Chas Wustum Mm., Racine, WI
1989, Sundered Ground, New York City
1989, Ruben Saunders Gall., Wich, KS
1988, Detroit Focus, Detroit, MI

Publications

Suzi Gablik, Michigan Quarterly Rev., Spring 1993, Vol. XXXII, No. 2, p. 231
The Artist As Enchanter, Suzi Gablik, COMMON BOUNDARY, Mar/Ap, 1992, Vol.10, Issue 2, p. 21
Garrett Holg, ART NEWS, Jan.1992, Vol. 91, No. 1, p. 135
The Ecological Imperative, An Interview with Shaffer and Anderson, Suzi Gablik, ART PAPERS, Nov. 1991
Michelle Grabner, NEW ART EXAMINER, Sept, 1991, Vol. 19, No. 1, p. 38
Review, David McCracken, CHICAGO TRIBUNE, May 2, 1991, Sec 7, p. 56,
The Re-enchantment of Art, Suzi Gablik, Thames & Hudson, 1991
The Reflowering of the Goddess, Perganon Press, Gloria Orenstein, 1990
Reweaving the World, Irene Diamond and Gloria Orenstein, Sierra Club, 1990
The World & I, Suzi Gablik, Dec.1988 Vol. 3, No. 12, p. 240
HIGH PERFORMANCE, Fall, '88, No.43
David McCracken, CHICAGO TRIBUNE, Oct.6, 1988, Sec. 5, p. 17, *Tempo*

Published

Healing Through, The Arts, CHICAGO MEDICINE, Epstein, M.D, Kaplan. PhD, Shaffer, MA, Vol. 94, No. 22, pp. 16–20, Nov. 21, 1991

Shaffer Studio
725 W. 18th St. Unit E
Chicago, IL 60616

Buster Simpson

The artist would like to express his thanks and appreciation to the following organizations and individuals who helped make these projects possible.

Host Analog:

Metropolitan Service District's One
    Percent for Art Program
The Oregon Convention Center
Portland Bureau of Waterworks
Fabrication Specialties, Inc.
Oregon Historical Society
U.S. Forest Service
Western Planning Associates
Wind River Nursery (U.S.F.S.)
Stevenson Co-Ply

Seattle George Monument:

Washington State Art Commission, Art
    in Public Places
Washington State Convention and
    Trade Center
Fabrication Specialties, Inc.
Portico Group

Exchanger Fountain:

Anaheim Redevelopment Agency,
    City of Anaheim
Anaheim Public Library - Historical
    Archives
Consolidated Studios
Blue Ox Mill

Alan Sonfist

Alan Sonfist's concern is for the fragility of Nature rather than for its sublimeness or monumentality. His continuing documentation of a repressed or forgotten natural history fits in with the interest in repressed and forgotten histories that is very much a part of contemporary art.

Awards (Selected)

1971–73, MIT Research Fellow,
    Center for advanced Visual Studies

Public Commissions

Earth Column, Greenvale, NY
Geological Time Line, Duisberg, Germany
Narrative Mural, Merrick, NY
Narrative Historical Mural, Belmore, NY
Four Seasons, Temple University, PA
Narrative Landscape, Liberty Park
    Museum, NJ
5 Time Enclosures with Forest Seeds,
    Boca Raton, Florida
Ice Age to Present, Tampa, Florida

Public Collections (Selected)

Albright-Knox Museum, NY
Art Institute of Chicago, IL
Berkeley Museum of Art, CA
Contemporary Art Museum, Los Angeles
Dallas Museum of Art, TX
High Museum, Atlanta, GA
Houston Museum of Fine Art, TX
Los Angeles County Museum, CA
Metropolitan Museum of Art, NY
Museum of Modern Art, NY
Museum of Modern Art, Paris, France
National Gallery of Art, Australia
Toronto Art Gallery, Canada

Bibliography (Selected)

Alan Sonfist, Michael Brenson, THE NEW
    YORK TIMES, July 13, 1990, p. C 23
The Ecological Art Explosion, Robin
    Cembalest, ARTNEWS,
    Summer, 1991, p.76
Situation Esthetics, Nancy Foote,
    ARTFORUM, January 19, 1980, pp.22–29
Nature's Boy, Grace Glueck, NEW YORK
    TIMES, November 15, 1970
Esthetics and Twigs, Helen Harrison, CUE,
    February 2, 1979
Carol Johnson, LANDSKAP MAGAZINE,
    Sweden, January, 1990
*Works by the Man Who Gave the Big Apple a
    Precolonial Forest*, Jo Ann Lewis, THE
    WASHINGTON POST, November 2, 1978

Represented by:
Nancy Drysdale Gallery
Washington, D.C.
Max Protect Gallery
New York, NY

James Turrell

The *Roden Crater Project* is being funded under the auspices of the Skystone Foundation, a 501(c) 3 public nonprofit foundation based in Flagstaff, Arizona. The *Roden Crater Project* has been generously supported by Count Guisppe Panza di Buimo, the McArthur Foundation, the National Endowment for the Arts, the Lannan Foundation, the Dia Foundation, the Canon Company, the Bohen Foundation, the Martin Bucksbaum Family Foundation, Dr. Pentti Kouri, Jean Stein, and numerous other friends and supporters of the *Roden Crater*. The Skystone Foundation welcomes any and all support to realize the *Roden Crater Project*.

The Skystone Foundation
POB 725
Flagstaff, AZ 86001

Mierle Ukeles

Space permits me to mention here a few, among many, who make my work possible. Overall:

To Jack, my beloved, my source of strength, my partner. To the blessed fruit of our lives: Yael, Raquel, and Meir.

To my beautiful mother, Bess Mallin Laderman, who shapes a big world for me. To my father, Rabbi Manuel Laderman, whose death four years ago only made me understand more clearly what a blazing path of hopefulness in loving community he had set out for me and many others.

To Ron Feldman and to Frayda Feldman, who stand for artistic freedom, who have believed in me forever, who have given me courage to continue to work. To Susan Yung who has made a field of coherence around my work with a devotion so fierce it amazes me. To all the staff of Ronald Feldman Fine Arts, who make art real and make being an artist a joyful enterprise.

Public Art Visionaries: National Endowment for the Arts: Bert Kubli; NYC Percent for Art Director: Thomas Finkelpearl; New York Foundation for the Arts: the late Arthur Kerr, Theodore Berger, Linda Hansen; Creative Time Inc. Founder: Anita Contini

The Men and Women of the New York City Department of Sanitation: Commissioner Emily Lloyd, 1993 onward, one of the most gifted leaders of the great social revolution against "Out of Sight Out of Mind;" earlier Commissioners of Sanitation: Stephen Polan, Brendan Sexton, Norman Steisel, the late Anthony Vaccarello: 1977–1993

Special Appointed Liaisons from Sanitation for my art projects: Kate Beeby, 1994 onwards; John Roweil, 1986–1993

I regret I cannot list others too numerous to name.

A Blizzard of Released and Aqitated Materials in Flux: Korea
Curators: Terrie Sultan; Yong Woo Lee; Young Sun Jin; assistants Mio Kim, Chong Suk, Jane Keller.

Turnaround/Surround for Danehy Park: Cambridge
Acting Director of the Cambridge Arts Council: Pallas Lombardi; Deputy City Manager, Richard Rossi; Landscape Architect John Kissida. For Glassphalt tests in NYC: former Commissioner of the NYC Department of Transportation Lucius Riccio; Glassphalt Plant Manager Bill Slater and his staff.

Tom Van Sant

Tom Van Sant is a sculptor, painter, muralist, architectural designer, and environmental planner. In forty years of professional work he has executed over seventy major sculpture and mural commissions for public spaces around the world including the central lobby of Honolulu International Airport, the Los Angeles International Airport, and the Taipei International Airport.

Tom Van Sant has had fifteen one-man exhibits in the United States, Europe, and Australia. His work is represented in both public and private collections around the world. He is also known for his innovative design of large-scale kites, which have been flown and exhibited in museums of art and museums of science around the world. Van Sant has done extensive work in environmental planning and architectural design, and has won three design awards from the American Institute of Architects. He served as Environmental Master planner for the Los Angeles Community Redevelopment Agency from 1967 to 1975, the city of Inglewood Civic Center, the Irvine Financial Plaza of Newport Beach, and the Davies Pacific Center in Honolulu.

Long recognized for his attention to issues of scale and perception, Tom Van Sant's interest in space and technology has resulted in unique environmental projects. In 1980 he created *Reflections from Earth* for the city of Los Angeles Bicentennial, in cooperation with NASA and the U.S. Geological Survey. At 1.4 miles in size, it is the world's largest man-made image. A year later, Van Sant created the world's smallest man-made image at one quarter micron high, *Ryan's Eye*. His *Eyes On Earth From Space*, a real-time zoom from a space satellite to the surface of the Earth, was commissioned by the Los Angeles Pacific Design Center in 1986.

In 1989 Tom Van Sant founded, with associates from the scientific and art communities, the California Non-Profit Corporation Eyes on Earth for environmental research and education, and the GeoSphere Project for dissemination of the products and systems developed by Eyes on Earth. The GeoSphere products include the GeoSphere Image, the Earth Situation Room Network, the electronic Global Visual Library and the Global Ground-truth Monitoring System.

The GeoSphere Project
146 Entrada Drive
Santa Monica, Ca. 90402

Vijali

I wish to thank the many friends and organizations that made it possible to complete the *World Wheel*: Andrew Beath of Earth Trust Found., Marion Weber of Flow Fund, Elizabeth Robinson and Morgan Trust Co., Skages Found., Anton Heart Found., Markell Brooks, Luisa Putnam, Pia Gallegas, Marion and Allen Hunt Badiner, Boo Beath, Oscar Janiger, and many, many other friends.

Thank you Nitai Gil for your assistance in many countries and Nyland Nido for your help in China and Patricia and Lee Sanders for your endless enthusiasm and help. Thank you Wata for your collaboration in Israel and Palestine, Dominique Mazeaud and Ichi Ikeda for your collaboration in Japan.

Mary and Eric Lloyd Wright for your land and Georgianne Cowen and Anne Mavor for your collaboration and great help in getting started.

Also my gratitude to Twylah Nitsch (Yewhewnode) for your knowledge of the medicine wheel and your wise grandmother support! Thank you all!

Biography

Vijali received her master's degree in fine arts from Goddard University. More than 500 of her art works are in private and public collections. Vijali created a sculptural amphitheater on the Pepperdine University Campus in California. She has lectured and given workshops for many years and numerous times has been represented on television and radio through out the world. Vijali's images have been used on book, album, and newspaper covers. Her work and life has been represented in the books: *Once and Future Goddess* by Elinor Gadon, *Reweaving the World* and *The Reflowering of the Goddess* by Gloria Orenstein, *The Feminine Face of God* by Sherry Anderson and Patricia Hopkins, and *The Box* by the Terma Foundation.

Vijali is presently working on a forthcoming book, *Doors of the Earth* and a feature for television, *World Family and Our Healing Planet*.

If you wish to contact me, please write to:
Vijali
HC-74
Box 4139
Mayer, AZ 86333
USA

Sherry Wiggins

Born 1955

Education
1988, B.F.A., Sculpture,
   University of Colorado

Selected Awards and Projects
1993, Creative and Visionary Award,
   AIA, Colorado
1993, Boulder Arts Commission, Major
   Grant, Boulder, Colorado
1992, International Airport, *Fenceline
   Artifact* and *Pivot Emblem*,
   with Buster Simpson
1991, Creative Fellowship Award,
   Sculpture, Colorado Council
   on the Arts
1990, Commissioned Artist, Farver
   Coll., *Water Works*, Woody Creek, CO,
1990, Artist Design Consultant,
   Denver Airport Art Program

Selected Exhibitions
1993, *Public Art for the 21st Century*,
   MSCD Center for the Visual Arts,
   Denver, Colorado
1992 *Midlands Invitational 1992:
   Installation*, Joslyn Art Museum,
   Omaha, NE, 1992
1992, *Art Outside*, Artyard Gallery,
   Denver, CO
1991, *Rites of Spring*, Connemara
   Conservancy Foundation,
   Dallas, TX,
1990, *Dream Chambers*, Arvada Center
   for the Arts and Humanities,
   Arvada, CO
1989, *Colorado Sculpture*, Aspen Art
   Museum, Aspen, CO
1988, *Sculpture in the Park*, Boulder Art
   Center, Boulder, CO

Wiggins Studio
Boulder, CO 80304

Phyllis Yampolsky

Painter, Public Events and
Program Designer

Art Teachers
Mary Sweeney, drawing, Phila. Museum
College of Art; who taught her students
everything they needed to know about
transposing three dimensional reality onto a piece of paper. Hans Hofman, who
taught his students everything they
needed to know about turning the flat
surface into three dimensional reality.

Collections (Selected)
Mr. and Mrs. Marcel Duchamp, Red
Grooms, Grace Glueck, Robert Graham
Sr., J.P. Lannin, Herbert Mayer, Dallas
Museum, M.C. Nay Institute, San
Antonio, Museum of Erotic Art,
Stockholm/ San Fransisco

Public Projects (Selected)
1960–61, *Hall of Issues*, First multi-
   media town hall, NYC
1965, *Kutsher's Art Follies*, one week of
   all-media events, Monticello, NY
1966, *Cartoon Performance*, First PaintIn,
   NYC
1966–67, Events-In-Open-Air (EIOA)
   nicknamed Hoving's Happenings, NYC
1967–70, *Portrait of Ten Towns (POTT)*,
   network of youth centers in ten New
   York State towns wherein the teens
   hosted the town in examining issues
1968, Youth Pavilion, San Antonio
   World's Fair
1969, *Impact*, Marylerose Academy
1970, *The New Millennium*, Bennett
   College, Millbrook, NY, Art curriculums
   teaching the basic creative process and
   transposing it into five media.
1978, *In the Event of Living Sculpture,
   (Who is Not a Work of Art?)*, fifty artists
   creating sculptures out of people, OK
   Harris and Susan Caldwell Galleries,
   NYC
1981, *Key in the Fugue of East*, Yoga lesson
   in the form of participation dance
   performance, for Arcosanti, Arizona
1982, *Toward a Grassroots Strategy for
   Peace*, Visual Town Hall Project,
   Vermont, NYC, and New Jersey
1985-89, *Summer Solstice Festivals,
   Visual Town Halls*, Robert Kennedy,
   Michael Dukakis, Bill Clinton
1993, *American Town Hall Wall at
   America's Reunion on the Mall*,
   President Clinton's Inauguration
Independent Friends of McCarren Park
   (IFMP), founder and president,
   organized to save McCarren Pool in
   Greenpoint, Brooklyn '89–?'

Patrick Zentz

Many people assisted me with the projects in this book and without their commitment and encouragement, none of
this work would exist.

   I would like to thank the Yellowstone
Art Center, for sponsoring the Day project, of which Creek Translator is a part.
Thanks to Gordon McCennell for his
thoughtful essay and Christopher Warner
for his design of the catalog. Thank you
also to Linda Burnham for giving a
broader profile to this physically isolated
work through her writing.

   Fred Albrecht, Director of the UNLV
Alumni Association, was phenomenal in
his support of all phases of the fabrication
and installation of Heliotrope, John
Labounty helped on site and I appreciate
his generosity. Bob Kountz, head of
Operations and Maintenance, was most
helpful. Dan Christian, Ray Turtle,
Robert Meads, Bill Quinn, and Richard
Hayes put in long hours. I am sincerely
grateful to them. Thanks to Heinz
Knocke, from the University's
Mathematical Sciences Department, for
assisting in the design and fabrication of
several components. Carl Cook, Jeanne
Davies, and Dixie Morrissey, all with the
Alumni Center, made our time at the
University enjoyable and productive.
Thanks finally to Maryann BonJorni for
her aesthetic talents, pickup truck, tools,
information, tours, and good cooking!

   The installation of Snake River
System in Oregon was facilitated by
Superintendent Ed Gates, who graciously
made sure our every need was attended
to. Much deserved thanks goes to Tom
Lester, Gretchen Ludwig, Jim Fugate,
Darla Cox, and Butch Warren. Their dili-
gent help enabled the timely completion
of this project. Phil Fugate's assistance
lowered stress levels significantly.
Thanks to Tommy Lee Kreshon for his
interest and assistance with the engineering specifications. My deep appreciation
to Tom Rudd from the Oregon Arts
Commission. His oversight of this project
was exemplary.

   There are many unnamed people
who have assisted me. I am grateful not
only for their help, but for the time I was
able to work with them. A rancher once
told me that the best way to get to know
someone was to fix a mile of fence with
them. I am happy when these projects
function like a "mile of fence."